7·99

EDUCATION FOR ADULT

Volume II: Educational Opportunities for
Adults

This reader is part of an Open University course and the selection is therefore related to other material available to students. It is designed to evoke the critical understanding of students. Opinions expressed in it are not necessarily those of the course team or of the University.

Education for Adults

Volume II: Educational Opportunities for Adults

Edited by
MALCOLM TIGHT
at the Open University

in association with
THE OPEN UNIVERSITY

First published 1983 by Croom Helm Ltd
Reprinted by Routledge 1990
11 New Fetter Lane, London EC4P 4EE

© 1983 The Open University

Typeset by Leaper & Gard Ltd, Bristol

Printed in Great Britain by
Biddles Ltd, Guildford, Surrey

British Library Cataloguing in Publication Data

Tight, Malcolm
    Education for adults.
    Vol. 2: Educational opportunities for adults.
    1. Adult education
    I. Title
    374   LC5215

    ISBN 0-415-05161-4

CONTENTS

Preface
General Introduction

to cn

PREFACE

This Reader is one of two collections of material published in connection with the Open University course E355, 'Education for Adults'. The course is designed for all those interested in the education of adults, whether adult educators, trainers, teachers, administrators, voluntary workers or members of the general public.

It is not necessary to become an undergraduate of the Open University in order to take the course. Further information may be obtained by writing to: The Course Manager, E355 (Education for Adults), School of Education, The Open University, Walton Hall, Milton Keynes MK7 6AA, Bucks.

GENERAL INTRODUCTION

This Reader and its companion volume have been prepared with the interests of a large group of people in mind: namely, all those who have some concern with the education of adults, in whatever form this may take. Though the stimulus for its preparation came from the needs of students taking a particular Open University course, it is hoped and believed that these students will constitute only a minority of those to whom the Readers will be of interest.

The general title chosen for the Readers, 'Education for Adults', reflects their broad concern. In the United Kingdom, the education of adults is still very much an emerging field of study. There are few journals devoted to the field, the subject is not commonly studied in universities or in other institutions of higher education, and much of the literature has either not been published or is not widely available. A considerable proportion of specially commissioned or previously unpublished material has, therefore, been included in these Readers. It is hoped that this selection will in its own way contribute to the further development of the field.

The selection and organisation of material in Readers is always to some extent arbitrary. Many items which could have been included here have had to be left out, and some editing of the longer articles has been necessary. Editorial interpolations and excisions have been indicated by square brackets.

The theme of this volume is educational opportunities for adults. In other words, it is concerned with the closely related questions of policy, provision and participation. Unlike its companion volume, the discussion centres almost entirely on patterns and practice in the United Kingdom.

The first section of the Reader presents an historical perspective on different aspects and areas of education for adults. The next four parts deal with present day patterns, looking first at the overall organisation of education for adults throughout the United Kingdom, then focusing successively on the opportunities which are available (or which are not available) to particular groups within the population, and on the structure and presentation of education for adults at-a-distance and face-to-face. The final section addresses future questions. As in the case of the first volume, both case studies and thematic chapters have been included, selected so as to illustrate the breadth of the field. This reflects a belief that the study and practice of education for adults can best be advanced by the deliberate adoption of a broad view.

I would like to thank all those who have helped in the preparation of this volume, particularly June, Bob, Martine and the other members of the Education for Adults course team, as well as the contributing authors.

Malcolm Tight
Water Eaton

Part 1

PAST

The history of the education of adults in the United Kingdom has been one of the more closely studied aspects of the field, though this study has tended to concentrate mainly on the narrower preserves of formal 'adult education' provision.

Thomas Kelly's opening article is a careful thematic synopsis of this body of historical research. In a broad sweep of narrative which ranges from the religious origins of education for adults in seventeenth-century Britain up to the 1980s, he identifies as successive major themes: education for vocation, education for civilisation, education for participation and education for recreation.

The chapter by Richard Johnson, considerably shortened here from its original version, is more narrowly focused. He is concerned with an aspect of educational history which Kelly, in the breadth of his coverage, barely touches upon; namely, the alternative and often critical forms of education available to, and pursued by, working-class adults in the early nineteenth century. Johnson indicates many links between education and wider social, political and economic trends and circumstances, some of which may still be observed today.

John Robinson examines the history of the use of one method, broadcasting, for furthering the education of adults in this country. He shows how the broadcasting media have aided and advanced the education of adults, always one of the underlying aims of the BBC from the date of its foundation, with varying degrees of success over the last 60 years.

THE HISTORICAL EVOLUTION OF ADULT EDUCATION IN GREAT BRITAIN

Thomas Kelly

Source: Copyright © T. Kelly 1983 (specially revised and expanded for this volume).

Education for Salvation

In the year 1657 George Fox, founder of the Quaker movement, addressed a meeting in the fields outside a small country town in Shropshire. At one point in his address his teaching was challenged by a member of the audience, whereupon Fox called upon the people to take out their Bibles and look up the relevant passage.

This little incident is one among many pieces of evidence which indicates that by the mid-seventeenth century literacy in England was fairly widespread. Once confined to the clergy and the upper classes of society, it had now spread through the middle classes and was reaching down to the level of the craftsman and the shopkeeper. None the less there remained whole groups of the population — the unskilled workers in the towns, and the great mass of the labouring people in the countryside — who were almost or completely illiterate.

This was regarded as quite natural, and did not become a matter of concern until the close of the century. At this period a new spirit of religious zeal — a reaction, perhaps, from the moral laxity of the Restoration period — led to the formation of a number of religious societies, of which the most notable was the Society for Promoting Christian Knowledge, founded in 1699. This Society promptly set to work to promote the education of the poor, establishing within the next 30 years some hundreds of free schools, supported by public subscription and providing generally a four-year course of elementary education. Steps were also taken, with the Society's approval and assistance, to place small libraries in the more remote country churches to assist the clergy in the task of educating their parishioners.

The first great adult education movement in Great Britain was an

3

outgrowth of this movement for primary school education. It was in 1737 that a fanatical Welsh parson, Griffith Jones of Llanddowror, embarked on what we should now call a literacy campaign among the poverty-stricken peasantry of his native land. His discovery in his early years of what he called 'the brutish, gross and general ignorance in things pertaining to salvation', led him to the conviction that unless the people could learn to read the Holy Scriptures they were inevitably destined to hellfire. He therefore collected money, gathered teachers, and established schools throughout Wales.

The method was very simple. The teacher established himself in a village, found accommodation for his school in the church, a barn, or any other building available, and announced his readiness to teach all comers, by day and if necessary in the evenings. The curriculum was limited to reading (in Welsh) and the church catechism, for, as Griffith Jones explained, 'It is by no means the design of this spiritual kind of charity, to make them gentlemen, but Christians, and heirs of eternal life'. After a few months, when all who wished had been taught, the teacher moved on to another village.

These 'circulating charity schools', as they were called, were attended by 'poor and low people of various ages, even from six years old to seventy, and sometimes parents and children together'. From the available figures I have calculated that in the years 1737-61, Griffith Jones's schools may have taught something like 100,000 children to read, and the same number of adults. In a country with a total population of about 400,000 this was an astonishing achievement. The work was continued for a time after Griffith Jones's death in 1761, but came to an end in 1779.

In England, in the closing decade of the eighteenth century, a similar task was undertaken, though on a smaller scale, by two pious sisters, Hannah and Martha More, who established day and evening schools, and Sunday schools, amid the poor miners, industrial workers and farm labourers of Somerset. 'My plan for instructing the poor', wrote Hannah, 'is very limited and strict. They learn of weekdays such coarse works as may fit them for servants. I allow of no writing. My object has not been to teach dogmas and opinions, but to form the lower classes to habits of industry and virtue.'

By this time the situation in the towns was even more alarming than in the countryside, owing to the unprecedented growth of the population and the tendency for the working classes to be concentrated increasingly in the urban areas. The great industrial and commercial centres such as Manchester, Liverpool, Birmingham and

Leeds expanded at a fantastic rate, and the influx of workers from the countryside, and immigrants from Ireland, quickly created slum conditions with which the existing educational facilities were quite unable to cope. These changes were, of course, associated with the onset of the Industrial Revolution, and it seems probable that one of the first results of this revolution was an actual decrease in the extent of literacy.

The poverty and ignorance of the poor stirred the conscience of the rich, and produced a new religious response. This response took several forms. One was the Sunday school movement, which became active throughout the country from the 1780s onwards; another was greatly increased activity both by the Church of England and by the Nonconformist churches in providing day schools for primary education; and yet a third was a new advance in adult education.

In the pioneering work we have so far described; both in Wales and Somerset, adult education was in a sense subsidiary to the teaching of children. Now for the first time adult education came to be thought of as something separate and distinct. The first school specifically for adults was a Sunday school for working women established in Nottingham in the year 1798.

It met from 7.00 to 9.00 in the morning and taught Bible reading, writing and arithmetic. A class for men was soon added. This time the inspiration came not from the Church of England but from the Quakers and Methodists. In 1812 similar schools were begun at Bristol, and from Bristol as centre the movement spread throughout England and Wales. The schools met wherever accommodation was available, if necessary in private houses. Meetings were usually held on Sunday mornings or afternoons, and were restricted to instruction in Bible reading. In many cases the scholars were turned out as soon as they could read the New Testament. A few schools followed the original Nottingham example by teaching also writing, arithmetic, and sewing, but this instruction was commonly regarded as unfit for the Sabbath and was provided for on weekday evenings.

This religiously motivated adult education, which I have named 'education for salvation', continued in spite of varying fortunes throughout the nineteenth century and in some degree into our own times. The Welsh Sunday school, even today, is a centre for education for adults as well as children. The English adult schools, as time went on, expanded their educational work to include more advanced subjects such as geography and languages, and gradually transformed themselves from schools to societies with a wide range of social and educational activities built round a central core of Bible teaching. They are now a dwindling number.

Education for Vocation

More significant, however, both in its extent and in its ultimate impact on English education, was the secular response to the Industrial Revolution, a response which found expression in the mechanics' institute movement. Though the factory system which was to be so characteristic of the Industrial Revolution had not yet developed at all extensively outside the textile areas, the growth of invention and the increasing mechanisation of industrial processes were creating by the end of the eighteenth century a demand for workmen with a good basic education and if possible some technical knowledge — men who could read not only a Bible but also a blueprint. It was this kind of education that the mechanics' institute sought to provide.

One of the most influential figures in the early years of the movement was Dr George Birkbeck, a London physician whose name has been perpetuated in Birkbeck College, which is now a centre for adult education in the University of London. In the year 1799, the young Birkbeck was a teacher at Anderson's Institution, Glasgow, a private foundation which has now been absorbed into the University of Strathclyde. Finding it necessary to have some scientific apparatus specially constructed for his first lecture, he was very struck by the keen interest in the subject displayed by the workmen, and it was this which led him to offer, in the following year, a free course of lectures on science specially designed for working people — lectures 'abounding with experiments, and constructed with the greatest simplicity of expression and familiarity of illustration'. He was convinced, he said, 'that much pleasure would be communicated to the mechanic in the exercise of his art, and that the mental vacancy which follows a cessation from bodily toil, would often be greatly occupied by a few systematic philosophical ideas, upon which, at his leisure, he might meditate'.

Two points are noticeable about this statement. The first is the use of the term 'mechanic', which at this time meant a skilled craftsman. Later, with the development of the factory system, it came to mean a machine operator, but in the mid-nineteenth century the word was often used to mean simply a manual worker.

The second point is that Birkbeck is not primarily concerned with the vocational value of his teaching, but rather with its cultural value, for the enrichment of the mechanic's mind. The spirit of the age, however, was too strong for him, and his mechanics' class became the starting point, in the 1820s, for a mechanics' institute movement which had a strongly vocational bias.

The first major institutes were at Edinburgh (1821), Glasgow (1823) and London (1823), and by 1826 there were already over 100 such institutions. The one in Edinburgh called itself the School of Arts (a name which calls to mind the *Conservatoire des Arts et Métiers* in Paris), and names such as Literary and Scientific Institution, or Society for the Diffusion of Useful Knowledge, were not uncommon, but the most usual title was that adopted at Glasgow, namely Mechanics' Institution. Some were founded by the efforts of the workers themselves, more by the patronage of the upper and middle classes. Motives were many and various: employers desired better educated and more industrious workers; politicians sought to train the people in self-government; social reformers wished to alleviate poverty; working-class radicals saw education as the key to political advance.

Only a minority of people regarded the institutes, as Birkbeck did, as a means to cultural education. In most there was at the beginning a strong emphasis on the vocational value of the education to be provided. As the banker Benjamin Heywood, one of the founders of the Manchester Mechanics' Institution, put it:

The object of this Institution, is to teach the workman (be his trade what it may) those principles of science on which his work depends; to show him their practical application, and how he may make his knowledge of them profitable; to enable him thoroughly to understand his business, and to qualify him for making improvements in it; to teach him how he may advance himself in the world, and to give him an honourable and delightful employment for his leisure.

Here the motive of personal enrichment does come in, at the very end, but only as a kind of afterthought.

The mechanics' institute movement continued to flourish throughout the greater part of the nineteenth century, in spite of occasional checks due to the depression of trade. By mid-century there were about 700 of them, in towns large and small throughout Great Britain, besides a host of other bodies — working men's libraries, mutual improvement societies, and the like, which were often very similar in purpose and organisation. The biggest concentration was in the industrial areas of the North of England.

In some ways the mechanics' institutes disappointed their founders. They did not, for example, prove attractive to the lower ranks of the manual workers, e.g. the factory operatives: their appeal continued to be, as it had been in the beginning, mainly to skilled manual workers and to clerical workers. Also, with a few exceptions in Scotland, the institutes had little success in what was originally regarded as their main task, namely the provision of systematic courses of lectures in chemistry, magnetism and electricity, and other scientific subjects. These proved too difficult, and soon gave place to miscellaneous programmes of lectures, concerts and social activities. Nevertheless many institutes did really solid educational work, not in the lecture-room but in the classroom. In 1851, for example, the Huddersfield Mechanics' Institution had 600 members in attendance at classes in reading, writing and arithmetic, commercial subjects, history and geography, literature and languages, music and elocution, chemistry and natural philosophy.

More systematic teaching in many of these subjects was encouraged when in 1856 the Society of Arts began to organise national examinations in commercial subjects, and when in 1861 the Government Department of Science and Art began to organise similar examinations in the basic sciences. The mechanics' institutes thus became the precursors of the technical and commercial colleges which were developed under the control of the local authorities after the passing of the Technical Instruction Act of 1889. Many institutes actually handed over their classes, their premises, and all their assets, to form the nucleus of the new colleges, and some of the most notable technical and university institutions of the present day originated in this way. Other mechanics' institutes, which had turned their energies in different directions, eventually became public libraries, or museums, or even day schools; and a few survive to this day as social clubs.

Education for Civilisation

The vocational emphasis of the mechanics' institutes led to a reaction in some quarters, and to attempts to provide a more broadly based curriculum which would give more rein to the imaginative faculties.

The first attempt in this direction began in 1842, in a whitewashed, unplastered garret in Sheffield, where R.S. Bayley, a Nonconformist minister, conducted what he called the People's College. Classes were held by candlelight at 6.30 in the morning and 7.30 in the evening, and were open to men and women at 9d a week.

Bayley believed that 'among the toiling masses of the town there might be a latent perception of the beautiful, an ardent love of the true', and he taught his pupils not only the usual elementary subjects but also literature, history, logic, Greek, Latin, and modern languages. Alas! in 1853, after Bayley's departure from Sheffield, it was decided that the curriculum was not sufficiently practical, and that there should be more classes with 'a direct bearing on the industrial pursuits that distinguish the town'.

In its brief life the Sheffield College did provide for a few people a glimpse of wider horizons, and this ideal of education for civilised living was taken up and developed by the Christian Socialist group, centring on Frederick Denison Maurice, which in 1854 founded the London Working Men's College. Christian Socialism was born among a group of university and professional people who were deeply shocked by the revolutionary events of the year 1848. The purpose of their socialism — not a secular socialism like that of Robert Owen but a doctrine deeply rooted in the Christian tradition — was to bridge the gulf between the middle and working classes, and unite all men in the pursuit of higher spiritual ideals.

The London Working Men's College was designed as a community of teachers and students, modelled on the Oxford and Cambridge colleges with which Maurice and his colleagues were familiar from their student days. The teachers (a distinguished band, including Maurice himself, Rossetti, Burne-Jones, Ruskin, and Kingsley) all gave their services voluntarily, and the emphasis was, as at Sheffield, on the humane studies.

The College did succeed in creating a real corporate life, but after a time financial difficulties arose, and in the 1870s teaching had to be reorganised to include 'useful' subjects such as shorthand and bookkeeping, carpentry and plumbing. A similar fate overtook most of the dozen or more provincial working men's colleges which were set up in imitation of the London one, and with the exception of that at Leicester they have now long since disappeared. The Leicester College, of which the motto was 'Sirs, ye are brethren', survived to become the extra-mural teaching centre for Leicester University. It is now known as Vaughan College.

The change that has taken place at Leicester is an appropriate one, for the spirit which animated Maurice and his friends was also the spirit which afterwards animated university extra-mural work. That work had its formal beginnings in 1873, three years after the most famous of all English Education Acts, and at this point it will be useful if we pause briefly to consider the significance of this Act.

By the middle of the nineteenth century the country was recovering from the worst of the social evils which followed in the wake of the Industrial Revolution. A mass of legislation had dealt with the reform of central and local government, public health, the poor law, hours of work in factories, the abuse of child labour, and a variety of other problems and thanks to a combination of voluntary and statutory efforts there had been a vast increase in the provision for education. The primary schools established in such numbers by the churches were assisted from 1833 onwards by the state, and their efforts were supplemented by private schools (good and bad), by Sunday schools, and by the impressive body of work now being done in the field of adult education. The main agencies of adult education at this time were the adult schools and mechanics' institutes, already described, and also the evening schools, mostly run by day school teachers, which became numerous about this time — the Census of 1851 records nearly 2,000 of them, with nearly 45,000 scholars.

It is safe to say that by mid-century most adults (though more men than women) had at least some schooling, if only in a Sunday school, and had at least some knowledge of reading and writing, though only a minority had any more advanced knowledge. The basic weakness was that primary schooling was still dependent on voluntary effort, and even though Government help was now available this meant that provision was patchy and uneven. The 1870 Education Act sought to remedy this situation by setting up a network of local School Boards to fill the gaps left by the voluntary organisations. It did not make education compulsory (this came only in 1876) nor free (this came only in 1891) but it did none the less substantially mark the beginning of universal education in England and Wales (a similar Act, for Scotland, was passed in 1872). It is for this reason that the centenary of the 1870 Act was celebrated in 1970 as an essential part of International Education Year.

It was, therefore, against a background of steadily increasing literacy that university extra-mural work began in the 1870s. Pioneering work had been done in this direction at the University of Glasgow as early as the eighteenth century, but the main movement was due to the initiative of a young Cambridge scientist, James Stuart of Trinity College, and was linked with the movement for the higher education of women. A group of women's organisations in the North of England invited Stuart to lecture to them, and although his subject was a difficult one — the History of Science — he was astonished at the enthusiastic response. Before long he had the same experience with audiences of working men, and in 1871 he approached the University of Cambridge with the request that lectures of this kind should be officially and systematically organised. This appeal, supported by petitions from women's educational organisations, mechanics' institutes, co-operative societies, and other civic and educational bodies, was granted, and in 1873 the university officially launched what came to be generally called 'extension' or 'extra-mural' courses.

London and Oxford Universities, and the newer English universities as they came one by one into existence, followed the Cambridge lead, and within 20 years there were reported to be over 60,000 students attending extension courses in various parts of England — in Scotland and Wales the movement was slower to take root. The courses offered, in a range of liberal studies from literature to the physical sciences, were short (6 to 12 lectures was customary) but very serious. They were accompanied by discussion and prescribed reading, and tested by examination; and students who took a systematic sequence of courses over a three or four years' period were entitled to special awards, including, at Oxford and Cambridge, exemption from the first year of the degree course.

No feature of English adult education has aroused at once so much admiration and so much criticism in other countries of Europe as this direct participation by the universities. Those who have themselves taken part in it have no doubt whatever of its immense value not only to the students but equally to the teachers. Of its significance in the history of adult education I have written elsewhere:

> At a time when many adult education movements were tending to drift in the direction of technical and vocational education, when even the working men's colleges were finding it difficult to resist the general trend, the universities clearly restated the concept of liberal study. In doing so they did not neglect the vocational needs of students, but they insisted that even studies directed to vocational ends should be undertaken in a broad humane spirit, and that the fundamental values and purposes of human life should be

kept steadily in view. Thereby the universities established a tradition of liberal study which has ever since been the distinctive mark and special pride of English adult education.

The work had, at this stage, one great weakness: it had no financial support either from the state or from the local authorities. Because of this it was necessary to charge such high fees that working people, whom the promoters particularly wished to interest, could not usually afford to come. When financial support was forthcoming, perhaps from an employer or from a co-operative society, so that it was possible to offer a course at a low fee, the response from the workers was tremendous: one Oxford extension lecturer, in an industrial town in Lancashire, lectured for nine successive years with an average weekly attendance of 650. This, however, was exceptional. In the main university extension teaching was supported by the middle classes, and it was not until the twentieth century that it became possible to provide on a large scale for the education of the workers. The change marked a new era, to which we must now turn.

Education for Participation

All the adult education movements we have so far described were promoted in the main by the middle classes. This is true even of the mechanics' institutes, for although some of these were founded by working men few could maintain themselves for long without seeking middle-class financial support. There were, it is true, radical working-class movements, such as chartism, socialism, and the co-operative movement, which were keenly interested in education, but none of them produced any enduring adult education institution. By the close of the nineteenth century, however, universal education and household suffrage (i.e. a parliamentary vote for every householder) had created among the working class a sharper awareness of their rights, abilities and responsibilities. The establishment in 1900 of the Labour Representation Committee, to secure the election of Labour representatives to Parliament, was a landmark. The time had come when it was essential that the working classes should be educated for the exercise of political power, for participation in the processes of local and central government.

It was to this task that the universities now addressed themselves, but they could not have accomplished it without the assistance of a new organisation, called originally the Association to Promote the Higher Education of Working Men, and afterwards, more simply and more appropriately, the Workers' Educational Association. It was brought into being in 1903 by Albert Mansbridge, a clerical worker in the co-operative movement and a former university extension student. Like Maurice he was a deeply religious man, and he preached education with all the fervour of the Salvation Army.

His Workers' Educational Association was based initially on the support of the co-operative movement, the trade unions, and the universities. Intended primarily as a consumer organisation, to promote extension courses for working men, it quickly developed a life of its own, and began to organise its own programme of classes. In this it was fortunate in having financial assistance, under regulations recently approved, both from the central government and from the newly established local education authorities.

This financial change at last made it possible to organise courses at a low fee for small groups of students, and the way was thus opened up for one of the most significant developments of twentieth-century English adult education — the tutorial class. This was a class organised by the WEA and carried out under the academic direction of the university. It was restricted at first to 32 students, later to 24, and met for twenty-four two-hour weekly meetings in each of three years. Regular reading and writing work were expected and the arrangements were supervised by a joint committee of the university and the WEA. There was no examination, and no certificate. The term 'tutorial' was used because the method of teaching was based as far as numbers would permit on the highly personal tutorial method of the older universities.

The first tutorial classes were opened in 1908, under the auspices of Oxford University. The movement was quickly taken up by other universities, and for a whole generation it became the major feature of university extra-mural work, and a most powerful instrument in the political education of the working class.

The work of the WEA was rooted in the liberal, humane philosophy of the universities. Though in a sense it functioned as the political wing of the Labour Party, it always remained officially neutral in all political and religious matters, believing firmly that differences could be resolved by impartial study and discussion. There was, however, a rival organisation which was not prepared to adopt this neutral attitude. This organisation, founded in 1909 under the title of the Labour College, and known later as the National

Council of Labour Colleges, based its teaching on the Marxian analysis of the class struggle, and offered an education 'designed to equip the workers for their struggle against capitalism and capitalist ideology'. Relying entirely on voluntary subscriptions and voluntary teachers, the college strove like the WEA to cover the country with a network of branches and classes. It poured scorn on the universities as the lackeys of capitalism, and denounced the WEA for its subservience to authority and its willingness to accept subsidies from the enemies of the working class. This contest between rival ideologies persisted until the dissolution of the NCLC in 1965, and had the unfortunate effect of splitting the trade union movement, which had it not been for this division could have brought powerful moral and material support to working-class adult education.

Looking at the picture as a whole, however, we see the universities and the WEA still dominating the adult education scene throughout the inter-war years. The mechanics' institutes and working men's colleges had mostly disappeared, and the adult schools were on the decline. The local education authorities were not yet actively interested in non-vocational adult education. Under new regulations formulated in 1924 both the universities and the WEA were able to secure financial support for their courses from the central government. At this period the relationship of the two bodies was close and intimate, but as time went on the relationship gradually loosened. The WEA, for its part, began to broaden both its student intake and its range of subjects, becoming less exclusively concerned with working-class students and with subjects of social concern such as history and economics. The universities, for their part, following the advice given in a famous government report of 1919 (the *Final Report* of the Adult Education Committee of the Ministry of Reconstruction), began to reorganise their extra-mural teaching and to look at their task less in terms of the needs of the workers and more in terms of the needs of society as a whole.

Education for Recreation

In Great Britain, as in other European countries, the years following the Second World War brought social, economic and educational changes of unparalleled rapidity. Standards of living rose, leisure increased, television and the motor car transformed people's daily lives. There was a veritable explosion in all forms of post-school education (including the universities), and alongside this there was on the one hand a growing demand from adults for refresher and training courses in subjects of professional interest, and on the other hand a tremendous upsurge of interest in hobbies, music and the arts.

The increase in the general tempo of life meant that the old-style tutorial class was no longer as popular as it had been, and in some parts of the country this type of provision shrank to negligible proportions. The universities and the WEA, however, maintained their special concern for the further education of the manual worker, and continued, either separately or in partnership, to seek ways and means of attracting this type of student. The approach that proved most fruitful at this period was through day-release courses arranged in collaboration with employers and trade unions. Such courses, which began with mine workers in the Midlands and were later extended to a number of other industries, involved the release of groups of workers for a half-day or a whole day a week for a period of ten weeks or more. The longest courses, conducted by the University of Sheffield for groups of mine workers, extended over three years, with one day's study per week for 24 weeks in the first year, and two days' study per week for 24 weeks in the second and third years.

Both the universities and the WEA have also expanded their provision of cultural courses for the general public in subjects such as history, literature, philosophy, psychology, music, art and biology, and there was a special growth of interest in subjects involving field work, such as local history, geology and botany. In addition many university extra-mural departments began to play an important role in the provision of professional refresher and training courses, frequently leading to a certificate or diploma. The demand for such courses came from teachers, doctors, lawyers, youth leaders, adult educators, and especially from social workers — a profession which was expanding rapidly because of the increase in social welfare provision. This kind of vocationally oriented extra-mural work, though common in North America, was new in Britain, but it was, of course, entirely in line with the traditional function of universities, which since the Middle Ages had combined liberal study with vocational training.

The most remarkable change in adult education after the war, however, was the emergence of the local education authorities as major providers in the field of non-vocational adult education. The evening institutes conducted by the authorities in the years before 1939 had been occupied mainly with low-level vocational work for adolescents, e.g. shorthand and typing, and with domestic subjects for women, e.g. sewing and cookery. Only in London had provision been made, through what were called 'literary institutes', for the higher non-vocational education of adults. After the war, however, the vocational work of the evening institutes was provided for in other ways, often on a daytime instead of an evening basis, and this left the institutes free to concentrate on courses for adults.

The Ministry of Education, in a pamphlet of 1947, urged that 'some place should be found in most areas for a college for adults which will provide a wide and varied choice of leisure-time interest and activities'. A later pamphlet (1956) stressed the need for 'gracious surroundings' and 'roomy and comfortable buildings'. Unfortunately no money was made available for these admirable purposes, so that most of the new adult education centres had to be improvised. Many were former evening institutes, in school premises; others were converted from schools or other buildings which had become redundant; others again were in special premises attached to new schools.

Under various names ('adult education institute', 'village college', 'community college', and so on) these centres offered a wide range of activities of which the main feature was provision for leisure and recreation, e.g. painting, pottery, sculpture, woodwork, metalwork, music, folk-dancing, ballroom dancing, cookery, dressmaking, flower arranging, football, bridge, yachting, motor-car maintenance, and foreign languages (especially for tourists). The response, especially from the more affluent groups in the population, was tremendous, and although government economy measures repeatedly forced local education authorities to reduce their programmes the number of adult students in evening institutes in England and Wales rose from 300,000 a year in 1947 to more than a million 20 years later. The boom in adult education for recreation, as in other forms of adult education, appeared to be limited only by the amount of money the providing bodies were permitted to spend.

By the close of the 1960s the structure of adult education in Great Britain was one of immense complexity. Vocational education was catered for in the main under the aegis of the local education authorities, by colleges of commerce, art and technology, inheritors of the tradition initiated by the mechanics' institutes. The edifice of non-vocational education was sustained by three main pillars — the local education authorities, the university extra-mural departments, and the Workers' Educational Association, all of them operating with financial assistance from the central government.

There were, however, many other organisations, both statutory and voluntary, which contributed to adult education in one way or another. These included the eight long-term residential colleges, mostly founded before the war; the 30 or so short-term residential colleges which had sprung up since the war; the public libraries, many of which were by this time directly or indirectly involved in promoting adult education; the BBC, which from the beginning had accepted an educational responsibility; the great women's organisations in town and country, with something like three-quarters of a million members; and an immense variety of other voluntary societies both national and local.

The Latest Phase

During the 1970s and early 1980s, unfortunately, the development of adult education has been overshadowed by the country's economic problems. Plans for a large-scale expansion of non-vocational adult education, put forward by a government committee (the Russell Committee) in 1973, have not been implemented: on the contrary, because of the financial constraints imposed by the central government, especially during the last few years, the local education authorities, universities, and voluntary bodies have found it increasingly difficult even to maintain their existing provision in this sector. In some areas, the gap has been filled by massive increases in student fees; in others, programmes have been drastically reduced.

Yet the picture has not been entirely black. During the early and mid-1970s some new initiatives were still possible. In particular the government made funds available to assist two important and continuing enterprises — the Open University, inaugurated in 1971, and the adult literacy campaign, launched in 1975. These and other recent developments, such as the Training Opportunities Scheme (1971), the Open College (1976) and the Northern College (1978) have woven new strands into the already intricate tapestry of British adult education. A great adult educationist, R.H. Tawney, once said that 'the administration of adult education must always be untidy because it has to make room for the initiative of the voluntary bodies and the special contribution of the universities.' Nowadays it has to make room for much more, but perhaps the time has now come when we should be attempting to relate its manifold activities more closely to some agreed national plan, and seeking some simpler and more economical divisions of functions among the participating organisations.

References

General

Department of Education and Science (1973) *Adult Education: A Plan for Development.* The Report of the Russell Committee, HMSO, London
Harrison, J.F.C. (1961) *Learning and Living, 1790-1960.* Based on a detailed study of the Yorkshire Region, Routledge and Kegan Paul, London
Kelly, T. (1962) *A History of Adult Education in Great Britain from the Middle Ages to the Present Day*, Liverpool University Press, 2nd revised edn, 1970

Adult Schools

Kelly, T. (1950) *Griffith Jones, Llanddowror.* On the Welsh circulating schools, University of Wales Press
Martin, G.C. (1924) *The Adult School Movement: Its Origin and Development*, National Adult School Union

Mechanics' Institutes

Kelly, T. (1957) *George Birkbeck.* A biography with a detailed study of the early history of the institutes, Liverpool University Press
Tylecote, M. (1957) *The Mechanics' Institutes of Lancashire and Yorkshire before 1851*, Manchester University Press

Working Men's Colleges

Allaway, A.J. (1962) *Vaughan College, Leicester, 1862-1962*, Leicester University Press
Harrison, J.F.C. (1954) *A History of the Working Men's College* [London], 1854-1954, Routledge and Kegan Paul, London
Smith, G.C.M. (1912) *The Story of the People's College, Sheffield, 1842-1878*, Sheffield

University Extra-mural Teaching

Burrows, J. (1976) *University Adult Education in London: A Century of Achievement*, 1876-1976, University of London
Kelly, T. (1950) *Outside the Walls*, Manchester University Press
Welch, E. (1973) *The Peripatetic University*, Cambridge University Press

Workers' Educational Association

Corfield, A.J. (1969) *Epoch in Workers' Education.* On work with trade union students, Workers' Educational Association
Fieldhouse, R. (1977) *The Workers' Educational Association: Aims and Achievements, 1903-1977*, Syracuse University, New York
Jennings, B. (1979) *Knowledge is Power: A Short History of the WEA*, Hull University Dept. of Adult Education
Mansbridge, A. (1913) *University Tutorial Classes*, Longman, London
Stocks, M.D. (1953) *The Workers' Educational Association — the First Fifty Years*, Allen and Unwin, London

Local Education Authorities

Allaway, A.J. (1978) *The Educational Centres Movement, 1909-1977*, National Institute of Adult Education and Educational Centres Association

Devereux, W. (1982) *Adult Education in Inner London*, Shepheard-Walwyn and ILEA

Jennings, B.K. (ed.) (1980) *Community Colleges in England and Wales*, National Institute of Adult Education

Williams, T.G. (1960) *The City Literary Institute*, St Catherine's Press

Recent Developments

Hutchinson, Enid and Edward (1978) *Learning Later: Fresh Horizons in English Adult Education*, Routledge and Kegan Paul, London

Jones, H.A. and Charnley, A.H. (1978) *Adult Literacy: A Study of its Impact*, National Institute of Adult Education

Lovett, T. (1975) *Adult Education, Community Development and the Working Class*, Ward Lock, London

Percy, K.A. and Lucas, S.M. (eds.) (1980) *The Open College and Alternatives*, Lancaster University Press

Perry, Sir Walter (1976) *Open University*, Open University Press, Milton Keynes

1.2

'REALLY USEFUL KNOWLEDGE': RADICAL EDUCATION AND WORKING-CLASS CULTURE, 1790-1848

Richard Johnson

Source: J. Clarke, C. Critcher and R. Johnson (eds.), *Working-class Culture: Studies in History and Theory* (Hutchinson, London, 1979), pp. 75-102.

Introduction

One of the most interesting developments in working-class history has been the rediscovery of popular educational traditions, the springs of action of which owed little to philanthropic, ecclesiastical or state provision. For a long time these traditions remained hidden, though they appear in some early social histories, especially those written in one period of radical education (1890s to 1920s) about another (1790s to 1840s).[1] But it was not until the 1960s that more fully researched accounts appeared, forming part of the general recovery of early working-class radicalism.[2] [...]

The radical press remains the obvious route of entry into popular educational practices and dilemmas. It was extremely articulate, indeed talkative, providing a weekly set of commentaries on everyday life and politics. Although it is the main source for what follows, this use is in itself problematic, posing additional questions which must be answered *en route*. For we cannot assume that the attitudes of radical leaders and writers were those of 'the workers' (any more than we can assume that radicalism was 'unrepresentative' or the downwards extension of middle-class 'ideas').[3] For one thing, radicals differed a lot on some essential matters. For another, popular opinion itself was not homogeneous. Moreover, radical leaders were clearly involved in a process that was part mediation or expression of some popular feelings, and part a forming or 'education' of them, an attempt to achieve, from very diverse materials, some unity of will and direction. This necessarily involved fostering some tendencies and opposing others. [...] It is important, then, to understand the particular position of leaders and journalists within radical movements and, more generally, within the popular classes as a whole. It is necessary, in other words, to face squarely the problem of the 'popularity' of radicalism. [...]

The Radical Dilemma

There were four main aspects to 'radical education'. First, radicals conducted a running critique of all forms of 'provided' education. This covered the whole gamut of schooling enterprises from clerically dominated Anglican Sunday schools, through Cobbett's 'Bell and Lancaster work', to the state-aided (and usually Anglican) public day schools of the mid century. It also embraced all the institutes, clubs and media designed to influence the older pupil — everything from tracts to mechanics' institutes. Plans for a more centralized state system of schooling were also opposed, a feature to which we will return. This tradition, then, was sharply oppositional: it revolved around a contestation of orthodoxies (and some unorthodoxies too) both in theory and practice. Nor was this critique limited to formally 'educational' institutions. In its later phases radicalism developed a practical grasp and a theoretical understanding of cultural and ideological struggle in a more general sense.

The second main feature was the development of alternative educational goals. At one level these embraced a vision of a whole alternative future — a future in which educational utopias, among other needs, could actually be achieved. At another, radicalism developed its own curricula and pedagogies, its own definition of 'really useful knowledge', a characteristically radical *content*, a sense of what it was really important to know.

Thirdly, radicalism conducted an important internal debate about education as a political strategy or as a means of changing the world. Like most aspects of counter-education, this debate was also directed at dominant middle-class conceptions of the relation between education and politics, especially the argument that 'national education' was a necessary condition for the granting of universal suffrage. But it expressed real radical dilemmas too.

Finally, radical movements developed a vigorous and varied educational practice. The distinctive feature was, at first sight, an emphasis upon informing mature understandings and upon the education of men and women as adult citizens of a more just social order. But radicals were also concerned with men and women as educators of their own children and they improvised forms for this task too. It might, however, be truer to say that the child-adult distinction was itself less stressed in this tradition, or in parts of it, than in the contemporary middle-class culture of childhood. This is one reason why, in what follows, no large distinction is made between the education of 'children' and 'adults'. Such a distinction is not found in nature by educators, but has actually, in large part, been constructed.

We can move beyond a rather descriptive listing like this by seeing these elements as aspects of a particular, lived, dilemma. This dilemma was not unique to early nineteenth-century radicals. It is arguable that it represents the *typical* popular educational dilemma under capitalist social conditions. Nineteenth-century radicals, however, certainly experienced it with a particular sharpness. On the one hand, they valued the acquisition of knowledge very highly indeed, often with a quite abstract passion. Knowledge or 'enlightenment' was *generally* sought: it was a good in itself, a use value. This passion can be traced in many working-class autobiographies in which the fervent 'pursuit of knowledge' always looms large, in the language and educational stance of the unstamped press, in the popular reception of quite abstract texts, and in an educational rhetoric as exalted and sometimes as high-flown as the more familiar language of middle-class liberals.

At the same time, however, radicals were aware of the poverty of educational resources to hand — a recognition often enforced by personal experience. This was partly a quantitative scarcity — lack of schools, lack of books, lack of energy, lack of time. But there was also a qualitative question involved. In the course of the period some of the quantitative deficiencies were supplied: certainly from the 1830s there was a growth, in real terms, of educational facilities of the provided kind, if not of opportunities for their use. Yet as 'facilities' grew, the dilemma actually deepened. The quality of what was on offer never matched the aspirations. Far indeed from promising liberation, provided education threatened subjection. It seemed at best a laughable and irrelevant divergence (*useless* knowledge in fact); or, at worst, a species of tyranny, an outward extension of the power of factory master, or priest, or corrupt state apparatus.... Schooling was not about 'political education' at all, not about 'rights' and 'liberties'; it was about 'servility', 'slavery' and 'surveillance', about government spies in every parish, about the tyranny of the schoolroom.

By the 1830s new forms of provided education had appeared, especially mechanics institutes, infant schools and the Society for the

Diffusion of Useful Knowledge (SDUK), some of which were less obviously 'knowledge-denying' than tracts or monitorial schools. Yet radicals maintained a critical opposition. The SDUK was universally ridiculed: infant schools were attacked by Owenites (as a corruption of Owen's ideals) and parodied in the Chartist press;[4] and mechanics institutes, the most popular of the innovations, were very cautiously evaluated and, on the ground, openly opposed or instrumentally used.[5] *The English Chartist Circular's* comment on the SDUK was typical: 'Their determination is to stifle inquiry respecting the great principles which question their right to larger shares of the national produce than those which the physical producers of the wealth themselves enjoy.'[6]

[...] It was '*really* useful knowledge', then, that was important. But 'education-mongers' offered the opposite. They didn't offer 'education' at all; only, in Cobbett's coinage, 'Heddekashun', a very different thing.[7] So how was really useful knowledge to be got? How were radicals to educate themselves, their children and their class within cramping limits of time, and income? The main answer for the whole of this period was by their own collective enterprise. The preferred strategy was substitutional. They were to do it themselves. A series of solutions of this kind were improvised, all resourceful, though none wholly adequate. Radical education may be understood as the history of these attempts.

Forms

The key feature was *in*formality. Certainly, Owenites and Chartists did found their own educational institutions and even planned a whole alternative system. Yet to concentrate on counter-institutions would be seriously to misread the character of the radical response and the nature of the transition in the practices of cultural reproduction through which working people were living. There is a danger, too, of separating out 'the educational' and constructing a story parallel to but different from the usual tales of schools and colleges.[8] Radical education was not just different in content from orthodox schooling: its formal principles were different. It was constructed in a wholly different way. There is also a temptation to exaggerate the extent and, especially, the permanence of such institutions in collusion with the invariably euphoric reporting of their activities.

Typically, then, educational pursuits were not separated out and labelled 'school' or 'institute' or even 'rational recreation'. They did not typically occur in purpose-built premises or places appropriated for one purpose. The typical forms were improvised, haphazard and therefore ephemeral, having little permanent existence beyond the more immediate needs of individuals and groups. Educational forms were closely related to other activities or inserted within them, temporally and spatially. Men and women learned as they acted and were encouraged to teach their children, too, out of an accumulated experience. The distinction between 'education' (i.e. school) and not-education-at-all (everything outside school) was certainly in the process of construction in this period, but radicals breached it all the time. As George Jacob Holyoake put it, 'knowledge lies everywhere to hand for those who observe and think'.[9] It lay in nature, in a few much-prized books, but above all in the social circumstances of every-day life.

Radical education cannot be understood aside from inherited education resources. It rested on this basis but also developed and enriched it. We mean the whole range of indigenous educational resources, indigenous in the sense that they were under popular control or within the reach of some popular contestation. Struggle of some kind was possible, of course, in every type of school or institute but there were also whole areas that were relatively immune from direct intervention or compulsion by capital or capital's agencies. We include, then, the educational resources of family, neighbourhood and even place of work, whether within the household or outside it, the acquisition of literacy from mothers or fathers, the use of the knowledgeable friend or neighbour, or the 'scholar' in neighbouring town or village, the work-place discussion and formal and informal apprenticeships, the extensive networks of private schools and, in many cases, the local Sunday schools, most un-school-like of the new devices, excellently adapted to working-class needs.

On top of this legacy, which in nineteenth-century conditions was very fragile, radicals made their own cultural inventions. These included the various kinds of communal reading and discussion groups, the facilities for newspapers in pub, coffeehouse or reading room, the broader cultural politics of Chartist or Owenite branch-life, the institution of the travelling lecturer who, often indistinguishable from 'missionary' or demagogue, toured the radical centres, and, above all, the radical press, the most successful radical invention and an extremely flexible (and therefore ubiquitous) educational form.

The product of these two levels of activity may best be thought of as a series of educational networks. 'Network' is a better word than 'system', suggesting a limited availability, fragile existence and a highly contingent use. The ability to use them, even at high points of radical activity, was always heavily dependent on chance individual combinations of more structural features. Accordingly, the working-class intellectual was (and is) a rare creation. The fully educated working man and, still more, working woman was, in Thomas Wright's phrase, 'an accidental being'.[10]

We have, however, many accounts of such people, for they often wrote about their lives.

Biographies

Parents, relations and friends were a crucial initial influence. [...] We might note that something more is suggested than the generalization that parental influence is enormously important in forming the interests and character of children. More interesting are the historical (and historically changing) conditions in which, say, fathers could quite commonly teach their sons to read, a practice which requires both an inherited literacy and time for its reproduction.

The educational resources of home and neighbours were invariably supplemented by some form of schooling. Schooling was common but took different forms, differently used. Dame schools and private schools, for instance, were quite casually used. When public or charity schools were also included they were used in much the same way, were changed often and were left early. Tutelage under any one schoolteacher in any one school was, in the total sum of educational experiences, usually quite marginal. The major exception here, in some cases, was Sunday schooling, which seems to have been more likely to create an abiding loyalty than any other form of contemporary schooling. [...]

One of the most interesting aspects of the relation of radicalism and the education of children is the quite pervasive figure of the radical schoolmaster or mistress. The common philanthropic distrust of the intelligent but unsupervised teacher of working-class loyalties undoubtedly had a basis in fact.[11] Schoolmaster was quite a common occupation among prominent radicals.[12] Teaching was indeed an obvious resource for an intelligent, self-educated man or woman especially if he or she had already fallen foul of employers or other authorities. [...]

Two main factors seem to have been important in maintaining an educational progression once the influence of parents or school-teachers came to an end. The passion for reading was sometimes expressed in a catholic appetite for print or in the desire to devour, and preferably to possess, a very particular book.[13] But the reading habit itself needed to be supported by some kind of fellowship in the effort to understand. This might be associated with religious questioning, a very common feature in youth, or with accounting for ordinary conditions of life, or might happen in a less self-conscious way in the course of ordinary sociality. For George Howell, for example, who learned his later liberalism within a radical culture, it was discussion with his mates in a shoemaker's workshop which provided the stimulus. The radical press, in this case as very often, furnished texts of debate, bridging a more private educational experience and the more public world of a movement.[14] From this point on 'the educational' becomes indistinguishable from more general current in radical culture and the approach via individuals distorts a more collective pattern, in which 'living' and 'learning' are hard to disentangle. The most important experiences were those that have been examined by students of the cultural life of 'infidelity', the more heterodox forms of religion and especially Sunday school teaching, the local life of radicalism, Owenism and Chartism. [...]

Press

It was, perhaps, the press, in each distinctive phase, that epitomized the forms of radical education. Its general historical importance is now well established. In the first phase it was the main source of unity: '1816-1820 were, above all, years in which popular Radicalism took its style from the hand-press and the weekly periodical.'[15] The unstamped press from 1830 to 1836 was both an educative force, developing much later Chartist theory, and a practical example of the struggle against unjust laws and oppressive government.[16]

The political importance of the press was closely linked to its versatility as an educational form. It was a resource that could be used with great flexibility. It could be carefully studied and pondered over, as the more expository parts of, say, the *Poor Man's Guardian* must have been. It could be read aloud in declamatory style in pub or public place as Cobbett's or O'Connor's addresses were.[17] It reached its 'pupils' at different levels of literacy and preparedness for study. We can take the *Northern Star* as the hardest case, the most newspaperly of the radical media and that with the strongest reputation for sheer demagoguery.

The *Star* was certainly a newspaper. It 'could compete with any adversary for coverage', using paid journalists and local correspondents.[18] Yet the *Star* was also saturated with an educational content, even if we interpret 'education' in the most conventional sense. It contained regular advertisements and reviews of radical literature, drew attention to travelling lecturers likely to appeal to popular audiences, noted prosecutions of flogging schoolmasters (presumably to warn readers off such offenders) and published Charles Dickens's exposé of boarding schools from *Nicholas Nickleby*.[19] It gave special attention to Sunday schools, noting the opening of new ones, reporting on meetings of Sunday school teachers and covering the doings of Sunday school unions in Chartist localities. It supported the fund-raising efforts of schools belonging to the more adventurous chapels and sects.[20] It carried reports of Sunday school festivals and outings. [...]

Content

Perhaps the phrase 'really useful knowledge' is the best starting point. It was more than just a parody of the Society for the Diffusion of Useful Knowledge. It was a way of distancing working-class aims from some immediate (capitalist) conception of utility and from recreational or diversionary notions. It expressed the conviction that real knowledge served practical ends, ends, that is, for the knower. A concern that knowledge should be relevant to the experienced problems of life was reflected in the criticisms of the SDUK and of the fare of mechanics institutes as trivial and childish.[21] A slightly different criticism was sometimes addressed to lecturers and to the more 'philosophical' of fellow radicals: a criticism of wilful abstractness or abstruseness, of the failure to speak plainly. [...]

Radicals, however, also argued that their conception of knowledge was wide, much more liberal than philanthropic offerings. Education should be comprehensive in *every* meaning of the word: widely available and extensive in content. The language of universal enlightenment occurs again and again in radical propaganda, the contrast being with the confining of knowledge by monopoly or control. [...] The 'practical' and the 'Liberal' were not seen as incompatible as they tend to be in modern education debates. For the practical embraced 'all known facts' and 'the attainment of truth'. Despite the stress on a relation to the knower's experience, there is no narrowly *pragmatic* conception of knowledge here. Knowledge is not just a political instrument; the search for 'truth' matters.

Radicals did distinguish, however, between different kinds of knowledge and the practical priorities between them. While a really full or human education, embracing a knowledge of man and nature, would certainly be achieved once the Charter had been won or the New Moral World ushered in, some substantive understandings had a special priority, here and now. Certain truths had a pressing immediacy. They were indispensable means to emancipation. These truths were several simple insights. Once grasped they provided explanations for whole areas of experience and fact. Once these truths were understood, the old world could indeed be shaken.

There were three main components in what we might term the 'spearhead knowledge' of early-nineteenth-century radicalism. For the radical mainstream, running from Jacobinism through Cobbett and the unstamped and into the Chartist movement, 'political knowledge' maintained its pre-eminence. [...] The primary strategic problem was how to secure a 'government of the whole people to protect the whole people'. This once achieved 'the majority' would be in a position to introduce 'Owenism, St. Simonism or any other -ism' that would ensure the well-being of the whole.[22] This was the core of what the *Guardian* called 'knowledge calculated to make you free'.[23]

Like 'political knowledge', the Owenite's 'social science' or 'science of society' incorporated a central ethical notion and a simple principle of social explanation. Owenism centred on 'community' and a rational altruism and the principle of the educative force of competitive social relationships and institutions. Social co-operation among equals-in-circumstances was the only enduring source of progress and happiness. But why was Society so unlike what Reason prescribed? The explanation hinged on the socializing force of institutions and, in the end, on a fairly mechanical environmentalism. To live in this old immoral world was to become irrational, to have one's character misshapen as competitive, disharmonious and violent, and to learn the great untruth that the fault lay with oneself. The competitiveness of the economic system was reinforced by a whole range of social institutions. There was little indeed which did not, in the Owenite analysis, count as an ideological resource. But it was in relation to three key institutions — the family, the church and the school — that Owenite ideas were most forcibly expressed: in Owenite feminism, in Owenite secularism and in Owenite educational theory.[24] Owenism, then, added whole dimensions to the analysis of privations and a much more rounded view of liberation. It also tended to counter the overwhelmingly conspiratorial view of ruling-class actions promulgated by most of the radical press. [...]

The third main element of spearhead knowledge concerned questions of poverty and exploitation. How was it, in the midst of the production of wealth, that the labourers remained so poor? Economic justice prescribed that the labourer should have the full fruits of his toil; 'labour economics' or 'moral' or 'co-operative political economy' showed how capitalists stole a proportion in the shape of a 'tax' called profit. Though such theories gave a central place to capital, unlike the older notions of poverty through taxation or land theft, the capitalist still tended to be understood in his role as factor, merchant or external organizer of production, and exploitation was still understood as something that happened in exchange. The characteristic solution was to attempt to cut out the middle man from the process altogether and subject production and distribution to communal control.[25]

When radicals spoke of 'really useful knowledge' they usually meant one or other or all of these understandings of existing circumstances. These understandings were very powerful. They embraced a theory of economic exploitation, a theory of the class character of the state and a theory of social or cultural domination, understood as the formation of social character. [...]

Popularity

It is difficult, perhaps foolish, to try to weigh the impact of the solutions we have discussed — their 'popularity' — in some simple quantitative sense. We have neither the conceptual means nor the evidence. We do not really know how to 'think' the 'circuit' of such effects: from the conditions from which radical theory arose in the first place, through the educational practices themselves, to success or failure in actually forming people's principles of life and action. Empirically, we might begin by establishing what David Jones has called 'the various indices of activity'.[26] We can assess the circulation of the presses, multiplying for collective readership. We can count and place geographically the more formal solutions of schools and halls. We can set this beside the overall geography of the movements themselves and an assessment of the extent to which they moved masses in different places and at different times. Beyond this there are really imponderable questions. How many working men followed Lovett's 'unpopular' advice to economize on drink and spend the surplus on radical journals?[27] How many talked politics with their wives in the spirit of equality advocated by radical women? How common was the practice of Sophia of Birmingham who gave her children a political education by telling them 'all we learn of good' and never shirking difficult questions?[28] How significant a contribution did radical education make to basic attainments — literacy for instance? What kind of effect did radical hostility to provided schooling have on popular patterns of school use?

From existing knowledge something can be said on some of these questions. The indices run very high at peak points of radical activity. The largest ever circulation for a radical paper was that achieved by the *Northern Star* in the summer of 1839 — perhaps 50,000 copies.[29] At such moments radicalism acquired a mass character. Radical ideas and organization could also penetrate into the most unpromising environments, under the noses, for example, of conscientious local paternalists.[30] But even Chartism had marked geographical limits. Whole communities, especially in the countryside and in the south and east, lacked organization, though it is impossible to assess sympathies.[31] In the north and Midlands, by contrast, many localities had a continuous history of radicalism throughout the period, often punctuated by major mobilizations. In such areas radical education in its various forms had a continuous and lively history, supported by groups of provincial leaders. It is also clear that radical politics and cultural activity secured, for thousands of individuals, some educational progression, providing a motive for learning. Yet it is certain too that radicalism's more formal solutions did not and could not match the provided forms in extent and solidity. The dream of Lovett and others, of a whole alternative system of education, remained a dream. One might guess, however, that the more democratic institutions had a greater effect on their pupils' consciousness of the social world than a more routine schooling. [...]

Shifts and Differences

The most important shift, over time, was a heightened awareness of the immense difficulty of sustaining radical education. We can, with the benefit of hindsight, see this as the beginning of a longer transformation in working-class educational strategies. From the 1850s and more surely from the later 1860s, the strategy of substitution — of an alternative working-class system — was replaced by the demand for more equal access to facilities that were to be provided by the state. This became the main feature of popular liberal politics and then of the Labour Party's educational stance.[32] Thus while radicals, Chartists and Owenites all opposed 'state education' except as the work of a transformed state, later socialists actually fuelled the growth of state schooling by their own agitations. The consequence of this adaptation was immense: it involved, for instance, accepting, in a very sharp form, the child-adult divide, the tendency to equate education with school, the depoliticization of educational content, and the professionalization of teaching. In all these ways the state as educator was by no means a neutral apparatus.

A study of discussions in the radical press from the later 1830s shows very clearly the preference for, but also the limitations of, a more independent route. Independence remained the central feature of the tradition. Most early radicals had accepted the Godwinian case against every authoritative direction of learning. Cobbett opposed 'national education' right up to his death in 1835. The *Black Dwarf* even opposed the setting up of national libraries on the ground that learning should support itself.[33] Owen himself sometimes, and rather rhetorically, called on government to supply (an Owenite) education: most Owenites probably agreed with Shepherd Smith about 'the folly of looking to governments for aid'.[34] The usual Chartist line was an inversion of that of middle-class reformers: 'national education' could and would follow universal suffrage rather than precede it: any education worth the name was unlikely and would probably be very dangerous beforehand. There was even some debate about the wisdom of a state organization of schooling after the Charter was achieved.[35]

As independence was asserted in still more class-conscious forms, difficulties multiplied. Radicals before the 1830s had tended to see the problem mainly in terms of monopoly. Secular and religious authority kept the people ignorant, ignorant even of the laws they were to obey. The task, then, was to spread knowledge where none had existed before — or only that lack of knowledge which Paine had called 'superstition': hence that unreasonable faith in reason and in their own presses, legacy in part from their own Enlightenment sources.[36] Besides, as Thompson has stressed, enlightenment seemed to work. But radicals of the 1830s and 1840s, faced by defeats, developed a greater sense of the ideological resources of competitive society, the need to 'un-teach' old associations and the significance, as positive sources of 'error', of institutions like the churches. The Owenite analysis of society's immense ideological weight, which in less sanguine times might have bred a deep fatalism, posed at least the problems of where to start.

The second set of difficulties concerned the material conditions for radical education. There was now much more emphasis on such practical limitations as lack of time, income, rest, and peace and quiet. A sense of these problems seems to have fuelled a move towards more collective and formal solutions, especially for children, different in kind from Cobbett's hearth-based remedies.[37] It was those media with readerships rooted in the industrial north and Midlands — the organs of the factory movement, the Birmingham and union-based *Pioneer* and the *Northern Star* — that seem to have responded most sensitively to new needs.

The factory movement itself is the most obvious example of the newer emphases, for it campaigned on matters of time and the reduction of the working day both for children and adults. It was also the first example of a working-class strategy of pressure on the state to secure well-defined reforms. Of course, the educational content of the movement should not be exaggerated: freedom from excessive toil as a human right or a Christian obligation was also stressed and the factory was attacked as a source of many evils. But the agitation over hours can certainly be read as an attempt to reinstate the educational importance of the family. The need for education was often cited as a motor of the movement and factory reformers put forward their own educational schemes. These sometimes had a Tory or Anglican character but the programme of the Society for Promoting National Regeneration, for instance, put forward a working-class alternative, similar to but more modest than later substitutional schemes.[38] [...]

Although all radicals saw education as an aspect of equal rights and a goal to be fought for, education was also part of a strategy or method. For Owenites, education (which always included the power of 'institutions', 'writings' and 'discourses' as well as schooling) was the principal means of agitation, but as J.F.C. Harrison has stressed, Owenism was 'not purely a movement to found schools and literary institutes'.[39] Similarly, in the political-radical mainstream, politics and education went together in a complicated web of means-ends relationships. Education without politics was deemed inadequate: it must be allied to some kind of power, some 'physical' or 'moral' force, some purchase on authority. But politics without education was also inadequate. Certain kinds of knowledge were immediate means to the Charter: all sections of the Chartist movement gave to 'intelligence' a key role in mass agitation. This in turn meant that all activity that led to a general raising of levels of literacy and articulacy was to be fostered. There was no division at all in Chartist ranks on this particular theme.

The unity of the compensatory and political aspects of educational enthusiasm did rest, however, on very particular conditions. The whole substitutional strategy was sustained by the belief that sooner or later the Charter or the New Moral World would be secured. Within the terms of this belief, the individual pursuit of knowledge or the general aim of 'improving' the whole class, or the desire to concentrate on the education of children, could all be held together. The task was to prepare for success and speed it. The larger education objectives, utopian indeed in existing circumstances, could be asked to wait. Soon, all would be achieved.

So when political challenges were blunted and hopes of immediate success began to fail, difficult tactical and strategic questions emerged. The commonest response was to hold the existing combination, limit educational ambitions, hope and work for some resolution at other (i.e. political) levels. But the history here is different within the Owenite and Chartist connections. Owenism was a protean movement that met frustrations by once more changing form, stressing yet another aspect of a very fertile repertoire. Chartism faced the problem of power, and had intermediate goals of great clarity (universal suffrage). Setbacks were correspondingly more traumatic, diversions more contentious and battles about strategy more ferocious and debilitating. None the less, somewhat similar debates can be traced within the two movements.

From the perspective of what remained the dominant tendency, the characteristic 'deviation' was to give to education schemes a priority independent of sensible tactical judgement. Since the commonest form of such schemes focused on the education of children, the threat was that radicals would become *merely* schoolmasters. [...]

It was natural that Owenites should wish to found their own schools to show the world how children really could be educated and to avoid using the schools of Church or Dissent. In its more usual forms — more improvised, combining adults and children, and connecting schooling with other activities — Owenite schooling, especially at the level of the local branch, was a widespread and sensible response. But the education projects often bear the mark of the crankier, more philanthropic aspects of the movement and invariably involved middle-class aid and, perhaps, a loss of independence.

The equivalent within Chartism was Lovett's plan to build a comprehensive system of counter-education eschewing the aid of 'irresponsible government' but allowing a role for middle-class sympathizers. The plan bore the stamp of Owenite influence, not least in its ambition: infant, preparatory and high schools in every place, reading rooms, lectures and libraries for adults in newly built district halls, agricultural and industrial schools for orphans, tracts, school-books, and a system for the training of teachers with at least one 'normal school'.[40] While mainstream Chartists continued more modest educational work and indeed increased its intensity, Lovett's association became a progressive but not too successful experiment in middle-class philanthropy. The founding of the first day school was delayed until 1848. By this time Lovett himself had actually become a schoolmaster.

But the orthodox Chartist route did not constitute a solution either. By the mid-1840s it had reached its limits. In the decades that followed and in the wake of the political defeats, independent working-class education continued; in the better-off sectors it may even have increased. But it took on more individualized forms ('self-education') or lost its connection with politics ('mutual improvement') or became the cultural preserve of the aristocracies. It certainly lost the ambition of being an alternative system, especially with regard to children. At the same time a new kind of educational agitation began to emerge, linked to popular liberalism and the anti-Anglican alliance. Working-class activists began to demand education through the state, even though initially, like the Chartist rump of 1851, they insisted still on some popular control.

Future Questions

[...] The educational story we have just described (not by any means the whole story of working-class education) corresponds to the economic experience of the small-producer-becoming-proletarian.

The main mechanism seems to have been the curtailment or interruption of the educative or reproductive autonomies of family and community through, primarily, the more complete subordination of labour (male, female and juvenile) in production. This pressure from the sphere of production and the enforcement of capitalist economic relations was reinforced, of course, by direct intervention in the reproductive sphere, of which the growth of state and provided schooling is the most relevant example. At the same time as indigenous educational resources were squeezed, alternative forms were offered or enforced. The erosion of an indigenous educational capacity seems to have occurred in different ways. It happened in a few trades through the concentration of production in the factory and, eventually, the separation of the household and the sphere of capitalist production. The employment of children, often a concomitant of factory production but occurring on an extended scale outside, had, itself, obvious educative effects. But perhaps the most important form of pressure on the family was through a deepening dependence of domestic outwork on the capitalist merchant, factor or middleman and the reduction of margins of time and income through the prolongation of the working day. Low income not only changed the (necessarily educative) relations within the family but also made the family more and more dependent on the labour of the children.

We may understand radical education as an attempt to expand and develop those areas of autonomy and control over reproduction which remained. If this is accurate, it is important to say that it was not a fully 'working-class' phenomenon: it did not rest on fully proletarian conditions of existence. Indeed, the material spaces which it occupied were actually shrinking. This was accentuated by the changing geographical basis of radicalism which was also a changing social basis. The early radical phases rested upon artisans, trades like weaving with relatively recent histories of some independence, and, perhaps, petit bourgeois and lesser professional groups, more modern analogues of the small producer. The spread of the factories, the deepening subordination of the outworkers, the growth of sweated trades, together with the geographic shift northwards in Chartism, gave to radicalism a more fully proletarian base. To such people some of the earlier solutions must have seemed grossly inapplicable. Yet it took time to find another route, appropriate to proletarian conditions, and a much longer haul to socialism. The priority, perhaps, *was* to build barriers to capital's appetite for labour and then to its tendency to intensify it. So far as education is concerned the period from the 1790s to the 1830s did *not* see 'the making of the English working class', did not see, that is, the development of the characteristic class strategies of later periods. *This* story really begins, thinly, with the factory movement and continues with the educational strategies of late Chartism, popular liberalism and the early-twentieth-century labour movement.[41]

Notes

1. E.g. A.E. Dobbs, *Education and Social Movements, 1700-1850* (Longman, London, 1919).

2. Brian Simon, *Studies in the History of Education, 1780-1870* (Lawrence & Wishart, 1960); J.F.C. Harrison, *Learning and Living 1790-1960* (Routledge & Kegan Paul, London, 1961); Harold Silver, *The Concept of Popular Education* (MacGibbon & Kee, 1965); E.P. Thompson, *The Making of the English Working Class* (Gollancz, London, 1963), especially pp. 711-45. Also important for first opening up many questions was R.K. Webb, *The British Working Class Reader, 1790-1848* (Allen & Unwin, London, 1955).

3. For the first of these faults see Simon, *Studies,* p. 275; the latter simplifications are commoner in conservative historiography.

4. For infant schools see *New Moral World,* 8 July 1837; and *Northern Star,* 7 January 1843. But for a more favourable view see the *Midlands Counties Illuminator* (Thomas Cooper's paper), 20 March 1841.

5. Even the most favourable assessments of the popularity of the mechanics institutes are open to the interpretation that the institutes were used for their 'really useful' content, e.g. the late acquisition of skills of literacy. See for example Edward Royle, 'Mechanics Institutes and the Working Classes 1840-1860', *Historical Journal,* vol. 14 (1971), where it is shown that elementary classes teaching the three Rs were the most popular aspect.

6. *English Chartist Circular,* no. 37, p. 145.

7. 'Heddekashun' was defined in Cobbett, *Cottage Economy* (London, 1850), p. 4.

8. For a similar argument see Yeo, 'Robert Owen and Radical Culture', in Pollard and Salt, *Robert Owen: Prophet of the Poor,* p. 108, note 2.

9. G.J. Holyoake, *Sixty Years of an Agitator's Life* (London, 1892), vol. 1, p. 4.

10. [Thomas Wright], *The Great Unwashed by a Journeyman Engineer* (1868; reprinted Cass, London, 1970), p. 7.

11. For this distrust see Richard Johnson, 'Educational Policy and Social Control in Early-Victorian England', *Past and Present,* no. 49 (1970), p. 114.

12. See for example, David Jones, *Chartism and the Chartists* (Allen Lane, London, 1975), pp. 30, 25.

13. For example Gutteridge's desire for *Culpeper* — a standard work of botanical reference; or Cobbett's encounter with *A Tale of a Tub.*

14. F.M. Leventhall, *Respectable Radical: George Howell and Victorian Working Class Politics* (Weidenfeld & Nicolson, London, 1971), pp. 6-9.

15. Thompson, *Making of the English Working Class,* p. 674.

16. For the best account of the unstamped as, itself, a political force see Joel

H. Wiener, *The War of the Unstamped* (Cornell University Press, 1969); for the best account of radical ideology in this phase see Patricia Hollis, *The Pauper Press* (Oxford University Press, 1970).

17. For Cobbett see Thompson, *Making*, especially p. 749; for O'Connor see J.A. Epstein, 'Feargus O'Connor and the *Northern Star*', *International Review of Social History*, vol. 21 (1976), part 1, pp. 51-97.

18. Ibid., p. 79.

19. For lectures see *Northern Star*, 5 May 1838, 2 June 1838, 28 July 1839; for schoolmasters see 25 August 1838; for Dickens see 1838, *passim*.

20. E.g. *Northern Star*, 6 and 13 January, 10 and 31 March, 21 and 28 April 1838.

21. For a typical attack on this score see *Le Bonnet Rouge* (journal of the neo-Jacobin, Lorymer), 16 February 1833.

22. *Poor Man's Guardian*, 30 November 1833.

23. Ibid., 14 April 1832.

24. The most 'authoritative' source for Owenite theory was the *New Moral World*, the 'official' journal of the movement. But see J.F.C. Harrison, *Robert Owen and the Owenites in England and America* (Routledge & Kegan Paul, London, 1969).

25. For a fuller account see E. Halevy, *Thomas Hodgskin 1787-1869* (London, 1903); R. Pankhurst, *William Thompson (1777-1833): Britain's Pioneer Socialist, Feminist and Co-operator* (Watts, 1954). For their influence on working-class theory see Hollis, *Pauper Press* and Thompson, *Making*.

26. Jones, *Chartism and the Chartists*, p. 170.

27. *Poor Man's Guardian*, 23 February 1833.

28. *English Chartist Circular*, nos. 22 and 27.

29. Epstein, 'Feargus O'Connor and the *Northern Star*', p. 69, for a discussion of various estimates.

30. E.g. at Benjamin Heywood's Miles Platting or at Crewe. See W.H. Chaloner, *The Social and Economic Development of Crewe 1780-1923* (Manchester University Press, 1950), pp. 233-4; Edith and Thomas Kelly (eds.), *A Schoolmaster's Notebook* (Manchester University Press, 1957), pp. 31-2.

31. See the maps of branches of the National Charter Association and the Land Plan in Jones, *Chartism and the Chartists*, for example.

32. This mutation is examined in Dan Finn, Neil Grant and Richard Johnson, 'Social democracy and the Education Crisis', in CCCS, *On Ideology* (Hutchinson, London, 1978).

33. *Black Dwarf*, 6 May 1818.

34. *Pioneer*, 21 June 1834. Senex was Shepherd Smith. See John Saville, 'J.E. Smith and the Owenite Movement' in S. Pollard and T. Salt (eds.), *Robert Owen: Prophet of the Poor* (Macmillan, London, 1971).

35. Lovett often put the case against state education; O'Brien the case for.

36. See also Thompson, *Making*, especially the discussion of Carlile and 'rationalism'.

37. *The Poor Man's Guardian* compared Cobbett's impracticalities with the enthusiasm with which the Co-operative Congress 'spoke of the formation of schools' (*Guardian*, 14 September 1833).

38. *Pioneer*, 7 and 21 December 1833.

39. Harrison, *Owen and Owenites*, p. 139. For the distinction between 'education', 'institutions' and 'writing and discourses' see William Thompson, *An Inquiry into the Principles and Distribution of Wealth* (Kelley, USA, 1970).

40. J. Collins and William Lovett, *Chartism, A New Organisation of the People* (reprinted Leicester University Press, 1969). There is a useful collection of cuttings and other materials on the scheme in the Lovett Collection, City of Birmingham

Reference Library.

41. This is not to deny the recurrent revivals of independent working-class education especially in the 1880s to 1920s. Nor is it to argue that there is nothing to be learnt from the radical experience. It could be said, indeed, that it is precisely the stress on education as an aspect of socialist politics that needs to be revived today. The inhibitions that remain are less material (though to be sure some exist) than ideological and political. They include, centrally, the obsession of British socialists with education of the most formal kind conducted through a system articulated through state or local state agencies. The exhaustion of this social democratic repertoire is very evident today.

1.3

BROADCASTING AND ADULT LEARNING IN THE UNITED KINGDOM, 1922-1982

John Robinson

Source: Copyright © The Open University 1983 (specially written for this volume).

The story of broadcasting in relation to adult learning — certainly in Britain over 60 years — has essentially been a development from simplicity to complexity. This is not to suggest, of course, that complexity is necessarily an improvement on simplicity; but in the case of broadcasting it has patently been both a beneficial and a quite remarkable progress.

The Main Elements in the Story

The development can be seen in all the central elements of the story and most notably in the following:

1. The changing concept of the body of adult learners.
2. The variety of purposes that broadcasting can serve in support of adult learning.
3. Variety of subject matter and particular content.
4. The blend of radio and television with other learning media in multimedia learning schemes.
5. Various forms of collaboration between broadcasting and the other adult learning agencies.
6. Both pragmatic and systematic forms of evaluation of the effectiveness of broadcasting in promoting adult learning.

These themes provide the central threads in the developing pattern of 60 years. They can generally be traced quite clearly, though sometimes they get lost in over-intricate design. It is worth keeping them in view together and noting how the pattern spreads and becomes more complex, as the concepts and the experience, the evidence and the technologies all move forward — till eventually we reach the 1980s. The situation then becomes so complex that it presents us with an entirely new range of challenges.[1]

The 1920s and 1930s

When the British Broadcasting Company was formed, in October 1922, and began broadcasting four weeks later, the body of adult learners appeared to be clear and simple. It was that committed minority of individuals who on their own initiative would seek to extend their knowledge and understanding, for their own benefit, for their immediate social class, and in many cases for the community as a whole. It was this minority which had been the main concern of the university extension and tutorial movements, of the Workers' Educational Association and the Educational Settlements Association, of Co-operative Education and the development of public libraries. The famous report of the Adult Education Committee of the Ministry of Reconstruction in 1919 had made an impressive appeal for adult education for all; but its practical considerations had had to concentrate on the same committed minority.[2]

Clearly this minority was of great importance. It provided the new cultural leaven in a dangerously doughish community and the new leadership in a broadening democracy. In both respects it was needed through all classes of society, but especially among the manual working classes, who had been educationally and culturally deprived throughout the country's history.

The adult education movement was seeking to strengthen this committed minority; and broadcasting was seen by most educationists as a valuable ally in this work. It could also help to extend the size of the minority. For one thing, many potential adult students found it difficult to attend regular evening classes, because of their working hours or their home location or even for financial reasons. The wireless could be a major boon to such people, bringing the lecturer or tutor to their very firesides. Some adult tutors saw this as unwelcome competition; but most had enough imagination to see it as a valuable extension of their work.

This initial concept of the contributions of broadcasting inevitably brought a didactic purpose to its provision; and this coloured all the early 'educational talks'. It was accompanied by an apparent assumption of widespread thirst for the quaint and the curious in the pursuit of knowledge. So the earliest talks during the first months of

1923 covered such topics as *How to catch a Tiger, The Discoveries in Egypt, The Ordainment of a Buddhist Priest* and *The Deathwatch Beetle*.

The appreciative response to these talks, both from listeners in letters to the *Radio Times* (which also began in 1923) and from adult educators in various articles, appeared to confirm the good sense of this approach. There were repeated references to 'people in rural areas', 'shiftworkers', 'women tied to the home' and other groups 'cut off from normal provision'; and to the benefits that wireless could bring to them.

This view was reinforced in 1924, when J.C. Stobart, a senior member of HM Inspectorate, was seconded to the BBC at John Reith's request to become Director of Education for the Company. He outlined his views about 'the adult student' in an article in *Radio Times* headed 'A Broadcasting University'.[3] It was also Stobart who first made it clear that broadcasting was not enough on its own; that the talks should be supported by written material specially prepared; that co-operation was needed with the public libraries and with the teaching bodies in adult education; and that broadcasting could work effectively with these other agencies. So the idea of collaboration developed early: collaboration for a committed body of adult students.

As broadcasting grew in confidence during the 1920s, it gradually became clear that it was able to interest a much larger cross-section of the adult population than had been attracted to more formal provision. It was not reaching them in the same depth and continuity of commitment; but it was stimulating scores of new interests among hundreds of thousands of uncommitted listeners, who began to discover the pleasures of good writing and good music, of social history and world geography, of science and politics, religious thought and philosophy, even of economics and industrial affairs.

By 1927, when the BBC and the British Institute of Adult Education appointed a Joint Committee under Sir Henry Hadow to make recommendations for the future of adult education through broadcasting, the power to extend the total body of adult learners was seen as one of their great responsibilities.[4] Unfortunately, perhaps, the Committee was equally preoccupied with the parallel need for two-way communication; and so they attached particular importance to the formation of wireless discussion groups. This became a central issue of policy and led to the appointment of a Central Council for Broadcast Adult Education, a plan for the creation of 14 Area

Councils (only four of which were in fact created), the production of special talks series for group discussion, e.g. *Modern Britain in the Making* and *The Changing World*, and the appointment of five BBC Regional Education Officers, to encourage the formation of groups. These appointments were all made in 1928; the Central Council lasted for five years; and the Education Officers began a chequered but unbroken tradition. The policy responsibility was divided in 1936 between a Talks Advisory Committee and a Central Committee for Group Listening, and seven Area Councils were appointed to cover the country.

Thus a formal structure of collaboration was established; but it operated almost exclusively with the 500-800 wireless discussion groups, as their numbers fluctuated from year to year. Thus, while the BBC's Listener Research Department (created in 1935) estimated the regular audiences for these talks series at around 5 million listeners, the number attending the discussion groups was never more than 20,000 in any one year. It was not only a minute proportion of the listening audience for these talks; it represented no more than 10 per cent of the numbers attending formal adult education. So, despite the first emphasis of the Hadow Committee's Report, collaboration was in fact being concentrated on a very small minority of listeners. It was to be another 12 to 15 years before many adult educators, both inside and outside broadcasting, began to take any systematic interest in the immensely larger home listening audience.

Two other results of the Hadow Committee's recommendations should be mentioned at this stage. One was the creation of an educational broadcasting journal, which led directly to the establishment of *The Listener*. This began production in January 1929 and has certainly made its contribution to adult learning. The other was the support given to political controversy in broadcasting, which helped Sir John Reith to persuade the Government to lift its formal ban on controversy.

The War Years and After

By the early years of the Second World War a number of adult educationists already saw the main value of broadcasting in extending the understanding of the whole listening audience — both service and civilian, at home and overseas. So Professor Julian Huxley and

Dr C.E.M. Joad, who had both been active for years in adult education, joined the team of *The Brains Trust* at the beginning of 1941; other adult education broadcasters, such as Vernon Bartlett, Harold Nicolson and Sir William Beveridge, became regular speakers in both the Home Service and the Forces Programme; W.E. Williams, Secretary of the British Institute of Adult Education, became Director of the Army Bureau of Current Affairs and co-operated energetically in special talks series for the Forces; J.H. Nicholson, as Chairman of the Central Committee for Group Listening, did a great deal to encourage group listening in the Forces, with the help of such lively series as *To Start You Talking* and *The World We Want*; and Dobson and Young, two Forces lecturers, became two of the most popular presenters of music on radio.

So during the war years the adult education tradition and the 20-year experience of broadcast talks gradually flowed together in a remarkable way. And the audiences for the programmes that resulted — *The Brains Trust, The World Goes By, In Britain Now, Music With a Smile, We Speak for Ourselves,* the Sunday evening *Postscripts* and many more — regularly exceeded 10 million listeners. Their educative influence was quite simply immense.

In addition to this widespread educative influence, there were vigorous and repeated efforts to make special provision for the armed services, both in Britain and overseas. The provision for the troops abroad was the responsibility of the BBC Overseas Service and included such popular series as *Over to You* and *Radio Newsreel.* The provision for the troops in Britain began with efforts to encourage group listening, largely through the co-operation of the BBC education officers with command and unit education officers. This was successful in a few pockets of the country, but in general it was a failure. It then occurred to many observers that special programmes during training hours might well prove more successful. From 1941, two half-hourly programme slots each week, on Tuesday afternoon and Thursday afternoon, were devoted to current affairs talks and series broadcast specially for the Services audience, under the title of *Radio Reconnaissance.* In September 1945, these were replaced by more extensive Forces Educational Broadcasts (six hours each week, planned on a wide curriculum, including English, science, languages, social history, economics and world affairs), a direct response to a War Office request for the BBC to help with education for demobilisation.[5] The broadcasts continued on a smaller scale from 1947 to 1952.

By 1952 the BBC was ready to launch an entirely new service of further education broadcasts, addressed to a widespread and varied home listening audience and not to any specialised audience. This provision was the result of a series of studies conducted between 1949 and 1951. In the course of two years, 14 detailed studies were carried out with various audience groups and programme elements, involving some 20,000 people in all, drawn from existing organisations or from population sampling. There were three main conclusions:

1. That many audiences with common interests, e.g. age, sex, occupation, leisure interests, were already well served by existing programmes.
2. That there was a case for a limited provision of special series for special audiences, e.g. occupational groups at a particular level of work and the young adult audience.
3. That there was a stronger case for a wide range of special series for audiences whose only common feature might be their interest in the subject chosen and their general level of understanding of spoken communication; and such audiences would best be reached as individual listeners at home and not through organised groups.

The new series began in the autumn of 1952 and continued with many similar features until well into the 1970s. They included series in history, science, literature, social studies and current affairs, for several years carrying the title of *The Wednesday Series* and generally supported by substantial pamphlets or textbooks; a limited number of modern language series, e.g. *En Voyage, Gute Reise,* with textbooks growing more substantial year by year; *The Younger Generation, Parents and Children* and *Talking About Music.*

And these developments were taking place while radio generally was enjoying perhaps its greatest days, with features such as *The Face of Violence* and *Under Milk Wood,* radio drama in *World Theatre* and *Stars in their Choices,* talks ranging from *The Reith Lectures* to *Any Questions?* and radio comedy in *Take It From Here, Hancock's Half Hour* and *The Goon Show.*

Meanwhile, television had entered the broadcasting scene. It had entered the London scene as early as 1936, but had still been limited to 25,000 homes around London when the service was suspended at the outbreak of war. The service resumed in 1947, but again for London and the Home Counties only; and it was not until the early

1950s that transmission was anything like nationwide. Even then the viewers were comparatively few, in relation to the multitude of radio listeners, with no more than 3.5 million television-licensed homes compared with 13.5 million radio-licensed homes, as late as 1954. But television was already making an important contribution to greater awareness and to popular enjoyment of a wide range of national events. The last field reached a new high level with the impressive coverage of the Queen's Coronation in 1953.

The early 1950s were also the period of the campaign for commercial television, which achieved success in 1954 with the passing of the Television Act. Independent Television had its opening night in September 1955; and it was soon clear that the broadcasting scene would never look the same again, however much Broadcasting House sought to keep it so.

The Years of Competition and Expansion

Just as complexity is not necessarily an improvement on simplicity, so competition does not necessarily mean expansion. Very often it leads to contraction; and that is what happened in British television, for several years, as far as breadth of choice was concerned. Both the BBC and the Independent Television companies were so concerned about capturing the popular audience (despite occasional protestations to the contrary), that they actually reduced the range of choice in programmes, though the hours of transmission roughly doubled. The educative potential of the medium was attenuated — in spite of some outstanding exceptions to the general fare, such as challenging documentaries from Granada and Associated Rediffusion, notable series in science, natural history and current affairs from the BBC, experimental drama in both channels, and the BBC's new-style television journalism in *Tonight*. More direct educational purposes stood no chance of acceptance at all.

Radio, meanwhile, had declined dramatically from its greatest period to one of mediocrity, with audiences falling, very few new ideas, no sense of adventure and a desperate need for new blood in its veins. Unhappily, one of the few decisive measures taken had a direct and crippling effect on the further education series — at the very time when they needed nurturing and supporting. This was the decision to take the first hour and a half of Third Programme time each evening and convert it into a network for minorities, to be known as Network

Three. If there was one way to ensure that minorities remained minorities, this was it; so what may have looked like special concern for minority interests was in fact a way of ensuring that they remained in a ghetto. Since further education was deemed to be one of the minorities, along with chess, dog-training and archaeology, all the series were transferred from the Home Service and the Light Programme and their audiences were decimated overnight — from around a million to less than 100,000. The transfer was fought every inch of the way by John Scupham, then Head of Educational Broadcasting, and by Jean Rowntree, Head of Further Education; and the Director-General, Sir Ian Jacob, was told in no uncertain terms, at a conference convened to explain the changes, what educationists thought of the new arrangements.

So, despite all the efforts of the BBC's educational staff, the educational prospects in relation to both media looked less promising than they had ever done before and relations with other educational bodies had reached their lowest ebb.

It was seven years, a director-general and a major broadcasting report later, before healthy growth really developed again, after the introduction of commercial television. The Director-General was Hugh Carleton-Greene at the BBC and the report was the Pilkington Report on Broadcasting.[6] Both had a major part to play in releasing new energies into programmes in general and in finding new resources for directly educational programmes. Hugh Carleton-Greene became Director-General in January 1960 and the Pilkington Report was published in September 1962, followed by an admirably speedy White Paper in October 1962. Their joint influence on programme development could be seen in television in many ways; in drama series such as the Shakespeare histories, *An Age of Kings* and *The Wars of the Roses*, the development of *The Wednesday Play* and *Armchair Theatre*; a new style of contemporary popular drama in *Z Cars*, *Maigret* and other new series; arts features by Ken Russell and John Schlesinger; documentaries such as Richard Cawston's *Television and the World* and Dennis Mitchell's programmes on Africa; a new dynamism in news and current affairs; the Saturday night satire programmes; comedy of the quality of *The Life of Hancock* and *Steptoe and Son*; and the whole new dimension of BBC-2 programme planning. These were to be followed within a few years by *The Forsyte Saga, Upstairs Downstairs, The Great War, Cathie Come Home* and *Civilisation*. An expansion both of choice and of quality was now quite evident.

Meanwhile, the new resources for educational programmes were the result of a clause in the White Paper which allowed both BBC and Independent Television to increase their transmission hours — over the existing limit of 50 hours per week — for the purposes of 'educational programmes for adults'. This meant that a definition must be agreed for such programmes and that advisory bodies would need to be appointed, to make recommendations to the Postmaster-General on the observance of this definition. This was the origin of the celebrated defining clause, which was composed by John Scupham in consultation with BBC and ITA management and with representatives of the adult education bodies. The definition read as follows:

Educational television programmes for adults are programmes (other than school broadcasts) arranged in series and planned in consultation with appropriate educational bodies to help viewers towards a progressive mastery or understanding of some skill or body of knowledge.

Both the BBC and the commercial companies (the latter strongly supported by the ITA), responded speedily to the new dispensation. Production staff and resources were allocated to the new provision and both organisations appointed advisory committees, in consultation with the principal adult education bodies. The ITA was in fact able to announce the start of its adult education service in January 1963, for an hour each Sunday morning, under the title of *Sunday Session*. The service started with three series of ten 20-minute programmes, *You Don't Say*, a course in spoken English, *Pen to Paper*, a course in written English, and *Mesdames, Messieurs*, a course in conversational French. The BBC introduced its service in the following October, with $E = Mc^2$, an introduction to relativity, *The Science of Life*, human biology, *Parliamo Italiano*, Italian for beginners, *Ten Modern Painters*, *Dressmaking for Beginners* and *Keeping Fit*. Six months later BBC-2 began and Tuesday evening was devoted almost entirely to professional education, with series for maths teachers, for industrial managers and trade union officials, for engineers and students of politics, all under the title of *Tuesday Term*. Within a year the specialist evening was changed to a pattern of programmes spread across the week; but the volume and range of content was in no way reduced.

The response to all this new provision, in audience figures, in sales of booklets and in correspondence back to the programmes was most encouraging. Clearly television education was reaching a varied audience of several million people: much larger than the total student body in adult education classes.

Further education by radio was also allowed to expand and it did so with notable enthusiasm. For the most part it remained within the third network, but its time was extended to one hour each evening, Monday to Friday, which enabled it to introduce a wider range of series, such as *Man and his Environment, The Elizabethan Nation, Colour in Britain* and *The Novel Today*, to increase the modern language series and the arts series, and to introduce a number of directly vocational series, particularly for business and office workers. The publications for some of these series became a great deal more substantial. In addition, the Ministry of Education invited the BBC to provide special help for married women teachers willing to return to teaching after the early years of bringing up children. BBC radio allocated three afternoon periods each week in the Home Service, under the title of *A Second Start*, and the response in audiences and in correspondence was again encouraging.

The expansion in provision was increasingly supported by expansion in the organised use and follow-up activity arranged by a variety of adult educators, from industrial trainers to the wardens of mid-week and weekend colleges. Study groups were organised all over the country for many of the new series; the use of the language series in language classes in evening centres substantially increased; there was an increase in broadcast use in both technical courses and general studies in further education colleges; and the arrangement of follow-up courses in the short-term residential colleges brought hundreds of new faces into organised adult learning. The old idea of the committed minority was being extended in a score of new directions.

There was also a significant development in the study of this varied body of potential learners. The BBC appointed a small team of further education officers and one of the first tasks entrusted to them was to conduct a survey of adult needs and interests, by wide consultation throughout the community. Soon afterwards the ITA conducted a questionnaire enquiry based on population sampling and this effectively complemented the BBC survey. Both revealed strongly the extent of practical and functional interests among the adult community, as opposed to 'academic' and 'subject' interests, and gave a new direction to the planning of provision.

These surveys added useful evidence to the systematic studies of researchers such as Joseph Trenaman and William Belson, whose work remains among the most valuable in this field.[7] None of it has pointed to any clear differences between those learning through broadcasting and those learning through traditional classes. Opportunity and convenience seem always to have been the main factors.

Clearly the whole of this expansion owed a great deal to the Pilkington Report. That Report may indeed be seen in retrospect as a major reinjection of community concern within the whole function of broadcasting. And this was a concern for the community as a complex and diversified aggregate of minorities' interests, not as an undiscriminating 'admass'. After the introduction of commercial television, broadcasting could have been dragged along a far less responsible course. It was the great contribution of the Pilkington Report that this did not happen.

Three other developments were of great importance during the expansive 1960s. One was the beginning of local radio, with twelve BBC local stations by 1970 and twenty by 1971. Each had a specialist educational producer on its staff and most also appointed an educational advisory panel. Since each was committed to a major concern with adult education and depended for this largely on the provision in the locality, each station became a new 'shop-window' for a wide range of adult learning activities and an opportunity for contact with a new body of learners for some hundreds of adult educators.[8]

The second development was the rapid spread of closed-circuit radio and television, both in local education authority areas, for example, Inner London, Glasgow and Plymouth, and in many universities and colleges of higher education. This meant, among other things, that hundreds more adult educators had their first regular involvement in education through the broadcast media, usually in co-operation with professional broadcasting staff who had moved across from the BBC and ITV.[9]

The third development was the emergence of the Open University from the long discussions about a University of the Air. This development included as central elements the political entrusting of the project by Harold Wilson to the redoubtable Jennie Lee, her long-lasting struggles with both the politicians and the educationists, the eventual appointment of the Open University Planning Committee, under the chairmanship of Sir Peter Venables, in September 1967, and the acceptance of the Committee's Report by the Wilson Government in 1969.[10] Perhaps the most important features for the present account were the clear acceptance of the value of radio and television as essential elements in the proposed multimedia learning system, the formal partnership between a national university and a national broadcasting organisation, and the working concept of a multi-skilled course team for each course, to make this co-operation a practical reality.

The 1970s and 1980s

In addition to the impressive development of the Open University, there were major advances during the 1970s in all the main elements of broadcasting and adult learning outlined at the beginning of this chapter. They could be seen clearly at work in the campaign for adult literacy, which developed during the middle years of the decade. No need could be more different from those of the articulate minority than the need of people who had been concealing for years a deep sense of educational inadequacy. The campaign also illustrated the variety of purpose to be served, for the one thing that delayed its proposal within the BBC was the recognition that television and radio could not teach people to read and write; and it was only when the purpose of motivating non-readers, of building their confidence and putting them in touch with local provision was formulated that the project seemed to have a future.

That meant seeking the collaboration of the adult education services in every locality; and this was done though a series of consultative meetings throughout the country. To the eternal credit of the local services, every one responded in a positive way; the BBC's Further Education Advisory Council gave strong support to the broadcasting project; and the Department of Education gave support to local tuition with a three-year grant of a million pounds a year and the creation of an Adult Literacy Resource Agency. The BBC set up a telephone referral service, with the financial help of the Ford Foundation, and the first programmes were transmitted in the autumn of 1975, under the now familiar title of *On the Move.*[11]

The literacy project, though it achieved the widest recognition, was not the only project to demonstrate the important advances of this decade. They were also illustrated in two radio courses linked with local study groups, *Living Decisions* and *What Right Have You Got?*, which sought to reach people who would not naturally think of themselves as students but were willing to commit themselves to some practical social learning, and which relied strongly on local group support. They were illustrated in *Trade Union Studies*, in which the BBC co-operated with the TUC Education Department and the WEA in seeking to reach members of trade unions through their interest in union activity and extend their understanding of its constructive role in the life of the country. They could be seen in Yorkshire Television's project, *Make It Count*, which sought to do something comparable to the literacy campaign in the important area of adult numeracy, with the particular co-operation of the National Extension College. There were also the short community education courses prepared by the Open University in addition to its degree courses, for example *The Pre-school Child*, in collaboration with the Pre-school Playgroups Association, and *Consumer Decisions* with the Consumers' Association. There were regular programmes in community and access television, such as *Open Door* and *Help*. There were the special series for ethnic minority groups, *Parosi* and *Speak for Yourself*, and also for the host community, such as Thames Television's *Our People*. There were projects such as *Contact* for the physically handicapped and *Let's Go* for the mentally handicapped. There were projects for the young unemployed, such as Westward Television's *Just the Job*, and for the over-60s, such as the BBC's *60, 70, 80 Show*. And there were scores of programmes in local radio in all these areas of special need and interest. By the later 1970s the pattern of educational programmes was quite transformed from the way it had looked even ten years before.

Many of these projects had been strongly influenced by the recommendations of the Russell Committee on Adult Education in 1973 and of the Alexander Committee in Scotland the following year,[12] but it should be said in fairness that they also developed from a strong tradition of social concern within broadcasting which was already producing recommendations of this kind, with the aid of the broadcasting advisory committees. There was, of course, a constant exchange of ideas; and the practical outcome was to be a rich harvest of adult education fortified by social concern..

So we come to the 1980s. The social challenges of the 1970s are now immensely complicated by technological challenges. Already we have Channel 4 in television, with a strong commitment to adult education. This is a major extension of opportunity; and it is clear that the opportunity is being vigorously seized. What should be the response of the other broadcasting channels — not forgetting local radio? What should be the response of the other learning agencies? What should be the response of both broadcasting and the other agencies to the possibilities opened up by the new technologies of audio and video recording, of television programmes on disc like LP records, of the possible choice of a hundred channels of programmes through cable or fibre-optic systems, of international exchanges through satellite broadcasting? Can we ensure that these new technologies are used to provide greater learning opportunities for all and not to open up further gaps between the 'haves' and the 'have nots' in knowledge and culture?

Having come so far in enlarging the scope and availability of adult learning, it is surely of the first importance that we should not go back to allowing exclusive minorities to monopolise the learning opportunities, but should make it our prime concern to see that the benefits of the new technologies are universally shared. That will only happen through our determined efforts.

Notes

1. J. Robinson, *Learning Over the Air* (BBC, London, 1982).
2. *The 1919 Report* (University of Nottingham, 1980). Reprinted with introductory essays.
3. *The Radio Times*, 13 June 1924 (BBC, London, 1924).
4. *New Ventures in Broadcasting* (BBC, London, 1928).
5. N. Luker, 'Forces Educational Broadcasting', *Adult Education* (British Institute of Adult Education, London, 1926), vol. 18, p. 163.
6. *Report* of the Committee on Broadcasting (HMSO, London, 1962).
7. J.M. Trenaman, *Attitudes to Opportunities for Further Education* (B. Litt. thesis, Oxford University, 1957); J.M. Trenaman in E. Hutchinson (ed.), *Communication and Comprehension* (Longman, London, 1967); W.A. Belson, *The Impact of Television* (Crosby Lockwood, London, 1967).
8. P. Baynes and D. Smith, 'Spanish on Local Radio', *Adult Education*, vol. 42 (1969), p. 226; A. Langford, 'Opportunities in Local Radio', vol. 41 (1968), p. 90; R. Shaw, 'Extra-mural Work with Local Radio', *Adult Education*, vol. 43 (1970), p. 102 (National Institute of Adult Education, London).
9. *Educational Television and Radio in Britain* (BBC, London, 1966).
10. W. Perry, *The Open University* (Open University Press, Milton Keynes, 1976).
11. D. Hargreaves, *Adult Literacy and Broadcasting* (Frances Pinter, London, 1980); H.A. Jones and A.H. Charnley, *Adult Literacy: A Study of its Impact* (National Institute of Adult Education, Leicester, 1978).
12. *Adult Education: A Plan for Development* (HMSO, London, 1973); *Adult Education: The Challenge of Change* (HMSO, London, 1975).

Part 2

ORGANISATION

The four chapters in this part of the Reader are intended to provide an overall perspective of the structure and organisation of education for adults in the United Kingdom at the beginning of the 1980s. As all four chapters indicate in their different ways, this is not an easy task, since there is no common, coherent, centralised 'system' of educational provision for adults in this country. Rather there are a number of overlapping systems, involving many organisations directly or indirectly in a great variety of roles.

The first three chapters deal with organisation in England and Wales, Scotland and Northern Ireland respectively. Arthur Stock's opening chapter introduces the main institutions involved — the local education authorities, the universities, voluntary organisations, distance education institutions, other private sector providers, informal educational providers, central government departments. These include some which have the education of adults as their sole or primary aim, and others whose interest in education (as opposed to, for example, entertainment or directly vocational training) is to them fairly minor, though still significant in the context of overall provision.

The chapters by John Horobin and Gordon Macintyre indicate that the structure, terminology and underlying philosophy of educational provision for adults is in some ways quite different in other parts of the United Kingdom, though many of the same institutions are involved. In both Scotland and Northern Ireland a considerable, but differing, emphasis is placed on the idea of community education (which is also dealt with in part of the accompanying Reader); and, because of the existence of a further tier of governmental responsibility, the pattern of organisation is more hierarchical.

The chapter by Keith Percy and his collaborators is based on an extensive survey of provision in one region of England. It presents a summary view of how the wide range of organised educational opportunities available to adults in that region appears to the potential participant; and indicates the overall level of response to them and the barriers preventing an increased response. This chapter gives an interesting picture of the inter-relationships, financial and otherwise, between the different providers, indicating the central role in the provision of education for adults currently held by the local education authorities and the Manpower Services Commission.

2.1

THE ORGANISATION OF EDUCATION FOR ADULTS IN ENGLAND AND WALES

Arthur Stock

Source: Copyright © The Open University 1983 (specially written for this volume).

Introduction

This brief essay is presented primarily from the perspective of the *provision* of education for adults. Adult education in England and Wales is essentially pluralistic, reflecting in many respects the society it serves. Whilst having the advantages of diversity and flexibility, the structure may appear confusing and arbitrary to the user or potential student. Indeed, in this latter respect much stress[1] has been laid in recent years on the need for information and guidance to enable fuller use of the range of services by a wider profile of the population, and to encourage more informed choice of and demand for appropriate educational experiences.

Traditionally, the organisation of education for adults is seen as a *partnership*. The involvement of local authorities, universities and voluntary agencies in the provision, under the benign leadership and support of central government, was the ideal projection promulgated in the famous 1919 Report[2] on Adult Education commissioned by the Ministry of Reconstruction as part of the planning for a better Britain following the First World War. Although elements of this Report were implemented between the wars — particularly in respect of the extra-mural work of the universities — the majority of its recommendations still awaited recognition and endorsement by central government at the beginning of the Second World War.

However, during that conflict the survival needs of the nation stimulated a great variety of adult educational activity; and it is likely that organised adult education was perceived by government for the first time as a significant 'service' (rather than merely a 'movement'). In any event, the great 1944 Education Act (England and Wales) steered through Parliament by Mr R.A. Butler as part of the necessary reforms of post-war Britain, contained several sections of major significance for the development of public education for adults.

The very first paragraph of the new Act established the responsibility of Government for the education of the population of all ages (not merely children), and devolved the organisation of this responsibility upon the local authorities.

> It shall be lawful for his Majesty to appoint a Minister ... whose duty it shall be to promote the education of the people of England and Wales and the progressive development of institutions devoted to that purpose, and to secure the effective execution by local authorities, under his control and direction, of the national policy for providing a varied and comprehensive educational service in every area.

That there should be a specific post-school responsibility — indeed a specific sector — was spelt out in Section 7 of the Act as follows:

> The statutory system of public education shall be organised in three progressive states to be known as primary education, secondary education and further education; and it shall be the duty of the local education authority for every area, so far as their powers extend, to contribute towards the spiritual, moral, mental and physical development of the community by securing that efficient education throughout those stages shall be available to meet the needs of the population of their area.

Note that this Section refers in some detail to the curricular range of provision (spiritual, moral, mental and physical development) required *at all ages*, and reinforces this comprehensive perspective by referring to 'community' and 'the population of their area'. These words, and other references in later Sections to the 'duty' which is laid upon local education authorities, are particularly significant in the light of current debates about whether LEAs have *duties* or merely *powers* in respect of the provision of education for adults.[3]

There are three more Sections of the 1944 Act (which, in spite of several minor or amending Education Acts in succeeding years, still stands) which are directly relevant to the structure and organisation of adult education, particularly to the *partnership* concept:

> 41. Subject as hereinafter provided, it shall be the duty of every local education authority to secure the provision for their area of

adequate facilities for further education, that is to say:

(a) Full-time and part-time education for persons over compulsory school age; and

(b) leisure-time occupation in such organised cultural training and recreative activities as are suited to their requirements, for any persons over compulsory school age who are able and willing to profit by the facilities provided for that purpose;

Provided that the provisions of this section shall not empower or require local education authorities to secure the provision of facilities for further education otherwise than in accordance with the schemes of further education or at county colleges.

Section 42, after laying down that local education authorities shall prepare and submit to the Minister for approval schemes of further education for their area, goes on:

42. (4) A local education authority shall, when preparing any scheme of further education, have regard to any facilities for further education provided for their area by universities, educational associations, and other bodies, and shall consult any such bodies as aforesaid and the local education authorities for adjacent areas ...

And Section 53 states:

53. (1) It shall be the duty of every local education authority to secure that the facilities for primary, secondary and further education provided for their area include adequate facilities for recreation and social and physical training, and for that purpose a local education authority, with the approval of the Minister, may establish, maintain and manage, or assist the establishment, maintenance, and management of camps, holiday classes, playing fields, play centres and other places (including playgrounds, gymnasiums, and swimming baths not appropriated to any school or college) ...

53. (2) A local education authority, in making arrangements for the provision of facilities or the organisation of activities under the powers conferred on them by the last foregoing subsection shall, in particular, have regard to the expediency of co-operating with any voluntary societies or bodies whose objects include the provision of facilities or the organisation of activities of a similar character.

In fact the Schemes of Further Education to which so much in Sections 41 and 42 relates, were never received from or approved for every local education authority. Moreover, even for those areas where submission and approval took place, the wholesale local government reorganisation of 1974, which reduced the number of local education authorities in England and Wales from 164 to 104, made nonsense of the Schemes as originally conceived; and as no further submission of Schemes has been required it could and has been argued that much of the public provision of further education not covered by other legislation is *ultra vires* (i.e. beyond the authorities' legal power). Nevertheless, the general pattern of local authorities 'securing the provision' by having '... regard to any facilities for further education for their area by universities, educational associations and other bodies' was implemented to a greater or lesser extent by the local education authorities.

The extent to which such organisational and partnership requirements should also extend to financial assistance by local authorities was never established; and in recent years, following the financial stringency imposed by central government, there has been a sharp cut-back in some local authority grants to voluntary organisations and university extra-mural department.

Specific Providers

Local Education Authorities

There are currently 96 local authorities in England and 8 in Wales exercising duties under the present Education Acts of Local Education Authorities (LEAs). The structure of their direct adult education provision varies greatly. Ideally, it should be the product of local needs-assessment and specifically designed provision. In practice, the pattern is frequently conditioned by historical traditions, the accidents of inherited buildings and institutions, the powerfully expressed beliefs of certain elected members or senior administrators, the local interpretation of national political and administrative fiats, reactions to local pressure groups and (more recently) the entrepreneurial capabilities of key organisers and professional adult educators.

For example, the fees per tutorial hour charged to local adult students during the 1981/2 academic year varied between 21 and 95 pence per hour with a mean of 51 pence per hour, and a median of 50 pence per hour. Many would argue that to have this degree of variation in the asking price for a similar educational product or experience — depending as it does on the accident of address of residence — is carrying local autonomy too far. Furthermore, the vast range in fees has contributed to the breakdown of inter-authority recoupment payments for students taking courses outside their authorities of residence. In turn, this has militated strongly against the freedom of movement and access for students to undertake courses of study wherever they deem appropriate and convenient.

In terms of the organisational and institutional forms involved in the direct LEA 'delivery' of education for adults, there are five major styles of operation:

1. Local Free-standing 'Area' Adult Education Centres, Colleges or Institutes. In this instance the institution for a defined area is designated specifically for the delivery of education services for adults and is staffed accordingly. There is usually a principal with a small number of full-time adult educators to assist in the programming, organisation, staffing, promotion and evaluation of the programmes. Increasingly it will have centrally situated full-time premises, often in buildings formerly used for other educational services, although it will certainly extensively use school premises during weekday evenings. Other 'out-centres' — parish halls, community centres, youth centres, may also be used. Allocation of space and time for university, WEA, other voluntary agency and possibly Open University usage is made by agreement with the respective organisations. When such centres develop a reasonable degree of student representation and involvement in the governance of the institution they qualify for membership of the Educational Centres Association, and there are currently some 155 institutions in ECA membership.[4]

2. Community Schools, Community Colleges, Village Colleges. In this organisational form a secondary school forms the structural nucleus for the attachment of additional provision for the organisation and specialist needs of adult education and also, on occasion, for the informal education of young people. Sometimes extensive 'leisure' facilities form part of the campus — sports hall, gymnasia, swimming pool, all-weather outdoor playing surfaces. The specifically 'adult' provision, whilst nominally being an additional responsibility of the head teacher, is often organised by an adult education/ community education head of department or tutor organiser. The administrative concept is to develop a multi-purpose campus, with the whole becoming more than the sum of the parts and having 'neighbourhood' contact with a local community.

3. Departments of Adult Studies, Adult Education or Community Education Departments of District Further Education Colleges. Again the administrative concept is to maximise the use of expensive plant and staff, to deploy the expertise and potential of a whole college for the education of adults whilst maintaining the traditional role of providing vocational education for young people in the 16-19 age range. As in the case of model 1, there is frequent use of school premises throughout the college's catchment area during the evening, and of other 'outcentres' as required. Specialist staff are engaged, with experience and qualifications related to education for adults, but other internal staff and 'outside' part-time tutors are also deployed as required.

4. Polytechnic and Institute of Higher Education 'Extension'. A fourth model may be identified having affinities to both the Further Education College model and to traditional university extra-mural provision, in that several public higher education institutions (such as polytechnics and institutes of higher education) are currently offering 'extension' courses for adults. These are often short-cycle updating or reorientation courses emanating from specific, often vocationally oriented, internal departments. In some instances an external public programme of general liberal academic education or of topical awareness public education is offered. Many polytechnics and institutes of higher education claim that they are, by their very nature, making a major contribution to the education of adults in that they have a much larger adult proportion amongst their enrolments on internal full-time and part-time courses than do the traditional universities. In the development of programmes specifically geared to the vocational, academic and cultural needs of adults they are certainly extending the range of opportunities available.

5. Residential Adult Education. Several LEAs, some in conjunction with others, operate short-term residential colleges where students can take up residence for periods from 2 to 20 days for concentrated periods of study. There are currently 27 such colleges operated by LEAs, with some half-dozen more of independent foundation receiving direct or indirect (e.g. student support) help from local authorities. Their development received great stimulus from the writings of Sir Richard Livingstone[5] who in turn was influenced by the experience of the nineteenth-century development of residential Folk High Schools in Scandinavia. In the late 1970s several local authorities closed their colleges as part of an effort to meet reduced budget demands. However, other authorities continue to see the colleges as important multi-purpose adjuncts of their total education service.

As well as these major institutional forms, LEAs also engage in other provision, often in collaboration with a department of central government or a voluntary agency. Thus, independent, experimental provision may be made through 'drop-in' centres (often set up in city centre shops), through Industrial Language Training Units (vocationally-oriented English as a Second Language for immigrant workers — paid for entirely out of Manpower Services Commission budgets), through Unemployment Centres (TUC and often MSC involvement), Prison Education (financed by the Home Office but with all the Prison Education Officers having a LEA collegiate base), Adult Training Centres — for the mentally handicapped (largely financed by the DHSS), long stay hospitals and other similar institutions (again financed by the DHSS). There is also increasing co-operation between LEA-employed adult educators and the professional health education specialists employed either by the local or regional hospital boards or by local authorities' social services departments.

The Universities

Many of the 34 English and Welsh universities (or university colleges) contribute to the education of adults by:

(a) accommodating full-time mature students on undergraduate and postgraduate degree courses;
(b) organising part-time or short full-time post-experience courses;
(c) promoting internally or externally part-time liberal education courses;
(d) organising part-time degree or diploma programmes at undergraduate or postgraduate levels;
(e) arranging full-time and part-time advanced diploma and higher degree courses in the subject of adult education.

However, in category (a) above the record of the universities is not brilliant as currently less than 20 per cent of home undergraduates beginning full-time degree courses are over the age of 21.

In respect of (d), the provision for part-time undergraduates is very limited with only 4,400 such students in 1979/80 (as compared to 11,600 part-time undergraduates in polytechnics and institutions of higher education) and 69,000 Open University undergraduates. By contrast, over 40 per cent of home postgraduate students were working part-time, some by research, others for taught higher degrees.[6]

Category (c) is the traditional mode of university provision for adults, dating back to 1873 when Cambridge University provided for a number of dons to travel to various parts of England to deliver public lectures of general cultural and liberal content. Although subject to many changes in organisational form and style, there is still a major commitment to public extra-mural provision by some 25 English and Welsh universities, which is recognised by the Department of Education and Science and the Welsh Office Education Department by direct grant of up to 75 per cent of the teaching costs of their public liberal education programmes. These university departments, together with the Workers' Educational Association Districts in England and Wales, and the Welsh Council of YMCAs, constitute the 'Responsible Bodies' as they are termed in the Further Education Regulations (1975). In addition these extra-mural departments also engage in 'extension education' often of a vocational or professional character, for example, short courses for management, trades unions, updating, reorientation. The remaining eight conventional universities not in receipt of direct grant for extra-mural work also contribute to the 'extension' or professional/continuing education of adults, with their programmes often being organised by an Extension Studies or Continuing Education or External Studies Department.

The majority of the liberal studies courses offered are in the arts and social sciences, with a minority in the sciences (and most of those in geology or biology). Most are provided on weekday evenings, and are conducted by academically qualified staff from internal university departments (about 40%), other higher education institutes (about 13%), from other professions or from amongst persons not in full employment. This liberal education programme currently enrols approximately a quarter of a million adults in England and Wales each year. There are currently twelve universities which provide for

the study of adult education as a discipline in itself (category (e)).
These, together with others in Scotland and Northern Ireland, and
with the Open University and research institutes such as the National
Institute of Adult Education, have formed the Standing Conference
of University Teaching and Research in the Education of Adults
(SCUTREA), to further the advancement of knowledge in this field.

In any consideration of the university contribution to adult education it is necessary to note the unique contribution made by the Open
University. This is the most 'adult' of all British universities, providing distance education courses leading to ordinary and honours
degrees. A growing range of post-experience and continuing
education courses is organised on a modular and shorter cycle basis.
The Open University has provided an enormous stimulus to the
whole range of education for adults not only by the development of a
judicious mixture of media, modes and methods in its teaching, but
also by the production of 'team written' teaching/learning units and
readers which are often models of resource at their various academic
levels. More specificially, the success of the Open University has
opened up novel perspectives on independent and open learning
which may well prove to be salutary for the further development of
continuing education forms and structures.

Voluntary Organisations

Today the Workers' Educational Association (WEA) is the leading
voluntary organisation specifically concerned with adult education,
and remains an essentially voluntary body with a relatively small
professional staff. It is, as it was designed to be, a 'bottom-up'
organisational structure, with the 900 branches forming the local
contact unit, these being federated into 21 Districts. Although the
branches are autonomous and self-governing so far as programme
formulation goes, the Districts are the employers of the full-time
tutor organisers under the direction of a full-time District Secretary.
Each District has the status of a Responsible Body and receives direct
grant from the Department of Education and Science or Welsh
Office Education Department accordingly. A National General
Secretary and a small headquarters staff are based in London, and
represent the whole Association in negotiations with central government and in links with other providers. It also publishes a biannual
newspaper and develops a range of teaching materials and resources.

WEA enrolments in England and Wales are currently around 150,000 per annum.

Besides the WEA, certain other voluntary organisations with a major interest in the education of adults also receive central government grants for the organisation of their educational programmes. These include the National Federation of Women's Institutes (NFWI), the National Union of Townswomen's Guilds (NUTG), the Marine Society (which subsumes the Seafarers' Educational Society and the College of the Sea), the National Council of YMCAs, and the Pre-Retirement Association. Others in receipt of small direct grants for development purposes are the Educational Centres Association and the National Association for Teachers of English as a Second Language. There is a much larger proportion of voluntary organisations which receives no regular direct grant but attracts local or central educational grants in respect of particular programmes or activities. Examples are the Gypsy Education Council, the Royal National Institute for the Blind and the National Federation of Voluntary Literacy Schemes.

Organisationally these voluntary bodies are very diverse. The larger women's organisations have county or district secretaries on a salaried basis as well as substantial headquarters staffs. The rural women's organisation (NFWI) also maintains a residential college (Denman College, near Abingdon). Other important national organisations with voluntary as well as professional staffing are the Trades Union Congress Education Department (with regional and national offices), the Co-operative Union (with branch, district and national structures and a residential college) and the National Federation of Community Associations.

In addition there are many informal, educative, special interest organisations such as the arts centres/societies, the sports and recreational bodies, the several social/supportive societies and groups, the organisations dealing with the multi-ethnic and multi-cultural nature of our society, and those engaged in attacking specific social inequalities or deprivation. All have a part to play; and increasingly the formal providers pay heed to their first hand knowledge and advice and seek to serve their interests.

A final category of voluntary organisations (but employing professional educators) worthy of mention are the Long Term Residential Colleges. In England and Wales there are eight of these: Ruskin, Woodbrooke, Fircroft, Hillcroft, Plater, Coleg Harlech and Northern College. Their major purpose is to provide opportunities for men and women with little or no formal education to undertake highly concentrated studies in applied social sciences and the liberal arts for periods of either one or two years. A range of certificates and diplomas is available, some of which are accepted as 'academic credit' equivalent to one year's initial undergraduate study at certain universities. Most colleges also organise highly focused short residential courses.

All receive direct grant from the Department of Education and Science on much the same basis as the voluntary colleges of education do for the training of teachers. Students accepted on their longer courses are entitled to mature student state bursaries for financial support during the period of their studies.

Although founded as a manifestation of the 'working-class movement' and its educational needs, they are increasingly perceived as second-chance organisations contributing a narrow (maximum 600 per annum) but alternative route either to higher education or to a significant career change.

Distance Education

This mode of provision, in its more primitive correspondence form, goes back almost to the inception of cheap postal services. Much of it (approximately half a million registered students per annum) is still in the hands of the private sector, particularly the many 'correspondence colleges'. Courses are provided, largely by print-on-paper at all levels of study.

Concern about the standards set by correspondence colleges — both educational and business standards — led to the establishment in 1969 of the Council for the Accreditation of Correspondence Colleges. Originally a 'trade' organisation, it is now recognised by the Department of Education and Science and the Welsh Office Education Department, and has five of its council members nominated by the Secretaries of State and receives a small grant for its administrative work.

During the last five decades the purely correspondence medium of instruction has been supplemented — but not entirely superseded — by the broadcasting media of radio and television. There is a requirement in law that all licensed broadcasting organisations in the United Kingdom should 'educate' as well as 'inform' and 'entertain'. Policy and programming to meet this objective is constitutionally built into the British Broadcasting Corporation's charter; and educational requirements, both in terms of time quotas and quality of production, also appear in the franchise arrangements of commercial broadcasters and are monitored by the Independent Broadcasting Authority.

More recently there have been several educational initiatives which have been essentially multi-media in nature but have been massively stimulated and promoted by a broadcasting 'lead'. Such was the nature of the adult literacy campaign of the middle 1970s.[7] In this as in other multi-media distance education initiatives, the initial broadcasting impact is often critical and substantial but tends to be ephemeral. In the longer term, as in the Open University experience, the 'correspondence' element related to local study centre tutor-counselling and/or residential elements will be perceived as of major importance.

Another major contributor to innovation in distance education is the National Extension College (NEC) based in Cambridge. As well as conducting correspondence courses, NEC publishes study materials for other institutions to use and has also collaborated actively with several broadcasting organisations.

Other Private Sector Providers

Commercial colleges, management colleges, special professional colleges (from agriculture to aeronautics), foreign language centres and general 'examination' colleges (crammers) — all are to be found as private, profit-making educational providers in the United Kingdom. Only if public money is involved is there a requirement for inspection. Various company, trading and advertising laws apply to these enterprises; but none of these covers the educational content, curriculum, standards or procedures. The few studies which have been conducted suggest that the range of quality is very wide: from the best available anywhere to abysmal and appalling procedures which amount to confidence tricks. In mitigation of this unfortunate state of affairs there was, until recently, a system of voluntary request for inspection by Her Majesty's Inspectors which could (if successful) lead to the title '... recognised by HMI as efficient'. This option has now been withdrawn by the Secretary of State as a cost-cutting move. Some self-monitoring bodies have been set up, sometimes attracting the support of a national institution (as in the case of the

English as a Foreign Language Schools in association with the British Council).

Informal Education for Adults

Teachers and even students in formal institutions of education often forget the marvellous educational resources which exist in the form of libraries, museums, art galleries, National Trust properties, National Parks and other taken-for-granted aspects of our cultural environment. It is often argued that these magnificent amenities which are easily accessible throughout the country — even in rural areas — should be deployed more systematically in the organised provision of education for adults.

To these informal, ubiquitous resources should be added the array of educative television and radio programmes (not merely those designated as educational), the local and community theatres, and the educative efforts of the recreation departments of many local authorities not themselves local education authorities (i.e. 'district' authorities, not designated as LEAs, but with responsibility for recreation and leisure facilities). Under this heading would also appear a large proportion of the activities of service and special interest voluntary bodies, e.g. clubs for the elderly, local units of St John Ambulance Brigade and Red Cross, many church organisations, amenity and conservation societies. These bodies tend to have structures and organisational forms different from the formal education providers. Professional adult educators have learned to identify the strengths and weaknesses of these community networks and amenities, make contacts as appropriate, and present their programmes accordingly.

Central Government Departments

Many of the major departments of central government now have programmes which can fairly be described as adult education, although in most cases they are not designated as such. Education or 'training' for adults is increasingly perceived as an essential dimension in national development efforts; sometimes mistakenly seen as a panacea for the ills of society. The Home Office, the Department of Employment, the Department of Health and Social Security, the

Department of the Environment, the Department of Industry and the Department of Energy, as well as the Department of Education and Science, all have major programmes with associated finance deployed in various ways towards the education of the public.

Several of these are of long standing, as in the Prison Department of the Home Office, where the commitment to the education of prisoners goes back over half a century. It could be fairly stated that Prison Education pioneered the early developments in adult literacy and basic education. The 1979 May Committee Report[8] indicated the need for much more investment in this aspect of the 'care and treatment' of prisoners. Organisationally speaking, the linkage between the prison education officers — crucial to the promotion and development of suitable programmes — and the 'outside' world of continuing education was much enhanced in the early 1970s by the collegiate attachment of every officer to a local college or centre. But in other respects the Home Office Prison Regulations sit rather uneasily alongside current notions of educational provision and environment, and several reforms are needed.[9]

The Home Office also contributes, through Section 11 of the Local Government Act 1966, to the amelioration of inner-urban deprivation and disadvantage. This has resulted in some excellent programmes in many cities.

The Department of Health and Social Security (DHSS) has for many years viewed sympathetically the needs of long stay patients in a variety of hospitals and institutions, and there has been a number of imaginative and innovatory joint appointments of adult educators to these institutions. The DHSS also funds the Health Education Council to engage in various direct public educational exercises, to support and inform the efforts of specifically designated health educators throughout the country, and to support the efforts of a variety of voluntary organisations with partly educational aims and procedures.

Perhaps the largest direct governmental impact on the education and training of adults is that channelled through the Manpower Services Commission (MSC) whose finances (£1.6 billion in the current financial year) emanate from the Department of Employment. MSC operate the Training Opportunities Scheme (TOPS) designed to retrain adults for new employment opportunities. In order to achieve a wider access to the scheme for those whose basic education is deemed inadequate MSC also operate a Preparatory Scheme (known as PRETOPS). Other specific programmes include

Wider Opportunities for Women, the Work Experience Programme and the Community Enterprise Programme. The largest current investment is in the Youth Opportunities Programme, designed to provide vocational training and related education for young people in the 16-19 age range. The recently published *New Training Initiative* indicates an enhanced commitment to the training of adults, although specific programme details and financial commitment have at the time of writing yet to appear.

In all these programme activities MSC contracts much of the work to LEA colleges of further education or other local authority institutions. In this respect, and in the case of the several other central government departmental programmes of adult education, there is a growing trend to directly influence the provision of the local authorities. The one Department unable to do this to the same extent is Education itself, as the central government component of finance for education is subsumed within the block grant to local authorities dispensed by the Department of the Environment under the terms of the Local Government, Planning and Land Act 1980. This education finance, although identifiable in global form at source, is not able to be 'earmarked' within the budget of each local authority. Consequently there is no guarantee that the respective education proportions of the grants to local government will be maintained at local level. It may thus be judged as no mere coincidence that central government places more of its specific 'educational' programme money in the Departments of State not so tied to the formulae of local government finance, thereby outflanking the traditional autonomy of local government to set its own educational objectives and levels of provision.

Servicing Bodies

In recognition of the need for a limited number of national servicing bodies for education, the Local Government, Planning and Land Act 1980 allows for the designation and grant aiding of certain organisations to carry out these functions. There are only four of these bodies at the present time; and three of them — the Further Education Staff College, the National Foundation for Educational Research and the National Institute of Adult Education may all be deemed to contribute to the education of adults, especially the last.

The Advisory Council for Adult and Continuing Education,[10] due to terminate its activities in October 1983, is appointed by the Secretary of State and has also contributed greatly to the necessary servicing and developmental function. Both the Russell Committee's Report on Adult Education in 1973[11] and the Venables Committee's Report on Continuing Education to the Open University in 1976[12] recommended the establishment of a Development Council to further the planning and reform of continuing education for adults. In the event the government of the day (i.e. in 1977) would only accept the formation of an advisory body without the necessary finance and staffing to institute new initiatives. Many would judge that some sort of developmental Agency will ultimately be necessary if the recommendations of the Advisory Council and its predecessor Committees are to be realised.

Notes

1. *Links to Learning*, Advisory Council for Adult and Continuing Education (ACACE, Leicester, 1979).
2. *The 1919 Report: The Final and Interim Reports of the Adult Education Committee of the Ministry of Reconstruction 1918-1919*, reprinted with introductory essays (Nottingham University, Dept. of Adult Education, 1980).
3. *The Legal Basis of Further Education: A Review*, N.B.W. Thompson, Chairman (Department of Education and Science, HMSO, 1981).
4. *The Year Book of Adult Education* (National Institute of Adult Education, Leicester, 1982-3).
5. R. Livingstone, *The Future in Education*, Current Problems Series, No. 6 (Cambridge University Press, 1941).
6. M. Tight, *Part-time Degree Level Study in the United Kingdom* (ACACE, Leicester, 1982)
7. *Adult Literacy: A Study of its Impact*, BBC/NIAE team report on adult literacy initiatives in England and Wales, 1975-7 (London, 1978).
8. *Committee of Enquiry into the United Kingdom Prison Services*, Sir John Douglas May, Chairman (Home Office, Cmnd 7673, 1979).
9. W.P. Forśter, *Prison Education in England and Wales* (ACACE, Leicester, 1981).
10. *Continuing Education: From Policies to Practice. A Report on the Future Development of a System of Continuing Education for Adults in England and Wales* (ACACE, Leicester, 1982).
11. *Adult Education: A Plan for Development*, Sir Lionel Russell, Chairman (Department of Education and Science, HMSO, London, 1973).
12. *Committee on Continuing Education: A Report*, Sir Peter Venables, Chairman (Open University Press, Milton Keynes, 1976).

THE EDUCATION OF ADULTS IN SCOTLAND

John Horobin

Source: Copyright © The Open University 1983 (specially written for this volume).

This article reviews the structure and organisation of education for adults in Scotland, concentrating on those areas where the arrangements differ from the rest of the United Kingdom. These differences occur because education, like the law and the church, has developed quite separately in Scotland.

Young Scots have traditionally enjoyed greater opportunities to proceed to higher education in Scotland than the same age group in the rest of the United Kingdom. There are more university places per head of the Scottish population and there has been a longer tradition of school education in Scotland coupled with relatively easy access to the Scottish universities. In the eighteenth century many university classes were open to the general public and lectures were often given at 7.00 p.m. for the convenience of workers. While such openness of the lecture rooms was partly based on a conviction that the Scottish people had a right to benefit from their universities, another cause was that the university staff received low stipends and were accustomed to supplement their incomes from students' fees.

This practice continued in the nineteenth century although those adults attending were drawn increasingly from the middle classes. Specific provision for women was introduced and university staff began to undertake lectures extra-murally. By 1887 all the Scottish universities had established programmes of extension lectures, but they lasted only for a few years and did not develop in the same way as similar programmes south of the border. The reasons for this are unclear, but the essentially popular nature of the Scottish educational institutions and the greater access that the people of Scotland had to university, technical and secondary education undoubtedly contributed to the lack of demand for an extension movement.

It is understandable, therefore, that the 1924 Adult Education Regulations did not apply to Scotland. They gave a great incentive to adult education provision south of the border, and provided exchequer grants to universities and voluntary bodies acting in adult education. In Scotland the Education Authorities remained solely responsible and although they were empowered to provide adult education classes they saw their main area of work to be in the provision of vocational classes for adolescents. Despite encouragement by the Scottish Education Department to widen their provision, the adult education service did not begin to develop until the 1934 Education (Scotland) Regulations empowered Education Authorities to co-operate with voluntary organisations, and defined a range of liberal education provision for those over 18 which would give a programme of continuous and progressive study.

The arrangements for funding liberal adult education are one of the ways in which Scotland differs from the rest of the United Kingdom. The Regional and Island Authorities are responsible for funding all the teaching costs for adult education, together with their responsibilities for primary, secondary and further education. This responsibility is interpreted in varying ways from an absence of any real provision to a substantial commitment of funds on a regular basis. The variety of response arises from the Education (Scotland) Act 1945. The Act has four main sections which concern adult education and these:

(a) require Education Authorities to secure that adequate and efficient provision is made throughout their area for all forms of primary, secondary and further education.
(b) define further education to include voluntary part-time and full-time instruction for persons over school age and voluntary leisure time activities of a cultural and recreational nature for persons over school age.
(c) require provision of facilities for recreation, social and physical training.
(d) require Education Authorities to have regard to the expediency of co-operating with voluntary organisations in the same area.

While the sections provide the basis for a diverse provision for adults they locate adult education firmly within the further education system, but do not specify the extent of the provision that should be made. The phrase 'adequate and efficient provision' is open to almost any interpretation that an Authority may choose. Furthermore the Authorities are only required 'to have regard to the expediency of co-operating with voluntary organisations'. They are not required actively to do so and they are certainly not required to make funds available if they do not wish to do so.

Thus there is no direct exchequer grant for adult education made to the universities or the Workers' Educational Association (WEA) in Scotland. The Scottish Education Department is, however, empowered under the 1952 and subsequent Further Education (Scotland) Regulations to assist 'approved associations' with their administrative, but not their teaching, costs and a number of Scottish universities, the WEA and other voluntary adult education organisations do receive finance in this way. In 1969 another Education (Scotland) Act widened the definition of further education to include more informal types of provision and omitted the phrase 'for persons over school age'. Thus informal further education as it became known could now be provided for any member of the community with little restriction on the subject of the courses. It was still, though, entirely at the discretion of the Education Authorities.

This was the legislative background for the 1975 report of the Alexander Committee into adult education, which complemented the Russell Report for England and Wales. Although it was constituted to report on adult education, the Alexander Committee was not faced with the diverse provision of adult education that faced the Russell Committee.

Community Education

The major recommendation of the Alexander Committee was that liberal adult education should be regarded as part of community education and, with the youth and community service, should be incorporated into a community education service provided by the Education Authorities. This stemmed from the Committee's belief that the educational activities of adults were so closely linked with their social, cultural and recreational activities that any attempt to distinguish between them or to deal with them in isolation would be undesirable even if it were possible. The Committee defined an adult as one who was over the statutory school leaving age, and recommended that statutory responsibility for adult education should continue to be vested solely in the Education Authorities, despite representations from the WEA for a status similar to the one they enjoyed south of the border.

The Committee made numerous recommendations for the

development of a community education service. It identified special groups such as young mothers, the elderly, those with literacy problems, immigrants, prisoners, the physically and mentally handicapped, and those working unsocial hours, for whom special provision must be expanded. It also stressed the difficulties of remote, rural populations and called for an increase in Scottish cultural subjects and classes in Gaelic.

Following the Alexander Report, the Scottish Office constituted a Scottish Council for Community Education to advise it on all aspects of community education. This body was superseded in 1982 by the Scottish Community Education Council which has a very different membership and an independent secretariat.

The first Council was concerned to distinguish the administrative structures which comprised the new community education service from its broader philosophy of community education, because it did not wish community education to become too narrowly defined. This presented a number of difficulties, because, while there was a general understanding that the activities of the existing liberal adult education and youth work agencies would in future comprise the community education service, the breadth of the Council's philosophy of community education was so great that it appeared to extend into most areas of human experience. The Council defined community education as any process affecting the individual learner. It recognised that the term 'community education' was a contradiction, because learning is an individual activity and there is no such thing as a communal mind, but felt that the community aspect of learning was achieved when individuals collaborated for their common good. In this way individual learning became an educational influence on the whole community.

Philosophically, therefore, the Council did not interpret community education as an educational structure or system. It recognised that a large number of educational organisations make contributions to community education but felt that there were other agencies, such as health and social work, whose contributions were also important.

However, such is the diversity among the constituents of even the more narrowly defined community education service, that much more thought needs to be given about how these should work together before attempts are made to develop a more extensive philosophy of community education. This will be one of the major tasks of the new Scottish Community Education Council.

The Education Authorities have restructured their departments to provide a community education service, and subsequent national agreements have produced a fairly uniform staffing structure throughout Scotland. Each Authority has a Regional Community Education Officer with responsibility for a number of Area Community Education Officers. The area team may comprise a number of workers with broad responsibilities for youth and adult groups as well as some with specialist skills such as sports coaching, craft work or adult basic education.

As liberal adult education provision has become part of the community education service there has been a decline in the number of traditional adult education classes. This reflects both the emphasis of the service on the relevance of its provision to the needs of local communities and the background of most community education staff, whose sympathies are often with the young and the disadvantaged rather than with the educated adults who were the main beneficiaries of the earlier service. There have been substantial increases in the numbers of buildings used solely for community education purposes, and in community schools to which the local population has been given varying degrees of daytime and weekend access.

It is, however, impossible to assess the full impact of the change to community education, for while the attendance at conventional classes has declined the more informal approaches of one-day conferences, or self-programming groups of adults working together with tutorial assistance, or voluntary associations determining their own courses of study, are more difficult to measure and assess. The benefits derived from participating in community groups, clubs and societies, or by working with young people are even more difficult to quantify. Some have argued that it is against the philosophy of community education to separate provision for adults, and that the use of the term 'adult education' merely indicates a refusal to recognise that things have changed. Others point out that the concept of community education is so broad that in practice it subdivides into different types of provision, and that one of these is learning opportunities for adults, either because some subjects are more suited to adults or because adults wish to be on their own. However, adult learning opportunities within the community education service are only part of what is available in Scotland and the work of, for example, further and higher education institutions, while it may come within the broad philosophy of community education, continues quite separately.

Organisation and Provision of Adult Education in Scotland

The emphasis upon community education has meant that there is presently little national concept of adult education in Scotland, and no statutory body with a remit to cover the breadth of adult education that is available. The Scottish Institute of Adult Education (SIAE) provides the only national focus for adult education in Scotland, although as a non-governmental organisation it is limited in its resources and in its scope for action. The Institute considers its work to be complementary to the community education service. It feels that within the latter there is a distinct area of adult education provision, but that there are other areas of provision, for example within the Colleges of Further Education or the universities, that are not a part of the community education service.

A number of different institutions exist that are essentially Scottish and they can be subdivided into four major categories: those receiving funds on a UK basis, those funded directly by the Scottish Office, those funded by local government, and voluntary organisations receiving funds from the Scottish Office or local government, or both of these sources.

In addition, the special programmes of the Manpower Services Commission are available in Scotland as elsewhere, the correspondence colleges offer their services throughout the UK, and the majority of adult education on radio and television is networked, although both the BBC and ITV companies provide some particular programmes for use solely within Scotland. The Open University also makes its provision throughout the UK, although Scotland constitutes one of its regions for administrative purposes and has concentrated on the special needs of students in remote areas. These UK bodies are not considered in any more detail here. In the sections that follow the statistics are drawn from the period 1980-2.

Scottish Institutions Funded from London

The eight Scottish Universities are funded directly by central government through the University Grants Committee (UGC), and offer the usual range of undergraduate and postgraduate studies. The Scottish University course lasts four years for an honours degree, and although the majority of the courses are full time, the modular nature of the Scottish degree can make it possible for adults to study part time.

In addition to their undergraduate and postgraduate teaching, the universities all make some special provision for adults through their Departments of Adult, Extra-Mural or Continuing Education. The Departments do not receive any direct funding that is comparable to that of their counterparts south of the border, and must compete within their institutions for a share of the UGC grant. With a total of 35,000 students each year, they are quite small, and while some receive administrative grants from the Scottish Education Department, the extent of their adult education provision is limited by the finance they have available to pay tutors' fees. This finance varies from nothing to substantial, so that the universities have tended to concentrate upon the areas which they felt were most important, while being quick to exploit other sources of funding and self-financing programmes.

Institutions Funded Directly by the Scottish Office

There are three main types of institution funded directly by the Scottish Office: the central institutions, the colleges of education and Newbattle Abbey College.

There are 14 central institutions. These are similar to the polytechnics south of the border in that they provide the majority of degree level courses outside the universities. Their degree courses are mostly validated by the CNAA, and, together with a number of diploma courses, are related to careers in industry, commerce and the professions. Although most of their 18,000 students are school-leavers taking full-time or sandwich courses, adult students may be admitted if they can provide evidence of recent study at an advanced level. Some central institutions make a special provision for adults on specific courses, such as social work, with entry restricted to older people and teaching only between 10.00 a.m. and 3.00 p.m. The central institutions also provide some non-vocational adult education for 2,000 students each year.

In Scotland all teachers employed in education authority or grant aided schools normally complete a course of training, which, apart from the University of Stirling, is provided only by the seven Colleges of Education. The courses range from three or four years for non-graduates to a one year postgraduate certificate, and the colleges have particular entrance requirements for adults wishing to enter the teaching profession.

In addition to their courses of teacher training some of the colleges of education provide full-time courses for some 200 students leading to a diploma or certificate in community education. This enables these students to undertake a wide range of duties within the community education service, and associated statutory and voluntary organisations. They also provide courses that offer a professional qualification in social work. For both community education and social work courses the colleges will relax their formal entrance requirements for adult applicants who can demonstrate previous relevant experience.

Newbattle Abbey College is the only adult residential college in Scotland and provides accommodation for 70 students eight miles from Edinburgh. The College provides a one year course and a two year diploma in Liberal Studies, with an emphasis on history, political theory, English, philosophy, economics and trade union studies. The two year diploma is accepted by the Scottish Universities as satisfying their entrance requirements and is becoming similarly accepted by universities outside Scotland.

Bodies Funded by Local Government

In Scotland the twelve Regional and Island Education Authorities provide the major educational opportunities for adults at a local level and they do so in two main ways: their colleges of further education and their community education provision.

Although many of the 54 colleges of further education provide non-vocational part-time adult education courses, their main provision is career-orientated, certificate courses in a wide variety of subjects. Some colleges specialise in commerce or agriculture, while others offer a range of courses including technical and craft courses for industry and training for a variety of trades. A few offer courses at degree level. The general education departments in many of the colleges offer courses leading to the Scottish Certificate of Education and the English General Certificate of Education, which provide a second chance to adults who wish to study for these qualifications.

College courses are both full time and part time, and although some may have entrance requirements which were probably written with the school-leaver in mind, there is discretion to allow adults within them to be admitted. The colleges also provide a number of distance learning courses designed for adults who are unable to attend a college on a normal basis. The courses lead to awards by either the Scottish Business Educational Council or by the Scottish Technical Education Council.

Some colleges have programmed learning schemes which enable adults to use a range of written, audio and video materials by appointment at the college. Pioneered by the Learning Resources Centre at Napier College, Edinburgh, these schemes allow students to work at their own speed and at times that are convenient, and provide access to a college lecturer for advice.

The Regional and Island Community Education Services provide educational opportunities for adults which are not related to qualifications or a career. These include both conventional non-vocational courses, often held during the evenings, and a range of opportunities of a social or recreational nature in which adults may participate either alone, or alongside or for the benefit of young people.

While evening classes are still primarily held in conventional schools or colleges, much of the more general community education provision is in community centres, school-linked centres or community schools, whose organisation and programme are determined by elected members drawn from the local communities that they serve. There are approximately 700 such buildings in Scotland. School-linked centres and community schools comprise about half of this total and are physically integrated to varying extents with existing schools. Community centres are freestanding buildings, which may have been purpose-built or are closed schools which have been converted for community use.

Physical activities, such as sports and Scottish Country Dancing, and practical subjects such as cookery and car maintenance, predominate in the community education courses programme, but there is a wide variation in the extent of the provision that is made by different regions. Although some regions have reduced their commitment to conventional adult education courses all have committed resources to the broader aspects of community education, encouraging participation in community-based activities and funding projects to help disadvantaged groups, as well as providing considerable support to voluntary organisations whose work involves adults. It is difficult to measure the total extent of this diverse provision but the best estimate at the present is that about a quarter of a million, or 5 per cent of the Scottish population, participate in some aspect of this service.

The District Councils are the second tier of local government in Scotland and although they have no statutory responsibility for education they do contribute to community education in a number of ways. Many districts have swimming pools, and some have community sports and leisure centres, which provide activities that are similar to those that take place in regional establishments, and some have designated community centres similar to regional community centres. The districts are also responsible for museums and libraries, which often organise local studies lectures.

Voluntary Organisations

The Workers' Educational Association (WEA) is the major adult education voluntary organisation in Scotland. Each of the three Scottish districts, which are based upon Glasgow, Edinburgh and Aberdeen, receives an administrative grant from the Scottish Education Department together with a varying amount of support from the Regional Authorities. The absence of national funding to meet the salaries of tutor organisers and pay part-time tutors has resulted in the WEA in Scotland being proportionately smaller than south of the border. In recent years the association has concentrated upon work with a variety of disadvantaged adult groups.

There are many other voluntary organisations that contribute to adult education in Scotland. Their range is so diverse that it is only possible to list some of the major ones whose work is primarily with adults. The three main churches in Scotland, the Church of Scotland, the Episcopal Church of Scotland and the Roman Catholic Church all provide education for adults wishing to participate more fully in their work. The Scottish Co-operative Education Association includes member education in its work, and the National Union of Townswomen's Guilds and the Scottish Women's Rural Institute provide educational opportunities similar to those of the equivalent bodies south of the border. The Scottish Field Studies Association has a field centre in Perthshire. The Scottish Pre-School Playgroups Association now includes a substantial adult education element in its work through the encouragement of parent participation. Within the broad concept of Scottish community education, organisations such as the Scout Association or the Scottish Association of Youth Clubs, which are primarily for young people but in which adults are very active, should also be included in a complete survey of the voluntary organisations.

Adult Basic Education

Following the national literacy programme in the late 1970s, when the Scottish Adult Literacy Agency and its successor unit were similar to the equivalent body south of the border, the Scottish Education Department established in April 1980, under the auspices of the SIAE, the Scottish Adult Basic Education Unit (SABEU), which was quite different in style and emphasis. The Department's memorandum described adult basic education as including 'not only literacy and numeracy but the basic competence and knowledge needed to cope with the demands of employment and adult life generally in a modern industrialised society'. The Unit was asked to respond to the demands made upon it, and was not constrained by a narrow or unchanging definition of adult basic education.

Because of this, adult basic education in Scotland has been able to adapt to changing social demands. Its work has not been solely the responsibility of Regional and Island Education Authorities, but has also involved action by social work, health, training, rehabilitation and other public services.

In practice, requests for adult basic education help from the public have included literacy, numeracy, communication and learning skills, basic managing skills, preparing people for a new start or a serious transition in adult life, and providing ways of raising self-confidence to deal with formal education, training opportunities, professional examinations or unemployment. In meeting this wide range of demands SABEU has collaborated with health board training colleges and institutions, Social Work departments, the Prison Service, the Scottish Health Education Group, the Scottish Consumer Council, the Regional and Island Education Departments, the media, the Universities, the Colleges of Education and industry. Although the major work with adults is undertaken by volunteers they need proper and regular training and administrative support. This has come primarily from the regional education budgets, but also from a variety of other sources such as the Manpower Services Commission and the European Community social fund.

The government has recognised the importance of SABEU's work and has announced that the Unit will receive additional funding to allow it to develop its pioneering work.

References

Horobin, J.C. (1980) *Community Education Statistics*, Scottish Council for Community Education, Edinburgh

Horobin, J. and Wilson, V. (eds.)(1980) *Handbook of Adult Education in Scotland.* Scottish Institute of Adult Education, Edinburgh

Scottish Adult Basic Education Unit (1982) *Report on The First Two Years' Activities*, Edinburgh

Scottish Council for Educational Technology (1982) *Open Learning Opportunities in Scotland,* Glasgow

Scottish Education Department (1975) *Adult Education: The Challenge of Change.* Report of the Alexander Committee of Enquiry, HMSO, Edinburgh

Shearer, J.G.S. (1976) *Town and Gown Together, 250 Years of Extra-Mural Teaching at the University of Glasgow*, Department of Adult and Continuing Education, University of Glasgow

2.3

EDUCATION FOR ADULTS IN NORTHERN IRELAND

Gordon Macintyre

Source: Copyright © The Open University 1983 (specially written for this volume).

This short article aims to describe four aspects of the education of adults in Northern Ireland during the last 15 years which are in some sense distinctive. These are the institutional foundations of the late 1960s and early 1970s, the growth of community education during the 1970s, educational guidance in the Province, and the work of the Council for Continuing Education. To highlight such development is of course to present a less than comprehensive picture, and in particular to do injustice to continuing work, such as that of the Further Education sector, industrial training, or the Department of Extra-Mural Studies of the Queen's University of Belfast, which is less novel.

Queen's Extra-Mural Department has in fact been providing classes throughout Northern Ireland, mainly at University level, since 1946; and from the same year there was a Northern Ireland District of the Workers' Educational Association promoting classes mainly at non-university level and based on a Belfast Branch formed in 1910 (it had a full-time District Secretary only from 1965). There was no residential adult education centre, and there are several reasons why most of the provision before the period with which this article is principally concerned was on fairly conventional lines. The size of the Province resulted in voluntary enterprises such as adult education being conducted on a correspondingly small scale and with a lack of internal competition and stimulation. Unlike Scotland, the tradition in Northern Ireland in educational matters has not been to develop a distinctive system or approach based on its own needs and institutions, but largely to follow English practice. This discouraged initiative and radical thought. Methods and curriculum in Northern Ireland schools have tended to be of a somewhat formal, conservative, and academic character. (Grammar schools and the 'eleven-plus' flourish still.) Good results within a relatively narrow focus are achieved by able children, but the style has been authoritarian, and

83

the attitudes and expectations thus instilled in successive generations have not encouraged participative, questioning modes of learning. Nor has Northern Ireland had an industrial working class which was either large or — in spite of isolated though significant events — consistently politically conscious: indeed it may be argued historically that when class mobilisation, especially by Protestants and Catholics together, was seen as a threat to the existing order, the forces of repression were quickly brought to bear.

Local authority provision was made mainly through the technical schools and colleges. The LEAs in Northern Ireland enjoyed considerably less autonomy than their counterparts in Britain: many responsibilities exercised by English LEAs resided in Northern Ireland with the provincial Ministry of Education, and in using such discretionary powers as they possessed the Northern Ireland Authorities tended to act in concert. (This remains true of the Education and Library Boards which replaced the LEAs in 1973 in relation to the contemporary Department of Education for Northern Ireland.) Thus there have been few examples in the Province of educational innovations or areas of special excellence being developed, as has often happened in England, through the drive and enthusiasm of a particular education officer or committee chairman. However, here too there has been evidence of change in recent years, symbolised by a change of title for most institutions to Colleges of Further Education. Their readiness to carry through the recent scheme for adult literacy is evidence of a changing concept of their role. The Belfast Education and Library Board has recently set up a Co-ordinating Committee for Adult and Community Education in the city with broadly conceived functions and membership.[1] This growing interest and commitment parallels the other developments now to be discussed.

New Institutional Foundations

Within the space of three years three major new institutions concerned with adult education came into being. These were the New University of Ulster, enrolling its first undergraduates in October 1968; the Open University, which started teaching in January 1971; and Northern Ireland's polytechnic, now known as the Ulster Polytechnic, formed from an amalgamation of existing institutions in April 1971.

Northern Ireland has been one of the Open University's regions, and its programmes of undergraduate, postgraduate, and non-degree courses have operated as in other regions of the UK; but the opportunity provided for part-time higher education in diverse disciplines was probably a more significant addition to the facilities previously available here than in most areas.

The foundation of both the New University and the Polytechnic was recommended by the Lockwood Committee, whose Report, *Higher Education in Northern Ireland*, was published in 1965.[2] However, the former may be seen as part of the general post-Robbins expansion (it was the last of the new universities), and the latter as part of the national movement initiated by the 1967 White Paper which introduced a new 'public sector' element into higher education. Compared with polytechnics in England and Wales, the Ulster Polytechnic has enjoyed additional strengths and freedom. It has an independent governing body, directly financed by the Department of Education (NI), and administers its own affairs with broadly the same freedom as an education authority. One of the Polytechnic's objectives has been the provision of a multi-level range of courses, and this has resulted in a notable enhancement of opportunity within the Province — the provision of courses leading to professional and academic awards at certificate, diploma, and degree level with full-time, day-release, block-release, and evening-only patterns of attendance. Courses are held not only at the Polytechnic in Jordanstown (some ten miles north-east of Belfast) but at out-centres throughout the Province. Its Centre for Continuing Education augments the provision with a community education programme and a range of short courses, many of which are mounted in response to requests.

So far as Continuing Education was concerned, the most novel of the new foundations arose as a by-product of the establishment of Northern Ireland's second university at Coleraine. For incorporated in NUU was Magee University College at Londonderry, and in 1972 the University established there the Institute of Continuing Education, thus anticipating several of the more significant recommendations of the Russell Committee on Adult Education about the future role of universities in the teaching of adults. Much of the Institute's work has been innovatory and exploratory; it has built up a wide-ranging programme of research, courses, conferences, and seminars, both full time and part time, residential and non-residential, ranging from postgraduate studies in Education through Diploma and

Certificate courses for teachers, social workers, nurses, and mature students to extra-mural-type courses in liberal studies and non-award bearing courses for industry, community associations, and the like. The Institute has a large experimental programme for unemployed workers, and serves to some extent as a long-term residential college for mature students on the Ruskin model.

Change does not stop. March 1982 saw the long awaited publication of the Report, *The Future of Higher Education in Northern Ireland,* by Sir Henry Chilver's Review Group,[3] and the simultaneous announcement by the Government of its decision to merge the New University of Ulster with the Ulster Polytechnic.[4] Steps to implement this decision have already been put in hand, but it remains to be seen what the character of the new institution will be, and in particular what implications this major development will have for adult and continuing education in the Province.

Community Education

The dramatic growth of community education in Northern Ireland during the 1970s was in part the result of Government action parallel with that taken elsewhere in the UK (the designation of priority areas, inner city programmes, community development projects), and of Government action taken with the specific aim of countering some of the conditions in Northern Ireland (poverty, unemployment, bad housing, poor recreational facilities) which were seen as contributory to the civil unrest of that period. At a deeper level it was more directly related to 'the troubles', for the appalling death and destruction of that decade and beyond were a catalyst for some things that were not malign: among these were that people in areas most affected were brought up in the sharpest possible way against many hitherto unquestioned assumptions about the nature of their society and the sources of power within it. Even some on the fringe of para-military movements came gradually to see that there were complex issues to which violence and counter-violence were no answer. Emerging community leaders wanted to know how to take effective action about the very real social problems of their streets and neighbourhoods.

Of course it can be argued that many of these problems, including drastic industrial decline and the highest rate of unemployment in the United Kingdom, are structural in a sense which precludes solution by any kind of community approach, and indeed that the promotion of community projects and the appointment of community workers, community development workers, community relations workers, and even community education workers, however well intentioned, was in effect largely cosmetic. Nevertheless it is a matter of record that many interesting and novel projects were launched and sustained in working-class areas.[5] Among these have been some pioneering projects and initiatives by women active in the education of adults in Northern Ireland (and especially Belfast). Sometimes they have broken across sectarian barriers. At the level of the personal and social development of the individual the aim was often to provide learning experiences which countered loneliness, depression, and lack of confidence through a friendly and supportive atmosphere. It also became clear that a small community education centre, when managed by local people, can fulfil a social function as well as an educational one, involving the entire age-span in the improvement of the cultural and recreational life of an area. Another role of community education has been found to be the provision of resources, information, and educational support for working-class organisations. This may well include the creation of a forum for debate and discussion on issues of local concern: community education is not just the provision of learning experiences but a stimulus to forms of social action and social change. The orthodox providers of higher, further, and adult education are less well placed to play this role, and tend to stand aside from the fundamental issues. They do so in order to preserve a necessary posture of detachment and 'neutrality', but incur thereby the danger of legitimising the *status quo*.

Recent innovations with their roots in community education include the Open College — not a similar concept to that of the same name in the north-west of England, but an independent, non-profit-making and experimental institution which opened in an old building in the centre of Belfast in 1979. It operates as a small and informal adult education centre with a special interest in the study of alternatives, basic skills training, practical craft skills (with week-end and day workshops), and the study of changes and the problems of life in the 1980s.[6] Another is the Ulster People's College, even more recently opened in Belfast, its Acting Director being Tom Lovett. It seeks to act as an independent, committed focus for the educational support of a wide variety of working class groups and organisations engaged in social and community action.[7]

Educational Guidance

In 1967 the Northern Ireland Council of Social Service started, as an experimental scheme funded by a charitable trust, an educational guidance service for adults. This service, which is still in being, now funded principally by the Department of Education, was unique in the United Kingdom because of its voluntary educational and counselling elements. With a Director qualified and experienced as an educational psychologist, the Service aims to help those who wish to change the educational or vocational choice made when they left school, to equip themselves for a career later in life, or to take advantage of new forms of further education or training, or those who are having difficulty in finding or keeping suitable employment because of a lack of appropriate educational qualifications at whatever level. Since its inception the Service has counselled many thousands of clients with a wide range of problems and backgrounds. Its ethos is that of an independent and informal agency, and it seeks to establish a personal relationship between counsellor and counselled.

The Education and Library Boards run a parallel Further Education guidance service which is concerned primarily with the provision of information about available courses. A Committee appointed by the Minister responsible for education in Northern Ireland recommended in March 1980[8] that the two existing services, modified as necessary, should continue to operate with the co-ordination of a central agency which would also encourage development and innovation. This has been broadly accepted, and the Council for Continuing Education, the subject of the next section of this article, will assume a general oversight of existing and further services. There is widespread agreement within the Province that the provision of educational guidance for adults is an important part of the education service.

The Council for Continuing Education

The Northern Ireland Council for Continuing Education met for the first time in October 1974, thereby pre-dating the Advisory Council for Adult and Continuing Education in England and Wales (1977) and the Scottish Council for Community Education (1978). Its terms of reference were to advise the Department of Education (NI) on various aspects of continuing education, with some limited executive functions notably in respect of publicity, and to act as a forum for the exchange and dissemination of information and ideas about continuing education in Northern Ireland. There were two interesting aspects of the Council's composition. One was that the Department of Education both serviced the Council and was in membership of it, and its Permanent Secretary was the Council's Chairman. The other, reflecting in part the relative intimacy of the Northern Ireland community, where representatives of all the major providers can sit round one table, was the breadth of interests invited to participate: they included the Universities, the Polytechnic, the WEA, all the Education and Library Boards (at member and officer level), the BBC and Ulster Television, the major museums, the Public Records Office, the Arts Council, the NI Council of Social Service, the NI Prison Service, the Department of Agriculture (which runs agricultural colleges), and professional associations of librarians and of teachers in Further Education. Thus the concept of a forum for exchange and dissemination has an immediate kind of reality, and some attempts at programme co-ordination have been made.

Specific issues so far considered by the Council through working parties have included adult literacy, the future of the Educational Guidance Service for Adults, the continuing education needs of released prisoners and detainees (a reference from the Minister of the day), continuing education for the socially disadvantaged (another request from a Minister),[9] the use of relevant resources in the Province,[10] the case for a residential adult education centre in Northern Ireland, paid educational leave, and, most recently, the educational needs of the unemployed. In November 1980 the Council's Development Committee published a discussion paper, *A Strategy for Development*[11] and this document aroused considerable interest and attention throughout 1981. A Steering Group appointed by the Council to promote and assess this debate produced a Development Plan which was submitted to the Council in March 1982. The Council immediately endorsed the first two recommendations in the Plan — namely, that the Council should be reconstituted as an advisory body for a four-year term, and that the Minister responsible for education in the Province should appoint an independent Chairman. The second of these proposals sprang from a recognition that the chairmanship of the Permanent Secretary, valuable though it had been in the early stages of the Council's life, had become somewhat anomalous, and that the Council needed to have and be seen to have a greater degree of autonomy. The Minister accepted both these recommendations, a Chairman has been appointed, and at the time of writing the reconstituted Council is about to hold its first meeting.

Clearly one of its first jobs will be to review with care its inheritance from its predecessor body — the Development Plan and the Strategy Report from which it derived. The latter argued for priority to be given to certain major tasks — industrial training and retraining; helping people to spend leisure in ways that are both personally enjoyable and satisfying and socially helpful and constructive; basic education; remedial work in relation to the traumas of recent years; attention to the special educational needs of women (who bear most of the social responsibility in adversely affected urban areas); and an educational approach to Northern Ireland's specific political and economic problems. The Report did not balk at proclaiming education as a component of, or a driving force in, regional development. By this it meant not primarily economic development, but a shift in the social purpose of education towards more important political, social and cultural development, with the aim of enabling people to articulate their view as to the character the regional development should take. If the new Council and its constituent bodies are prepared to accept this challenge, they have before them an ample and profoundly stimulating challenge for the 1980s.

Notes

1. For the background to this, see Belfast Education and Library Board, *Adult and Community Education in Belfast*, Report of a Working Party (Belfast, 1981).

2. *Higher Education in Northern Ireland*, Lockwood Report (Cmd. 475, HMSO, London, 1965).

3. *The Future of Higher Education in Northern Ireland*, Chilver Report (HMSO, London, 1982).

4. *Higher Education in Northern Ireland — the Future Structure*, Department of Education for Northern Ireland (HMSO, London, 1982).

5. See, for example, *Report of a Community Education Project 1976-79*, a research project attached to the Department of Further Professional Studies of the Queen's University of Belfast (Ronan Press Ltd, Lurgan, n.d.).

6. See *The Open College — Report 1979-1982* (Belfast, 1982).

7. For the background, see *Community Education and Community Action in Northern Ireland*, The Final Report of the Community Action Research and Education Project (New University of Ulster, 1982).

8. *Educational Guidance for Adults in Northern Ireland*, Jackson Report (HMSO, London, 1980).

9. *Continuing Education in Socially Disadvantaged Areas of Northern Ireland* (HMSO, London, 1978).

10. *Resources Available for Continuing Education in Northern Ireland* (HMSO, London, 1979).

11. *Continuing Education in Northern Ireland — A Strategy for Development,* a Discussion Paper issued by the Northern Ireland Committee for Continuing Education (Bangor, 1980).

2.4

POST-INITIAL EDUCATION IN THE NORTH WEST OF ENGLAND: MODELS OF PROVISION, BARRIERS TO PROVISION

Keith Percy, Stephen Butters, John Powell and Irene Willett

Source: K. Percy, S. Butters, J. Powell and I. Willett, *Post-Initial Education in the North-West of England* (Advisory Council for Adult and Continuing Education, Leicester, 1983).

[This article has been compiled from the final report of a research project which aimed to survey the provision of post-initial education for adults in the North West of England, and which was sponsored by the Advisory Council for Adult and Continuing Education and funded by the Department of Education and Science.

The research team set themselves three main objectives:

(i) to delineate a model of the whole range of post-school educational institutions and agencies and their interrelationships, in the North West of England.
(ii) to identify the barriers to the development of increased provision.
(iii) to deduce from the descriptive and analytical evidence of the model, key indicators affecting the growth and development of post-school educational institutions and agencies.

The team defined their area of concern as involving:

(i) adults aged 18 years and over
(ii) individuals making systematic attempts over time to learn and to retain what is learned
(iii) learning materials and/or a framework for regular study/ practice/participation made available by a 'provider' (but a 'provider' might be, e.g., a club, a self-directed study circle, an animateur, or a TV educational series, as well as an LEA or RB class)

(iv) purposes which are distinguishable from those of the Initial Education System (which prepares pupils and students for publicly recognised social roles by means of a series of teaching/ learning activities related to age-graded curricula administered by schools, colleges, and initial vocational training agencies).

On this basis, the research team developed a detailed taxonomy of providers of interest (see Table 1), and estimated the total numbers of participants involved in each sector in the year 1978-9 (see Table 2).

The following article summarises the research team's conclusions relating to their first two main objectives, the delineation of a model of provision and the identification of barriers to provision.]

Models of Provision

... Figure 1 attempts to describe the field of post-initial education through the resource flows between providers and their sponsors. It seeks to answer the questions 'who provides?', 'who decides and who guides the decision on what is provided?' and 'who pays?'. It emphasises in simple graphical terms the multitude of sponsors and providers in the field of post-initial education; and the central and crucial position of the Manpower Services Commission (MSC) and the local education authorities as intermediate sponsors and providers and, consequently, the manifold effects which their withdrawal from the web of funding relationships would cause. [...]

Figure 2 is the Project's attempt to model the working relationships between providers, basing the model on the local education authorities and the MSC as the key agencies in a network of relationships. The model shows seven kinds of interaction between agencies (indeed, because of its complexity, it only shows the most important ones). Three kinds of sponsorship relations are incorporated and the various elements of inter-agency co-operation and collaboration are compounded into two forms of co-operation ('limited' and 'extensive'). Some, but not all, competitive relationships are included.

Figure 2 also illustrates the manifold nature of the relationships among providers, their non-systematic manner, and the central position of the local education authorities and the MSC. The model in Figure 2 is not descriptive; it is analytical in the sense that it demonstrates judgements about degrees of co-operation and the presence of

Table 1: Taxonomy of Providers

(i)   Public Authorities

a   Local Education Authorities
b   Responsible bodies
c   Locally administered services other than education (e.g. libraries, leisure, social services)
d   Cultural/leisure sponsors (e.g. Arts Council, Craft Council, Film Institute, Sports Council)
e   Universities and direct-granted colleges
f   Media: TV and Radio
g   Co-ordinating and support agencies (North West Regional Advisory Council (NWRAC), North West Adult Education Association (NWAEA), Merseyside and District Institute, etc.)

(ii)   Voluntary Organisations

a   National voluntary organisations created for an educational purpose
b   Other national voluntary organisations with some educational functions (including Churches)
c   Regional voluntary organisations
d   Local voluntary organisations

(iii)   Vocational Training Agencies

a   Manpower Services Commission (MSC) and Industrial Training Boards (ITB)
b   Confederation of British Industries (CBI) Educational and Training, and Employers' Federations
c   Trades Union Congress (TUC) Education Department, and Affiliated Trade Unions
d   Validating and examining bodies (Technician Education Council (TEC), Business Education Council (BEC), Council for National Academic Awards (CNAA), City and Guilds, etc.)
e   Activities of Further Education (FE) and Higher Education (HE) establishments provided at full cost to employers and others
f   Employer provided education and training
g   Professional associations
h   Armed forces

(iv)   Community Development Agencies

a   Community Associations and Neighbourhood Councils
b   Community development projects
c   Community arts and community education ventures

(v)   Private Agencies

a   Correspondence colleges
b   Private local schools — many categories: e.g. driving, music, language, dancing, sport, office skills, crafts, etc.
c   Private local tutors — as above.

Table 2: Provision of Post-Initial Education in 1978-9
(Estimated Numbers of Participants in Each Sector in the North
West)

	(thousands)	
Public Authorities		
Adult education centres and Adult Basic Education	176	
Non-vocational course enrolments at Colleges of Further Education	68	
In-service training for teachers and youth workers	10	
Responsible Bodies (*except* TUC courses)	27	
Open University	7	
Cultural, recreational, leisure services (Local Authorities)	36	
Social services (Local Authorities)	15	
Health services (Area Health Authorities)	49	
Police, fire, ambulance and other public services	24	
		412
Voluntary Organisations Sector		
Training courses for volunteers and leaders	25	
Pre-packaged study/discussion courses	55	
Organised sequences of lecture/discussions (etc.)	120	
		200
Vocational Training Sector		
Training Opportunities Scheme	15	
Training Services Division direct training services	5	
Industrial Training Boards direct training services	2	
Employers' provision of in-house training	150	
Employers' provision of Paid Educational Leave for college courses	50	
Self-financed participation in college courses	26	
TUC scheme enrolments	8	
Trade Unions member education enrolments	8	
		264
Community Development Sector		
Community development projects		
Local self-managed associations		
Community arts and other 'animateurs'		50
Private Agencies Sector		
Private colleges and schools plus correspondence courses administered in the North West		100
Total (with no adjustment for double counting)		1,026

competition. It serves, moreover, to show that private agencies are located in the model chiefly through the representation of competitive relationships and that voluntary organisations are recipients of sponsorship and co-operation from other agencies to a considerable extent. One effect of drawing the model in this manner is to highlight the multidimensional position of the Open University in the complex of inter-agency interaction. A national 'neutral' agency such as the Open University — able to relate across all five sectors of provision and high on status and achievement — is able to act as a powerful catalyst for development. [...]

A crucial need for policy determination in post-initial education is a systematic means of identifying deficiencies, omissions, gaps in the totality of provision by all agencies for which there is (or would be, or should be) a demand by individual adults, particularly those who are socially disadvantaged in some way. However, the construction of an adequate normative model, which would guide such an identification of need, is fraught with difficulty because of the judgements of value and the conceptual definitions that are necessary.

Figure 3 is an example of a simple approach to the problem. The two axes on which it is based — curriculum area and social grouping — are 'liberal adult education', gradated from basic education to postgraduate level, and the specimen social groups of 'ethnic minorities', 'working class' and 'elderly'. The list of such social groups which adult educators conventionally regard as 'special' or 'disadvantaged' is, of course, considerable, although the labelling is pragmatic rather than philosophically sound. Moreover, the axis of 'curriculum area' could equally be 'vocational', 'cultural or recreational' or several others.

In the boxes created by the two axes in Figure 3 are entered the post-initial agencies which are successful (as far as we know in the North West) in attracting an identifiable or even substantial proportion of the relevant social grouping to the particular level of liberal adult education. But it is the *empty* boxes which merit special consideration. Should they be filled as a matter of policy, and, if so, by which providers, and how?

Finally, Figure 4 is the Project's attempt to construct a model showing the inter-related characteristics of different kinds of post-initial education providers and of the provision they make. It is a typology of agencies which seeks to abstract from reality the key aspects of the agencies so as to define the differences between them — differences in sponsorship and purposes, administration and

Figure 1: Provision of Post-initial Education: Sponsorship and Funding

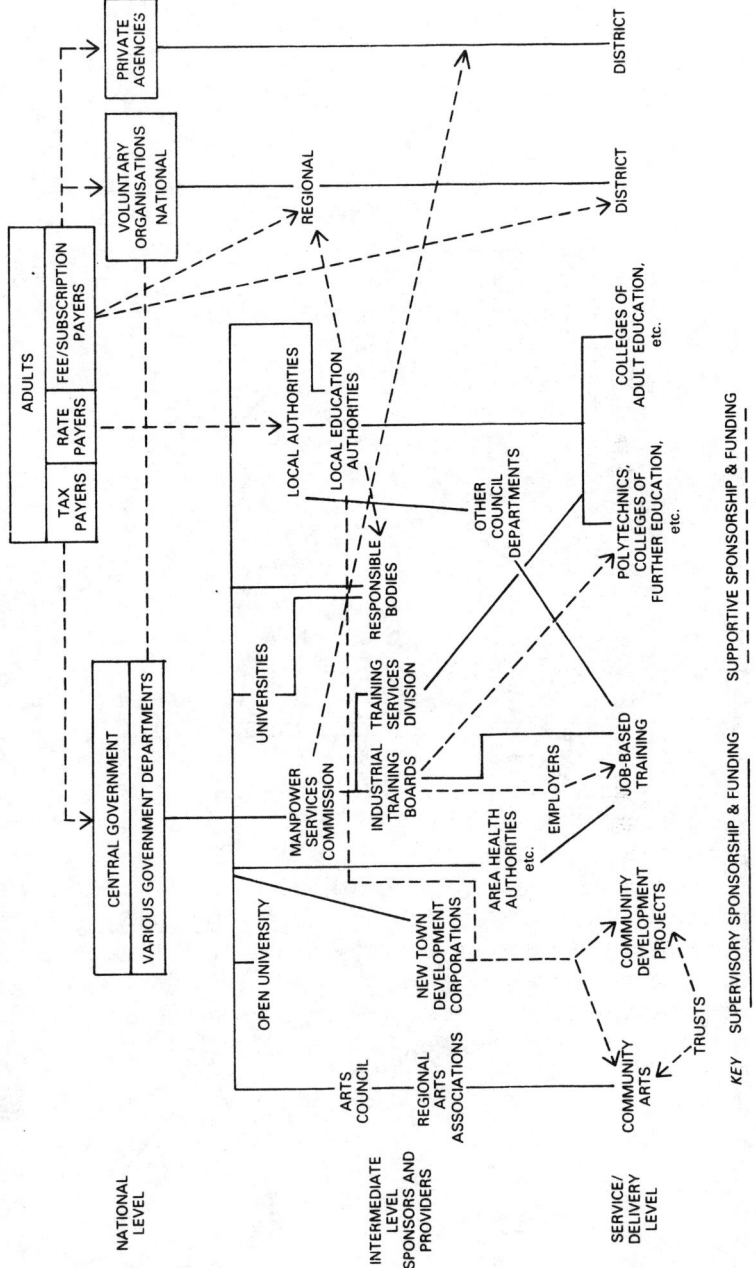

Figure 2: Working Relationships Between MSC, LEAs and Other Providers

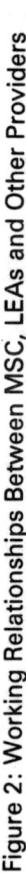

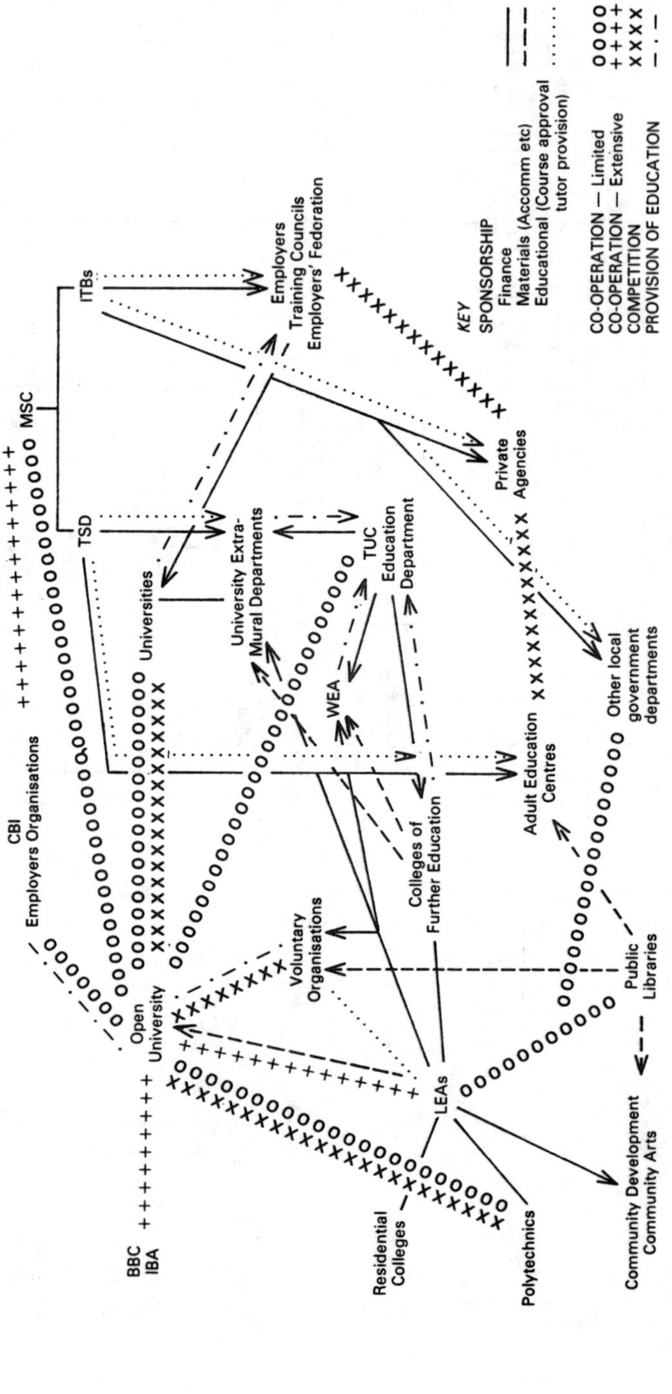

KEY

SPONSORSHIP
Finance
Materials (Accomm etc)
Educational (Course approval
tutor provision)

CO-OPERATION — Limited
CO-OPERATION — Extensive
COMPETITION
PROVISION OF EDUCATION

management, and the kind of adult learner and learning context to which they are directed. Few individual agencies fit exactly into the typology, but almost all agencies can be identified with one sector — that is the nature of typologies. Figure 4, then, has a heuristic purpose; it seeks to promote understanding of the nature of agencies and the relationships (real and potential) between them by taking an analytical stand on the characterisation of major types. Figure 4 is not a causal model; that is to say, it provides no guidance on whether to argue causally from the top of the model or from the bottom. One could hypothesise equally well that the nature of sources of finance and of legitimation determines the learning situations and type of adult learning which develop in an agency; or that the characteristic teaching and learning to be found in an agency determine the legitim-ations which are appropriate and the sources of finance which are forthcoming.

Barriers to the Development of Increased Provision

Introduction

An attempt to identify the 'barriers' to 'increased provision' immedi-ately brings into play a particular metaphor of adult participation in learning opportunities (and it is an undimensional and rather mechanistic one). It is a 'steeplechase' or 'assault course' metaphor: remove or lower the barriers and post-school agencies and institu-tions will be able to race on to wider and greater provision.

However, that said, this kind of metaphor has a clear use in identifying issues about institutional provision and makes possible a relatively straightforward ordering of those issues. The remainder of this section therefore works within the framework of this metaphor.

Societal Barriers

The Project data shows that barriers to the development of the pro-vision of post-initial education are manifold and are both diffuse and concrete. It is useful to conceptualise them in terms of social institu-tions and the sector of post-initial educational agencies taken as a whole.

Social Attitudes

Attitudes in society towards the education of adults are the major barrier to the development of increased provision. Despite the high

Figure 3: Educational Provision for Adults in Special Categories:
Liberal Adult Education

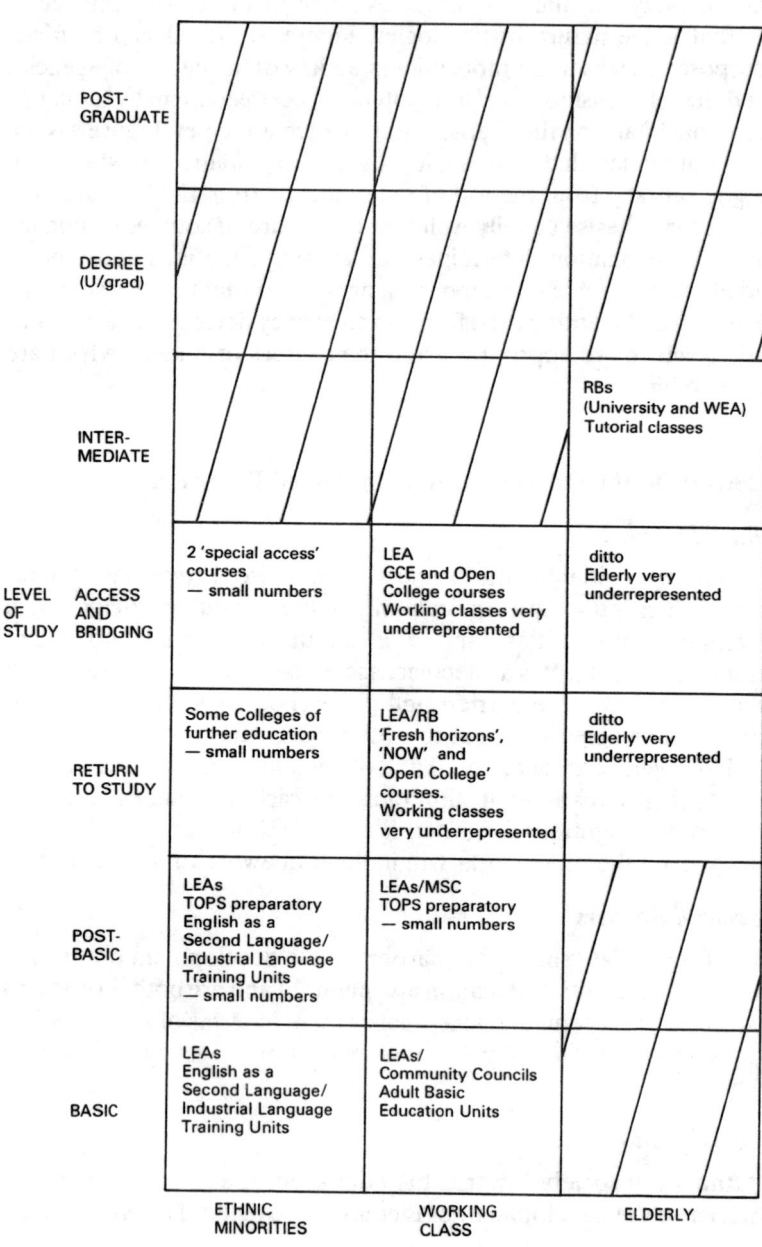

		ETHNIC MINORITIES	WORKING CLASS	ELDERLY
	POST-GRADUATE			
	DEGREE (U/grad)			
	INTER-MEDIATE			RBs (University and WEA) Tutorial classes
LEVEL OF STUDY	ACCESS AND BRIDGING	2 'special access' courses — small numbers	LEA GCE and Open College courses Working classes very underrepresented	ditto Elderly very underrepresented
	RETURN TO STUDY	Some Colleges of further education — small numbers	LEA/RB 'Fresh horizons', 'NOW' and 'Open College' courses. Working classes very underrepresented	ditto Elderly very underrepresented
	POST-BASIC	LEAs TOPS preparatory English as a Second Language/ Industrial Language Training Units — small numbers	LEAs/MSC TOPS preparatory — small numbers	
	BASIC	LEAs English as a Second Language/ Industrial Language Training Units	LEAs/ Community Councils Adult Basic Education Units	

SOCIAL GROUPING

Figure 4: Typology of Post-initial Education Agencies

	Type I\nThe educational service agency	Type II\nThe participant member agency	Type III\nThe training programme contracting agency	Type IV\nThe community project developing agency	Type V\nThe private sector agency
Sponsorship\nFINANCE	ALLOCATION from central & departmental budgets	LOCAL AND REGIONAL MIXED FUNDING (self-help plus subsidy)	PROGRAMME BUDGETING SYSTEMS	PROJECT BUDGETING (with supervision)	PROFIT-MARGIN BUDGETING
LEGITIMATIONS	Public Service ideologies: stressing learning process values	Philanthropic ideologies: stressing collective and altruistic values	Managerial ideologies: stressing design and product values	Participation ideologies: stressing community & self-awareness values	Market ideologies: stressing 'value for money' values
Management\nFOCUS	Deploying given resources within imposed limits	Mobilising members or volunteers to secure provision	Meeting cost and effectiveness targets	Developing a strategy for social animation	Identifying and filling market gaps
FORM	Bureaucratic management plus professional elements	Elective representative management plus advisory elements	Corporate management	Idiosyncratic management	Commercial management
User\nMARKET	Universal entitlement but specified priorities	Bringing together of those of similar interests	Specified training target groups in specified numbers	Positive orientation to the culturally & educationally deprived	Supplying demand where profit can be maximised
STATUS	LEARNER	MEMBER	CLIENT	PARTICIPANT	CUSTOMER
Learning Mode\nCONTEXT	Class	Club	Course	Workshop	Group/Home Learner
STYLE	Teaching	Skill exchange	Training	Facilitation	Instruction

levels of participation in educational activities, provision of educational opportunities for adults is marginal to the public consciousness. This marginality is embedded deep in our social history; the difficulty of eradicating it must be related to the alienating impression made on many adults by the initial education system. The level of informed public knowledge about the variety of education opportunities open to adults and the means of access to them is poor.

If social attitudes could be changed, if a major value of our society was acknowledged to be the education of its adults, then political will and financial resources supporting post-initial education would be transformed and the majority of the barriers to development discussed below would melt away.

Political Parties

One or other of the political parties, when in government, has the ultimate power (if it chooses to exercise it) to determine the ground rules for much of the provision of post-initial education and does determine the economic context in which decisions about central government financial resources for post-initial education aré made. But there are no votes in post-initial education. If political manifestos, or even the all-party parliamentary lobby, consider the education of adults it is in terms of some of its more salient features: the Open University, increases in LEA non-vocational fees, the WEA, the MSC, etc.

A major barrier to the development of increased provision must be both the lack of detailed knowledge of post-initial education (and, partly in consequence, the low level of priority attaching to it) among those who have ultimate political responsibility for central government resources and the management of the legislature. The heterogeneous world of post-initial education, which the Project has documented, is badly handicapped by the absence of a political will to update the 1944 Education Act so as to ensure the existence of a comprehensive and co-ordinated provision of educational opportunities for adults.

Central Government Departments

The Project has shown that the Department of Education and Science and a range of other central government departments (for example, Home Office, Welsh Office, Department of Employment, Department of Health and Social Security, Department of the Environment, Ministry of Defence) are involved in directing and/or financing the provision of post-initial education. We were not aware of close inter-departmental co-operation and collaboration in this provision: this appears to be a significant barrier to the rational development of provision and to the maximisation of the return on related central government investment. We had no way of adding up the total of central government funds directed to the providers of post-initial education in the North West, but, if all sources are identified, the volume is very great. Our impression was that at certain times one government department would be lavish in its endowment of one area of provision while another department would restrain expenditure among the providers for whom it was responsible. There seems to be a good case for an inter-departmental evening out. [...]

A major barrier to the development of provision (whether or not the relevant clauses of the 1944 Educational Act are revised) is the absence of co-ordinated and coherent guidance to public providers from the Department of Education and Science and the Welsh Office in particular, in the form of memoranda, circulars and notes of guidance about points of provision. The relevant part of the Schools Inspectorate can and does provide a crucial role in promoting good practice, innovation and development in post-initial education. But the number of HM Inspectors is limited.

Providers of Post-initial Education

A significant and obvious conclusion from the Project research is that, while there is a very wide range of providers of post-initial education, there is no *system* of provision. That is to say, no provider is aware of the presence of all the other providers and knows the total range of opportunities, levels, types and modes of provision, resources and developments which we have observed in the field. There is not a comprehensive system of post-initial education visible with agreed sequencing of the existing different levels, types and modes of learning opportunities for adults. Without such a system the gaps and the deficiencies in provision, the instances where what is available does not adequately match 'need' and 'demand' often go unrecognised. Similarly overlaps and duplication in provision can be observed to occur. Competition between agencies in provision may or may not be a good thing if it occurs in the full knowledge of each party. Otherwise it is wasteful.

What we have, of course, is the result of unco-ordinated and piecemeal historical development; it could never be completely

Figure 5: Major Societal Barriers to the Development of Increased Provision of Post-initial Education

Social institution/ agency	Barrier to development of PIE	Action that may remove or lower barriers
Social attitudes	Education of adults marginal to public consciousness	Can only be changed over a long period. Providers of PIE should devote resources to positive promotion and self-advertisement
Political parties	Ignorance of, and lack of priority attached to, PIE	Lobbying and promotional activities by PIE providers and committed students
Central government departments	Lack of liaison between departments over direction and funding of PIE	Formal mechanisms for inter-departmental co-operation and collaboration
Department of Education and Science	Lack of central guidance and advice to PIE providers	Generation of departmental circulars, etc. as with Schools sections. More HMIs
Providers of post-initial education	Absence of comprehensive system of provision of PIE; absence of inter-agency communication flows and working relationships	Generation of co-operative and other relationships by providers themselves and national, regional and local intermediaries

unravelled and rationalised. However, the absence of systematic communication and interaction between providers (particularly bodies in receipt of public funds and voluntary organisations) is an important barrier to the development of increased provision. Analysis elsewhere suggests that both 'co-operative' and 'authoritative' strategies will help overcome this barrier; but intermediary bodies may have to become active in order to stimulate the inter-agency relationships necessary. Figure 5 attempts to summarise the major societal barriers to the development of increased provision discussed so far in this section and also indicates in general terms action that may remove or reduce some of the societal barriers discussed.

Local and Institutional Barriers to Development

It is difficult to systematise the information available on local and institutional barriers to the development of increased provision, particularly if the attempt is to be made to include all providers and agencies in the analysis. It is, in fact, tempting to concentrate on barriers occurring in the post-initial education provision of the local education authorities (because they are the pivotal provider in any locality). However, Figure 6 attempts to give an overview of barriers to development as they affect selected providers. Explanatory notes follow; they give more emphasis to a consideration of the situation of the local education authorities. [...]

Figure 6 interacts with Figure 4 in a number of ways. As types of providers can be differentiated according to the nature of their financial sponsorship, the ideologies with which they are legitimated, the form and focus of their management structures and the adult market on which they are targeted, so the significance will vary of such barriers to development as availability of finance, clarity of goals, administrative flexibility and regularity of feedback and monitoring.

Limited Educational Scope

This factor relates to the curriculum range in which providers are willing to involve themselves. In one sense, the more limited and fixed the scope of provision, the greater is the barrier to development. Thus, private agencies limit their provision to subjects for which individuals will pay the price and from which profit can be made; community arts projects are limited by definition of the areas of experience appropriate to them; trade unions (apart from their correspondence courses) concentrate on health and safety and worker representative studies; employer-provided education is confined to job related courses. If, of course, employers were prepared to finance or to provide courses of more general, or non-vocational, orientation then a significant barrier to the development of provision for workers would be removed. Voluntary organisations potentially cover every subject in the post-initial education curriculum, whereas the university extra-mural departments and the Workers' Educational Association (WEA) — although primarily concerned with liberal studies tuition in the 'great tradition' — actually have a relatively broad curriculum scope (including industrial relations and trade union studies). The educational scope of local education authority provision is very wide. It has grown steadily in the last 20 years and in some areas clearly overlaps that, for example, of the WEA. For the LEA it is the least significant barrier to the development of provision.

Figure 6: Presence of Barriers to the Development of Increased Provision as they Affect Selected Providers of Post-initial Education

Provider:	Presence of Barriers to the Development of Provision Relating to:							
	Limited educational scope	Lack of clarity of goals	Finance	Accommodation	Support services (e.g. clerical)	Administrative inflexibility	Quality of staff (training, morale etc.)	Feedback and monitoring
Private Agencies	High[a]	None	Not Relevant	None[c]	None	None	Medium[b]	None
Community Arts Projects	High	Medium	High	Medium	High	None	Medium	High
Trade Unions	High	None	Medium/ None	None	Medium	Medium	Medium	Medium
Employers	High	None	Medium	Medium	Medium	High	Medium	None
Voluntary Organisations	None	High	High	High	High	None	Medium	Medium
WEA	Medium	Medium	High	High	High	Medium	Medium	Medium
University EMDs	Medium	None	Medium	High	Medium	Medium	Medium	Medium
LEAs	Medium/None	High	Medium	Medium	Varies	High	Medium	High

Notes: a. 'High' indicates *significant presence* of barriers to the development of provision.
b. 'Medium' indicates *some presence* of barriers to the development of provision.
c. 'None' indicates *no significant presence* of barriers to the development of provision.

Lack of Clarity of Goals

This factor touches on the coincidence of 'social' and 'educational' goals in the programmes of some providers. This is evidently an issue for many voluntary organisations: indeed there is room for debate about the depth of the educational goals of many of these organisations. Moreover, it was clear from our interviews with LEA organisers and tutors that they disagreed over the relative importance of 'social' and 'educational' goals.

This factor also relates to questions about the level of study and the kind of teaching which is appropriate for the provider. The extra-mural departments and the WEA (in its general programme) aim for an academic level and for tutorial teaching — although there are grounds for suggesting that WEA tutor-organisers are not always certain of the educational rationale for their choice of programme and the levels of student performance expected. The Project identi-fied clear disagreements over fundamental educational philosophies between protagonists in certain WEA districts.

The employers aim for the level of skill and learning style appro-priate for the operative/employee. Private agencies adjust their offerings to what satisfies their customers and, if they are not satisfied, the provision ceases. In community arts projects the level and nature of the learning experience is informal and, in one sense, shapeless. Trade union studies are mainly orientated to a specific range of levels of skills and knowledge areas necessary for worker representatives.

Lack of clarity about goals is, we suggest, bound to inhibit the providers' willingness and capacity to develop provision. It makes it problematic to discern potential new areas of development and, because there is no single clear frame of reference, response to demand may be sluggish, uncertain or ill-directed. The interviews with LEA organisers suggest to us that they were not clear about their educational frame of reference and that they were cautious about their capacities to discern and satisfy new educational markets.

Finance

Availability of finance must obviously be included in any model of barriers to the development of provision, but it is important that it should take its place in due proportion to the other factors. Clearly, a dramatic increase of funds flowing to any of the providers would enable it to increase the volume, if not the range, of its provision or to make its provision in a more lavish manner. But if none of the other factors in Figure 6 was changed, then incursion of extra funds would have a limited or distorted effect on some of the providers.

In some respects the factor is irrelevant to the private agencies; they increase provision to the extent that their market will stand. We did not have a strong sense that trade union education had been inhibited in the late 1970s by limitations of funding. Similarly the community arts projects had been well endowed with Arts Council and Regional Arts Association (RAA) monies; Figure 6 shows finance as a significant barrier for these providers simply because of the volatility of their sources of income: it is all short-term money. Finance for employer-provided education seems likely to ebb and to flow with the state of the economy and the profitability of various sectors of industry and commerce. Voluntary organisations, dependent on subscriptions, donations, fund raising and short-term grant-aid are necessarily inhibited by their dependence on uncertain finance. University extra-mural departments and the WEA have their Responsible Body grants, but still have to find about 25 per cent of their costs from other sources. For the WEA subscriptions from members and affiliated societies are only a limited source of income. WEA districts in the North West have considerable financial problems, particularly when certain LEA grants are discontinued.

Collectively, of course, the LEAs dispose of considerable budgets for provision of post-initial education. Nevertheless, each year the post-initial education budget is subject to the local authority's fate in relation to the level of the Rate Support Grant and its own decisions on the rate income to be secured. Not only is the uncertain volume of the financial budget a barrier to development, but also associated problems such as timing of financial decisions, changes in the levels of local authority ancillary staff and in the rules about the heating, lighting and opening of local authority buildings — all matters that may be aspects of general council policy and not in the purview of the Education Committee and its officers.

Accommodation

Private agencies, as far as we could tell, hired a range of accommodation and normally costed it into their fees to customers. Accommodation was shown in our surveys to be a significant barrier to development for the voluntary organisations, the university extra-mural departments and the WEA in the sense that, in a period of public expenditure restraint and inflation, their traditional dependence on hiring other agencies' accommodation made them vulnerable to escalating letting charges. Although LEAs have access to the evening use of day school premises, our surveys show clearly that limited availability of prime use and of day accommodation for post-initial education is a significant barrier to its development.

Support Services

LEA heads of centre and WEA tutor/organisers in particular devote large proportions of their time to clerical, minor administrative and routine tasks. If they had greater access to clerical support, they would evidently have more time available for matters involving professional expertise. We were aware that the various district and regional administrative offices of the TUC Education Department and the WEA appeared to have inadequate clerical and administrative support.

Under the heading of support services as they might exist for all providers (except perhaps the commercial providers) we include: library services, publicity, and educational guidance services. We explored the provision of library services in the North West extensively: in most districts it is a professional and comprehensive service which can supply post-initial education providers with such support as book boxes, book list preparation, display space and information retrieval (particularly if — as librarians emphasised — given more resource), yet this support service is under-used by post-initial education providers in many districts and that under-use constitutes a barrier to development.

Publicity is relevant not only in providing information to existing students and attracting new students, but also in raising public awareness and institutional morale. Yet it is generally poorly done, particularly by public authority providers. We would stress the importance of shared publicity as a back-up service for all providers.

The importance of the general development of independent educational guidance services for adults has also been emphasised. The absence of a systematic provision of such services in all local education authority areas not only inhibits the access of individual adults to educational opportunities but also deprives providers of a useful form of feedback about gaps in provision and of a purposeful network of inter-agency contacts.

Administrative Inflexibility

Figure 6 identifies significant problems of administrative inflexibility in employer-provided education and, in particular, the LEAs. With employers this merely implies the evidence which we have been given of the (understandable) wish only to release employees in work-time for training under stringent and formal conditions and with concrete expectations of real benefit to the company.

The Project formed the view that the barriers to development in the LEA provision of post-initial education which involve administrative inflexibility over structures, regulations and procedures are very considerable — indeed, that this should be a major area of re-assessment and reform.

Many of the areas of concern are self-explanatory. The most important seem to be:

(i) Inflexibilities and inadequacies of financial procedures, such as:
— Heads of centre, etc. having no freedom to innovate (and possibly maximise income) through operating variable minimum class size/average class enrolment figures and rarely having 'free' 'pump-priming' funds (e.g. by retaining profits).
— Heads of centre, etc. being bound by centrally fixed scales of letting charges and concessionary fees.
— Heads of centre, etc. being obliged to manipulate all forms of adult learning (even those not class-based) to a formula related to class enrolments.
— Ironically, attempts to improve efficiency and to calculate the 'real cost' of a non-vocational class which, in those LEAs which apply it, will make much provision inaccessible to adults.
— Various effects of the applications of Burnham Committee regulations in colleges and centres offering advanced and non-advanced further education, e.g. the temptation to maximise the ratio of senior staff by increasing the programme of vocational advanced courses potentially at the expense of outreach and innovative adult courses.
— Notifications of budgets late in the year and retrospective implementation of financial restraint.
(ii) Inflexibilities and inadequacies of administrative procedures and regulations, such as:
— Limited mechanisms for co-ordination and joint planning between different local authority departments.
— Limited mechanisms for inter-LEA (e.g. sub-regional) *provision* of adult classes or other forms of adult learning.
— Difficulty, if not impossibility, of centres being open at week-ends and outside term; evidently relates primarily to conditions of

service of teaching and support staff and cost of heating buildings, etc.

— Inflated significance given to artificial and non-educational curriculum considerations through the forced division of subjects into vocational and non-vocational.

Quality and Conditions of Staff

— Absence in some LEAs of sufficient full-time organising and tutoring appointments for adult education to secure a 'critical mass' for educational innovation and development.

— Inadequate 'educational leadership', i.e. insufficient senior staff advising and helping in programme development and tutor supervision.

— Absence of a 'professional identity' shared by all those who teach adults. In a local education authority, teachers of adults can be found in a number of different kinds of educational establishments and combine adult teaching with a range of other teaching duties.

— Where full-time staff are involved in the teaching of adults, particularly in colleges, class contact teaching loads (e.g. Lecturer I at 21 hours) leave limited time for educational innovation and professional development.

— Organisers, both full- and part-time, appear not to have developed certain relevant skills, e.g. management, marketing, programme development and evaluation and monitoring. The implication seems to be that briefing and training, where available, is often deficient.

— In some places where all local authority provision is based in, or organised from, a college, the relationships between the 'department of adult education' (or equivalent label) and 'internal' departments are often marked by rivalry or lack of understanding. The common cause is the feeling that so-called 'non-vocational' adult classes are not 'serious' and are 'entertainment'.

— The employment of a large body of part-time tutors requires considerable professional support. Not all who did not possess teaching qualifications in the LEAs of the North West had access to basic training modules but, perhaps even more importantly, not all were in centres or colleges in which it was the practice to gather part-time tutors together occasionally for a general information and feedback session. Part-time tutors could, therefore, easily be isolated and poorly informed although — for their adult students — they were the front-line representatives of the local authority adult education service.

Feedback and Monitoring

Our survey of private agencies indicated that the larger concerns, at least, recognise that their commercial survival depends on monitoring customer satisfaction and researching areas to which provision might be extended. Commercial reasons also encourage employers to have formal methods of training course quality control by instituting job performance reporting procedures on the work of former trainees.

Other providers, particularly the LEAs, were in our view limited in their monitoring of student satisfaction and of the teaching/learning transactions in college, centre, course and classroom. Some were also näive in their methods (if they had any) of estimating 'demand' for new areas of study from potential students. Many LEAs might reject this observation and point to the supervisory functions of organising and advisory staff. However, methods likely to be employed by these personnel are, we think, too informal and too likely to be put aside because of pressure of time in completing other, more formal, requirements.

The Project believes that feedback and monitoring information on the provision of, and demand for, post-initial education could be gathered in a systematic and sophisticated manner and that its absence is a significant barrier to the development of provision. [...]

Part 3

PROGRAMMES AND TARGET GROUPS

The four chapters in this section deal with different, though overlapping, groups of the adult population, and with the kinds of educational programme or opportunities that have been offered to them, might be offered to them or ought to be offered to them.

The opening chapter by Arthur Jones and Alan Charnley chronicles the experience of the adult literacy initiative in the United Kingdom over the first five years of its existence during the 1970s. One of the most significant developments in this country in recent years, in the education for adults field, the literacy programme represented one aspect of a trend away from 'normal' adult education provision towards provision for 'disadvantaged' groups. Yet, as Jones and Charnley indicate, the programme was launched and sustained on a low budget, and has relied heavily on large numbers of untrained or quickly trained volunteers. Other interesting aspects are the range of media used, and the involvement of central and local agencies in the provision made (cf., the chapter by Paulo Freire on the Brazilian literacy programme in the accompanying Reader).

Ian Bryant deals with another 'disadvantaged' group, currently more topical and likely to be far more difficult to ignore in the foreseeable future, the unemployed. As Bryant argues, there has not yet been a coherent response from the educational services to the problems and potentials of the unemployed; nor, perhaps, given the underlying structural causes and conditions of unemployment, can there be, at least until there is a notable change of opinion on the part of both government and the general public. Yet, as Bryant has identified, there are a number of interesting small-scale initiatives under way in the field which may provide useful guidelines for future practice.

Jane Thompson's chapter is much more polemical in style,

113

taking as its subject the group, slightly more than half of the adult population, which constitutes the majority of participants in the more traditional forms of adult education: women. Thompson argues that, despite this majority interest, these forms of provision remain largely controlled by men and, as a result, the curriculum on offer reflects men's perception of women's role: namely, as home-maker, cook, flower arranger, clothes-maker, foreign holiday translator, slimmer, etc. Such activities are all too easily dismissed as trivia, and Thompson sees part of the explanation for the marginal position of adult education in this state of affairs. The chapter ends with a plea for a greater involvement of women in the organisation of their own and others' education, and describes a number of local programmes which are working along these lines.

The final chapter in this section is concerned with another pressing social 'issue': race. John McIlroy argues that not only should educational opportunities for adults be available to allcomers regardless of their racial origin, but that they should, through the adoption of a sensitive curriculum and approach to this issue, help improve, albeit in a limited way, race relations amongst the adult population of the country. This, McIlroy argues, would be in line with the traditional, egalitarian principles of adult education.

THE ADULT LITERACY INITIATIVE, 1974-1979, UNITED KINGDOM

Arthur Jones and Alan Charnley

Source: A. Kaye and K. Harry (eds.), *Using the Media for Adult Basic Education* (Croom Helm, London, 1982), pp. 114-44.

Origins

The adult literacy initiative emerged in 1974 for a variety of reasons, which, taken together, produced a uniquely favourable climate for innovation in the adult education service.[1] [...]

However, laudable educational plans are not always translated into action; to answer why adult literacy initiatives succeeded in 1974, we must consider the politics of the situation. Though central government was already attempting to limit educational expenditure, a good deal of political support was secured for the 'Right to Read' campaign and hence Gerry Fowler, then Minister of State for Education and Science, was able to announce a special grant of £1 million to provide the resources for a rapid expansion of literacy teaching.

Through the services of the National Institute of Adult Education (NIAE), an Adult Literacy Resource Agency (ALRA) was created to administer the grant. Some local education authorities, fearful of yet further demands on their restricted budgets, were less than enthusiastic about venturing into this field and there is no doubt that their compliance and the government's action in making the grant were precipitated by the BBC's determination to proceed. That in itself, however, had a political aspect, for the prospect of a fourth television channel was beginning to emerge and in the discussion about its allocation the concept of public-service, or 'social action' broadcasting became prominent. Hence the broadcasting authorities, and not just their education staff, were favourably disposed. In this way a combination of educational vision, social purpose and political realism released an enterprise which again proved in the words of the Alexander Report that 'supply may well stimulate demand and acts of faith must increasingly be a feature of pioneering adult education'.

In other words, what the British experience shows is the way in which dedicated educators could engage the media, not only as a prime contributor of educational resources, but also as a major means of extending public consciousness about the problem to be tackled and of reinforcing the political will to release the funds.

It would however be simplistic to speak of a decision at this stage to adopt a multi-media solution. The three major participants — the BBC, the government, and the local educational agencies — shared the same objective (the eradication of illiteracy) but they held different views about the means. The BBC's initial concern was for an independent initiative by television and radio, with no more print materials than would normally accompany a substantial educational series; the government's intention in setting up the Adult Literacy Resource Agency was to provide resources (which in the first instance were thought to include much audio-visual and other equipment) for teaching, and the education authorities' emphasis was on schemes of local face-to-face tuition using volunteers.

Early on, however, two general problems emerged that changed the base-line for planning. The first was the recognition that individual learning from a broadcast was not likely and that therefore the main aim of the broadcasts must be to stimulate the target population to come out and seek help; and the second was that virtually no teaching materials suitable for adults existed. Out of the first grew the referral service, and out of the second grew the BBC's publications in support of the broadcasts, and ALRA's switch of emphasis from equipment to publication, and to training for the production of teaching materials.

The referral service was set up, after great difficulty over finance, by the creation of the Adult Literacy Support Services Fund, with a major grant from the Ford Foundation and smaller amounts from other major sources.[2] This was necessary because BBC licence revenue could not be used for this non-broadcast activity. Telephone referral points were established in London and Glasgow, and for a short time in one or two provincial centres, and the numbers were prominently displayed on the TV screen. Those who rang were asked to give their name and address and this was passed to the appropriate local education officer for follow-up. Hence the link between the broadcasts as a recruiting medium and face-to-face tuition became much closer. Moreover, as many of the local schemes in the early days turned to the BBC workbooks when they found children's reading material inadequate, the relationships became even closer and a multi-media project evolved almost by accident.

The NIAE research team found little perception of this inter-dependence among the students and volunteer tutors. The main impact of the broadcasts was in recruitment of both students and volunteers. But it was also found that the popularity of the 'On the Move' television programmes had a considerable influence on the general public's awareness of adult illiteracy and their attitudes towards it, and there can be little doubt that this change of public attitude in turn affected the frame of mind in which people sought or offered help. There was therefore more mutual support among the media and agencies involved in the work than was generally recognised by the participants.

Indeed it may be said that, without the BBC's initial decision to move into this field, little of the provision made by either central or local authorities would have happened and adult literacy could well have remained a tiny minority concern of a handful of voluntary bodies.

Target Population

In the original plans the target population was visualised as illiterate adults, barely able to read or write beyond a few words. The BBC envisaged a double role, to give such people enough of a start at home to enable them to join a class if they so wished and to help in attracting adults into tuition by removing the social stigma attached to illiteracy. But the general experience in the first year — as the NIAE research team found — was that the severely illiterate adult was either not common or was reluctant to come forward, for the constituency embraced quite a varied range of the semi-literate. Despite the much publicised claims of the 'Right to Read' campaign, which fastened on the figure of two millions, both the extent of adult illiteracy and its nature were guessed at rather than known.

The received wisdom at the time was that individual tuition was the only effective method, chiefly because the students would be so shy and shamefaced about their deficiencies that they would shun any kind of public appearance, even in a small class. This notion could be translated into action only if sufficient volunteers came forward to help, all over the country. Thus, the BBC also produced programmes and materials designed to attract and inform volunteer tutors, and training programmes for them were broadcast on radio.

The numbers involved year by year are given in the annual reports of ALRA and its successors. Certain general features may be noted:

1. Although the proportion of the putative two millions that has so far been recruited is small (not more than ten per cent overall), all the students have by definition never been involved in adult education previously and this must count as evidence of successful outreach.

2. In the early stages four-fifths of the students were men and four-fifths of the volunteer tutors were women. More recently these ratios have become less extreme, but the majorities remain as they were.

3. A graph of the age distribution would show a very flat arc, with roughly equal proportions in the 25-35, 35-45 and 45-55 ranges and considerably fewer in the younger and older groups; though collaboration with the Manpower Services Commission in the last two years has brought rather more young students into tuition.

4. As already indicated, the proportion of the totally illiterate has not been large (the NIAE research team estimated it at less than 30 per cent in the first three years), and over a quarter of the students have been 'spellers' (that is, with reasonably adequate reading skill but poor writing and spelling). There is some evidence that the number of virtual beginners has increased in recent years.

5. Although the concept of disadvantage has been at the heart of this whole initiative, the students have not all shown the features of social disadvantage. Many are holding jobs of some intricacy and even of responsibility; many have come forward because they have been offered advancement at work that would require greater literacy than they possessed; many show astonishing ingenuity in evading discovery of their deficiency and in evolving strategies of their own to cope with their daily lives. Although there is an appreciable minority of slow learners, and some mentally sub-normal, the majority are of average ability and intelligence and their lack of literacy cannot be ascribed to dullness.

6. As far as is known, there are no major discrepancies of social class, intellectual ability or motivation as between urban and

rural literacy schemes. But in a few inner-city areas there is a preponderance of the socially deprived.

7. Finally, it is of interest to note that, especially during the first two years of the telephone referral service, an identifiable number of callers seeking help with their reading were schoolchildren.

The characteristics of those joining the scheme cannot be defined with any precision. The standards of literacy skills of those seeking help vary so much, as do the other indicators of social or occupational status, motivation, and so on, that the NIAE research team concluded that the only workable definition of an adult illiterate was, 'one who thinks he is'. That is, the perception by the individual of his need for improved literacy skills is the criterion for his inclusion in the target population. This finding, of course, raises very extensive questions about the demand for literacy — and other forms of basic education — in our society.

Literacy Materials

Introduction

[...] In the extensive consultations they undertook about the content and format of the programmes, the BBC project team was able also to gather experiences and expectations about the learning materials needed and their Students' Workbook and Tutors' Handbook were the result. These were sold in large numbers, but the evidence for their actual use is unclear. There was much criticism of their level of approach, but that may reflect more upon the variations of expectation in the field than upon the material itself. One of the most important elements in the raising of public consciousness, however, was the copyright-free material made available by the BBC and distributed mainly through the Tesco Supermarket chain during October-November 1975 (as the first broadcasts began): 1,200,000 units of this material were issued. Another was the well-known literacy symbol which was first displayed on posters in supermarkets and bookshops at this time. [...]

Equal care was shown in piloting the television programmes.[3] The difficulty at first was that there were relatively few literacy schemes to consult and their participants were not the isolated non-readers that the programme sought to reach. These early consultants were often highly critical and even hostile to the proposed programmes and their reactions were very different from those found later by the NIAE research team among students who had seen the programmes and been influenced by them. In part this is due to the sensitivity with which the BBC team reacted to the field comments they received.

Adult Literacy Resource Agency (ALRA) and its Successors

[...] The work of the Agency in creating resources could not be completed in one year and its life was extended for a further two years (1976-8). When it came to an end, it was replaced, following heavy pressure from the field, by the Adult Literacy Unit (ALU), with a much reduced budget, for two further years (1978-80). That in turn has now been succeeded by the Adult Literacy and Basic Skills Unit (ALBSU) with a wider remit than just literacy and a somewhat larger budget (approximately £½million). There has been some continuity of staff between the three bodies and a serious attempt to maintain continuity of policy.

These agencies have had certain important effects:

1. They have been the major influence on the materials and methods used in teaching and learning.
2. They have stimulated and often directed the training of local organisers and tutors and have thus established some comparability of standards across the country.
3. By their ability to fund special projects they have stimulated innovation and experiment and have directed the attention of the local education authorities towards unrecognised areas of work: for instance, basic education for the young unemployed. [...]

The Local Education Agencies

[...] What the LEAs have had to provide includes:

1. a referral officer to whom telephone referrals from ALSSF or elsewhere can be passed
2. a local organisation for the recruitment and disposition of volunteer tutors and the placing of students
3. accommodation for this organisation and for tuition where required
4. resource centres from which materials may be distributed and sometimes produced
5. training schemes for volunteer tutors. These have changed considerably since 1975 as knowledge of the student has accumulated, and different LEAs have developed their own styles of training. [...]

Library Resources

Most schemes also involved their local library, where simple readers were provided, special sections containing series of such books were mounted and special measures to welcome students were arranged. The public libraries also acted as referral centres and it may be that the number of 'spellers' in the local schemes came largely from this source.

Conclusions

The element of distance teaching came, thus, from two main sources, the BBC and ALRA. In contrast to the Open University, which has specific student groups following a course determined by the course team, those organising literacy tuition were faced by a student body which required individual tuition, the need to proceed at an individual pace and above all, the right to specify individual objectives. This is the crux of dealing with the educationally disadvantaged. Thus both the BBC and ALRA provided examples of materials, types of materials which would lead to the development and use of further materials as chosen by a student in consultation with a tutor, or by the student alone in the light of his or her own needs.

In general adoption of one-to-one tuition by volunteer tutors increased the pressure towards this flexibility of teaching styles and materials, for the crucial element in the student's progress was the personal relationship that was created. Unless the tutor could see that the student was making progress, frustration and disappointment soon broke up the partnership; but similarly, unless the student could see the relevance of what was being attempted, motivation flagged. Everything depended on the tutor's ability to sense the student's need and to respond to it by the sensitive and ingenious selection of learning materials. The repertoire from which the selection could be made was indicated by the materials produced centrally. In this way an unusual and sophisticated form of distance teaching was developed by ALRA and BBC together, with the major responsibility placed on the student and tutor; and the local training courses, stimulated by both bodies, have come to concentrate very much on the production of home-made materials, using the central materials as starting-points.

A corollary of this is that notions of standard diagnostics, testing, progress schedules and specified objectives, generally inseparable from courses of further or higher education, are quite inappropriate for students who are sharply aware of their individual needs but equally sharply aware that eight to ten years of compulsory and conventional education have failed them.

Media and Methods

[...] Generally, there were three types of tuition on offer:

(a) on a one-to-one basis, in either the student's or tutor's home;
(b) on a one-to-one basis in a group environment;
(c) in a small class at an adult education centre or similar locale.

In the home-based situations it was difficult for organisers to know what methods and progress were present, and there has been a strong tendency to bring as much as possible of the teaching into a group environment. Here the opportunity for student to learn from student, even when still accompanied by a personal tutor, and for tutors to learn from one another about the use of materials or different approaches, has been found of great value.

Much of the early teaching was undertaken by school-teachers (or ex-teachers) and there was a tendency to apply school-based concepts of a 'reading scheme' in which all aspects of literacy are successively covered. More recently these concepts have given way to the kind of individual planning already described. With the move towards group tuition, however, and with the increasing trend towards courses of basic education (as distinct from simple literacy) these notions of a consistent scheme are being reinforced. The experience of success in individual tuition, however, is so strong that a large element of flexibility is retained even in groups or formal courses, and it is clearly important for this disadvantaged clientele that that should be so. [...]

The Student Operating System

Student Enrolment

The system can be seen as a series of stages.

The first stage is the enquiry, which might result from a variety of sources. By mid-August 1978, some 49,000 would-be students had contacted the ALSSF referral points in London, Glasgow, Cardiff and Belfast. A close study of the figures week by week reveals how influential was any mention of the literacy scheme on a popular TV or radio programme, especially disc-jockey shows on radio, for the number of enquiries shot up after every such occurrence. Clearly the target group is to be found in the listening audience for such programmes.

Enquiry could also be stimulated in other ways. In some areas local radio had great influence; the literacy symbol or 'logo' displayed in the window of a shop or house brought many enquiries; social services, probation officers, clergy, district nurses and health visitors all encouraged people to approach their local schemes for help. In some parts more than two thirds of the enquiries came from sources other than the BBC referral number, but there was no clear geographical distribution. The expectation that, with only a London number to ring, the enquiries would diminish with the distance from London proved not to be the case.

The second stage was the transmission of name and address of enquirer to the local scheme. Local organisers spent much time in following up an enquirer, sometimes with no success, and many of them came to face a stark choice between contacting only those who were easily found, and spending inordinate time in pursuit of the rest, to the detriment of the area tuition that was their primary charge.

It is therefore necessary to distinguish between enquiry and enrolment. Whilst the media — broadcasting and press — were most effective in stimulating enquiry, some other influence was often necessary for that enquiry to proceed to active enrolment. The influence was most commonly personal contact, either from the area organiser, from a friend, from some other student, or frequently from a member of the family.

The third stage was placement in tuition. In the early days, when the tender susceptibilities of students were much talked about and absolute confidentiality was thought to be essential, there was great concern about 'matching' — that is, the selection of a volunteer whose personality would fit with the student's. Some schemes had elaborate selection and vetting procedures for this purpose. In the event it was found that most tutors and students were much more adaptable than that attitude suggested, and pairings are now effected by what one organiser has called 'common sense and geography'.

The fourth stage is in the progress of the tuition. Most organisers attempt to keep in regular contact with their pairs, even the home-based ones, but monitoring and support are much easier when there is a common meeting-place. Progress is usually self-assessed, and in recent times attention has been given on tutor-training courses to techniques whereby the student can make his own week-by-week assessment of his learning.

Record-keeping is therefore sometimes a problem. Records of both volunteer tutors and of adults with literacy difficulties are usually held at local levels, by the local voluntary schemes and adult centres. Calls for detailed records have often met resistance from volunteer tutors; though many are conscientious in maintaining records, most volunteer tutors are equally concerned to keep such records confidential to protect their students. Here again the problem is best met where the student is actively involved in the maintenance of the record.

A further problem that arises at this stage is that of drop-out, an extremely difficult matter to define. Home-based pairs in particular may lapse into a pattern of sporadic meeting where it is not possible to say that the student has dropped out but yet little progress is being made, and because of the isolation of such pairs and the tutor's understandable reluctance to 'inform' on the student, the organiser may be unaware of the situation. Great efforts however are made by most organisers to encourage lapsed students to return, generally by means of an offer of a change of locale or of tutor. Recently there has been some evidence that more students who had dropped out of tuition have been returning; and there is also evidence that drop-out is less likely among students who have settled into a group environment.

Not all students who cease from tuition are drop-outs. The fifth stage of the student's progress is graduation, and instances are on record in which a student's self-set objective — it might be the passing of a driving test — has been achieved and he has retired satisfied. Unfortunately, not much is known about this stage with the majority of students, for there has been little opportunity of following up their progress after leaving literacy tuition. Subjective impressions among tutors and organisers are that the access of confidence known to have been experienced by the great majority of students will have led to more satisfactory relationships at home and at work and to a greater ability to order their daily lives. But hard evidence is scanty.

Some ex-literacy students however have gone on to other forms of study. Many of the classes in basic numeracy are comprised of such students; a number have been able to take vocational training courses; and some have progressed into examination classes for 'O'

Level GCE or other qualifications.

What is clear from the successful students' experience is that progress is nearly always slow and the period of attendance envisaged by the system must be measured in years rather than months. Expectations of over-rapid progress in the mind or either student or tutor lead only to frustration.

Student Support

This may be given by the paid professional staff, by the volunteer tutors, by other students, and often also by the student's family and friends, but the critical link is that between the professional organiser and the volunteer tutor.

The ALRA report for 1978/9 notes the gradual increase of trained paid staff to 1,603 by that year but draws attention to the wide variation in practice between local education authorities and remarks that this is a 'cause for concern'. Where there are few trained professional staff the support systems for volunteer tutors cannot be adequate and it is then the students who are likely to suffer. Even in the best staffed areas, the numbers of volunteers to be supervised by one organiser, and their geographical spread, mean that there cannot be fully adequate support for volunteer-tutors in one-to-one home schemes.

A measure of this problem can be seen by examining the volunteer force involved and comparing it with that slow growth to 1,603 professional staff.

Recruitment of volunteer tutors in most schemes was initially through the established adult education networks, through voluntary bodies and through school notice boards. However, volunteer tutors came to learn of literacy schemes from many sources — broadcasts, the Workers' Educational Association, church groups, the local press are all mentioned — or from friends who were already tutors. Sometimes, more than one source of information is quoted but the local press has seemed to be the most influential, especially in articles about the BBC's plans in the early stages. The exact influence of broadcasting in recruiting volunteers cannot be identified, for it appears often to have acted at second or third hand, or as reinforcement of an interest originating elsewhere.

The volunteers are given training and often the training course was used as a screening process: not a few volunteers found that the commitment demanded of them was more than they had expected and withdrew at that point.

By February 1977, some 45,000 volunteer tutors were engaged in various schemes, about 41,000 of them under local education authorities. By 1978/9, the number of volunteer tutors in post had fallen to about 37,000. In part this reflects the growing tendency to organise the teaching in groups with a trained teacher, rather than one-to-one with a volunteer. But over the period more than 75,000 volunteers had been trained and engaged. Therein lies the measure of the problem of adequate support.

A common pattern now is for volunteers to act as ancillary helpers to a group tutor. They are still engaged in one-to-one teaching and can still adapt to the individual purposes and needs of the student, but they have the benefit of continual advice and support. Moreover they have regular contact with other volunteers and can discuss their discoveries and their difficulties with their peers.

The nature of adult basic education requires that such support be readily available, for individualised tuition requires constant adaptation. As problems arise they must be solved, otherwise momentum and motivation are lost. This is again why conventional distance-learning methods are inapplicable: a package or a broadcast can give only generalised advice.

In some schemes, especially in rural areas, regular telephone contact between tutors and organisers is required. In this way a measure of continuing support can be given. But, as we have said, organisers are under heavy pressure and cannot be always at the end of a telephone. There is no doubt that the education service as a whole has seriously under-estimated the resources needed to maintain and support a volunteer scheme.

This description of the machinery for tutor-support is of course based on the premise that the link between organiser and volunteer is the essential ingredient of effective student-support, though this is more evident for home-based pairs, where the tutor may be the only means of contact with the whole scheme that the student ever has.

Where a good group exists, the benefits already described for the volunteers apply even more to the students. The supervision and support of the professional teacher, the opportunities to see other students and their tutors at work, and especially the stimulus of mixing with other literacy students, all conduce to greater regularity of attendance, more awareness of progress, and above all the confidence that comes from a feeling of belonging to a purposive group activity. This confidence was identified in one of our research enquiries as the most important achievement of the students[4] and as affording the psychological release that made skill-learning possible.

There is also evidence that where active support is given by the student's family, or by friends or workmates, this can be of great value in sustaining motivation. The desire to keep up with the family is often stated by students as a reason for joining: for instance, to read to the children, to help with their homework, to be able to write a note to school, or simply not to appear foolish before the children as they reach reading age. Moreover, it was often the wife of the student who telephoned the referral service or made the first enquiry, and the student's subsequent progress is seen as a shared achievement. Here again is evident the highly individual nature of the learning objectives and the need for the operational system to allow for this.

Assessment and Evaluation

The individual nature of the learning makes any external or standardised assessment very dubious. In some schemes opportunities are given to students, if they will, to undertake the assessments that have been introduced experimentally by the Royal Society of Arts or the City and Guilds Certificate in Communication. Relatively few candidates have emerged for these examinations and there is little prospect of their coming into general use.

Rather more students wish to prepare for other forms of assessment. Trade and occupational tests are often quoted, usually as set by an employer; some students wish to enter TOPS or other vocational training courses and require basic general education to do so; and an appreciable number need to be able to read the Highway Code and other such material in preparing for a driving test or heavy goods vehicle licence.

The problems are revealed in some of the evaluative research that has been published.[5] This demonstrates that skills of literacy are acquired only slowly by these adults who have already experienced many years of failure. How far they use their skills depends on the building up of their self-confidence. 'Confidence', a word often used in literacy education and in adult basic education schemes, is shown to be a complex notion; the role of the volunteer tutor is interactive and the success with which confidence is built up largely determines progress in literacy skills. Perhaps the major lessons to emerge from this study are the need to appreciate the time taken by adults with literacy difficulties to make any secure progress, and the realisation that progress can be defined only in terms of the student's individual abilities, potential and objectives. [...]

At least two thirds of the adults with literacy difficulties who came forward were of average or above average intelligence. For such a population the explanation of their failure to learn cannot be sought in the conventional formulae of education, and the application of standardised literacy tests or intelligence tests is of very questionable utility. The whole concept of normative reading ages is inapplicable to adults whose linguistic age may be close to their chronological age, whatever their lack of skill in reading and writing. [...]

So far as literacy provision in general is concerned, it is clear that the existence of ALRA as a central agency prompted local education authorities to find matching resources of their own. ALRA was not a centralising body removing local responsibility: it was a focus of resources pushing out to local areas and receiving from localities ideas and information. Its financial subventions were often necessary to start local initiatives but these moneys were always given after full consultation with and often after the request from local areas. Moreover, the fact that applications for funds in later years would be viewed in the light of ALRA's assessment of what had already been done made possible a kind of running evaluation that had widespread effect.

The main impact of the broadcasts was upon recruitment and upon public awareness, two crucial areas for the success of the whole enterprise. Moreover, the light and entertaining style of 'On The Move', and its association in the public mind with popular entertainment personalities, helped to avoid those associations of dreary rectitude that commonly accompany educative efforts. There can be no doubt that any initiative towards general basic education for adults must be able to count on a major and positive contribution from the media, especially television and radio. This is equally true at the level of local transmission as at the national.

Finally, an evaluation must be made of the quantitative success of the literacy project. As already shown, if the target population is indeed two million, less than one in ten has been reached. But the absolute numbers are impressive and they show that 'submerged minorities' can be reached by multi-media collaboration. Nevertheless, the demand for basic skills in a complex and changing modern society becomes more insistent and not less. [...]There remains therefore much still to be done in the provision of basic learning skills, among which literacy is the most essential. [...]

Yet we cannot but be encouraged that society in the UK has recognised the problem of semi-literacy and has found the political will to allocate resources to its alleviation. What the history of the adult literacy project shows is that:

1. outreach to a submerged and disadvantaged population is feasible
2. the combination of broadcasting and other forms of tuition is possible and highly effective
3. there is a great resevoir of voluntary goodwill waiting to be tapped for socially desirable ends
4. a substantial initial investment can bring about a notably cost-effective service
5. a national multi-media enterprise can be created in which full play can be given to the personal need and circumstance of the individual student
6. a project of this kind can have widespread influence on the public mind about a particular form of social and educational deprivation.

Notes

1. H.A. Jones and A.H. Charnley, *Adult Literacy: a Study of its Impact* (National Institute of Adult Education, Leicester, 1978), pp. 12-19.
2. Jones and Charnley, pp. 14-15.
3. D. Hargreaves, *Adult Literacy and Broadcasting: The BBC's Experience.* A Report to the Ford Foundation (Frances Pinter, London, 1980).
4. A.H. Charnley and H.A. Jones, *The Concept of Success in Adult Literacy* (Huntington Publishers, Cambridge, 1979), pp. 174-8.
5. Ibid.

3.2

EDUCATIONAL INITIATIVES FOR THE ADULT UNEMPLOYED

Ian Bryant

Source: Copyright © The Open University (specially written for this volume).

Introduction

Mass unemployment presents the greatest possible challenge to adult educators. They are not currently equipped to serve the needs of adults on the scale required to make a significant difference to the lives of more than a small minority of those who are jobless, either by enhancing their employability or by offering rewarding alternatives. There are important historical and philosophical reasons for this state of affairs which are embedded in the structure and operating assumptions of the major providing agencies. Whereas children's educational needs are determined by their elders, this cannot reasonably be so for adults whose status requires that they be heard. Yet this is not generally the case when they lose their jobs. Collective or self-representation of adult educational interests is made doubly difficult by the isolating and demoralising consequences of unemployment. So the 'needs' of the unemployed continue to be determined by those who are in work and not by the unemployed themselves. The latter are rarely equal, let alone dominant partners in decisions about the content of learning programmes. Jobless adults do not articulate learning needs in a way that is convenient to curriculum planners or allocators of resources; and the resources which support further education and training are concentrated on the young.

Current and envisaged 'educational initiatives' for the adult unemployed — the term itself is significant as suggesting programmes which are dynamic and purposeful but which must operate in a general socio-economic climate of stagnation and uncertainty — can perhaps best be discussed in terms of whether they support or reject particular philosophies regarding the proper function of adult education. The problem of evaluation is thus a threefold one: (a) to discover the underlying *principles* governing the provision of

130

facilities to unemployed learners; (b) to determine the extent to which existing adult education *provision* actually reflects those principles; and (c) on the basis of prevailing theory and practice, to assess what *prospects* jobless adults have of obtaining relevant educational assistance. The history of educational policy at all levels is one of pragmatic and piecemeal reforms. Given that, projections concerning the future of education for the unemployed are bound to be speculative. But they can only be reasonably realistic if we try to understand what is happening now, and why.

Principles

There are five overlapping areas of debate about the kind of educational service that could be offered to the unemployed, each illustrating that particular principles are at stake.

The first issue concerns that of *identifying and responding to need.* Should educators give priority to individual, social or labour market requirements? They are not necessarily incompatible: for example, both individual and market needs for particular kinds of employment may be satisfied by offering the unemployed (re-)training. Also, educational responses to a group disproportionately affected by unemployment, such as the disabled or an ethnic minority — possibly through some form of 'positive discrimination' — would be expected to benefit individuals within those groups. But where individual, social and economic needs are *not* compatible, priorities will be drawn that are reflected in resource allocation governed by cost-effectiveness. Training will not meet individual needs and will represent 'wasted' expenditure if the labour market cannot absorb its products. Educational initiatives in the form of vocational training are therefore limited by the capacity of the economy to support a particular level and diversity of employment.

Collective or social need can be squeezed out of the debate about what individuals want, what the market can support and what educational interventions are therefore relevant. The personal experience of joblessness is not just an individual one but is also shared, even when unrecognised, so that common difficulties and requirements can be grouped. The second kind of argument is thus concerned with the *targeting of particular audiences* for educational assistance. Identifications can be made according to a number of criteria, such as age, sex, race, disability, geographical location, parental status, educational qualifications and former occupational status. These serve as both qualifiers and disqualifiers for particular adult learning programmes for the unemployed. The balance of existing initiatives is likely to be weighted in favour of the most socially visible and/or vocal groups within the heterogeneous jobless population.

The third set of principles concerns *access to learning programmes* for the unemployed. Issues here include convenience (timing and location of courses), qualifications for admission, fees and subsidies. In practice, further and higher educational institutions operate a system of entrance controls which does not permit either the unemployed, or any other group of students for that matter, unqualified rights of access to courses. There is an unresolved argument about whether unemployed adults should have such a right, with or without qualifications, and how it might be secured. The nominal availability of different types of learning opportunity does not necessarily mean that they are actually available to those without the means to take advantage of them.

The *determination of the curriculum* is a fourth issue involving two sets of questions: (a) the extent to which learning programmes are to be targeted exclusively towards the unemployed or particular groups therein; and (b) the role of the jobless in determining programme content. Answers here will depend upon adult educators' characterisation of potential demand, or on how 'need' is perceived. A labour market definition of need is more comfortable to the idea of a pre-set or imposed curriculum; individual and collective interpretations of 'need' provide more scope for a negotiated or learner-controlled curriculum.

Finally, there are questions which concern the *overall purpose* in providing any kind of educational opportunities at all to those out of work. These are pre-eminently questions of value. Given that no educational service can directly solve what for the unemployed is their major 'problem', i.e. a lack of paid work, what then is the function of educational initiatives for the unemployed? Is it simply to reconcile people to their condition, or to offer constructive adaptation, or to offer critical insights and hence socially transformative potentials? These are not questions which concern only those adults without jobs, but they are ones that mass unemployment casts into sharp ideological relief and which for adult educators will not disappear however much they may be avoided.

Having identified the major areas of debate, it is now possible to locate different kinds of adult education practice, if not definitively then at least in terms of the provisional answers that they are presently offering to the above questions. It is also possible to categorise the various learning programmes available to unemployed adults by agency type, sponsorship and funding of educational services. Statutory and voluntary bodies are making some contributions to providing the jobless with educational options, but there are wide differences in their terms of reference and operating methods. Collectively they do not represent an 'educational solution' to unemployment, but individually they can alleviate the problem for some of those affected. In discussing the recent research into adult education initiatives and projects for the unemployed in the UK, Charnley and his colleagues pointed to the nub of the dilemma faced by providers and the inherent tension in the most carefully planned schemes, i.e. that whereas 'the numbers of unemployed seem to require a macro-solution, the clientele demand and need a micro-service'.[1]

Provision

(a) Manpower Services Commission (MSC). Existing educational provision for the unemployed is dominated, in terms of the numbers of adults reached (60,000 in 1981), cost (£260 m.), and public knowledge of the service, by the Training Opportunities Programme (TOPS) of the MSC. The Commission recognises that (re-)training *per se* does not offer an automatic solution to adult unemployment, especially since post-TOPS job placement rates are now less than 45 per cent.[2] Nevertheless, as an agency of central government, it continues to operate a labour market demand philosophy according to which the acquisition of new, and ideally transferable, instrumental skills, as required by industry, is considered to offer the best hope to the jobless in the long term. In present economic circumstances, it is misleading to speak of conventional TOPS programmes as 'initiatives'. The demand for such programmes exceeds availability, so that there are now long waiting lists for most courses. Also, the capacity for training (assessed via an entrance test) requires a level of confidence and competence that many unemployed adults may not possess. More than half of all economically active manual workers aged 20 years and over have no educational qualifications,[3] yet it is manual workers who bear the burden of unemployment.[4] Belief in one's ability to train, especially for this group, is not automatic.

Within the TOPS scheme, but as a comparatively small component of it, are non-vocational courses which address themselves to issues of a 'basic' educational nature, and which are planned to serve altogether some 8,000 adults at a cost of £17 m. in 1982-3.[5] These include Wider Opportunities Courses (job acquisition and skill sampling), Vocational Assessment Courses (employability and trainability assessment), preparatory courses in literacy and numeracy, and English as a Second Language course. They are intended to reduce the relative disadvantages of particular groups among the unemployed, for example, non-English-speaking immigrants, and to start them on the road to skill acquisition or other learning options. A not inconsiderable benefit of such TOPS administered courses is that an allowance is paid to students which at least provides the semblance of a wage, while social security benefit entitlements are retained. Such courses are likely to prove attractive to some unemployed adults on these grounds alone. Recently, under the auspices of TOPS, a number of short experimental job search and confidence-building courses based in further education colleges have begun to offer some unemployed adults the chance to develop generic skills and the opportunity of self-evaluation in a relatively informal but supportive context. For example, twelve-week intensive courses for the long-term unemployed are offered at Blackpool and Fylde College of Further Education. A full-time three week job search, presentation and linked self-assessment course, using video playback for developing interview techniques, has recently been provided for 60 adults in three intakes at Reid Kerr College, Renfrew. It is too early to assess the effects of such intensive but small scale programmes. In MSC terms they are admittedly costly, and for that reason alone are likely to remain fairly peripheral to its major training input. As 'marginal' educational enterprises they are, however, extremely valuable. There is evidence of considerable indirect benefit quite apart from their central purpose of improving employability, and of a demand for more courses of this nature which would manifest itself if they were given better publicity.[6]

Two other MSC schemes are of potential benefit to the unemployed in educational terms. The Voluntary Projects Programme was launched in August 1982, at a cost of £8 m. per year for two years, to support the unemployed in 'constructive activities', and can make funds available to local authorities and other organisations providing adult education as long as this is 'directed to training for or obtaining work'. It is intended to support a variety of basic educational initiatives in this way, and to encourage local authorities to provide the unemployed with easier access to their educational facilities, as a way of overcoming the inactivity of the jobless. It remains to be seen how this will work.

The Community Programme, announced in the summer of 1982 is a more controversial initiative. It is intended to offer full- or part-time work, of benefit to the local community, by paying sponsors to employ 130,000 persons in its first year of operation (from October 1982) at a total cost of £550 m. Rates of pay are to be lower on average (£60 per week, full time) than under its predecessor, the Community Enterprise Programme, and there is no specific budget either for training or general adult education. This is likely to be provided only on an *ad hoc* basis and funded either out of allocations for wages (thus reducing average wages) or from employers' overhead subsidies. The scheme has few supporters in adult education circles since it contains no separate educational element despite the comparatively high cost of the programme.

Although any comparative educational evaluation of the above schemes would be difficult to make, even when they are operating at full steam, it can reasonably be said that the position of the MSC as an educational agency is somewhat paradoxical and that many unemployed adults are bound to suffer from the contradiction. As an institutional provider and facilitator of adult education for the unemployed, its most visible and costly programmes in *overall* terms may be less effective than those few experimental courses that are offered in response to the identified needs of particular groups of adults, but whose *unit* costs are higher and whose products may still be difficult to place in jobs. In the present economic and political circumstances, it is unlikely that the more adventurous programmes worthy of the description 'initiatives' will be anything other than marginal activities.

(b) Workers' Educational Association (WEA). Nationally, the provision of the Workers' Educational Association includes the traditional liberal academic mix of social, political and economic education, as well as citizenship and community role education of a practical kind. Together with industrial and trade union education, this still accounts for the bulk of all WEA class offerings. Individual Districts of the WEA exercise considerable autonomy in the provision of adult education classes, but since the publication of the Russell Report the National Executive of the WEA has attempted to

define particular development areas, including work with the unemployed.[7] Charnley reports that 'student recruitment policies which do not identify with the special problems of the unemployed do not attract unemployed students'.[8] It is not known how many unemployed adults are actually served by the WEA, since some Districts consider formal registration or detailed record-keeping to be incompatible with voluntary attendance.

Marginal groups, including those particularly prone to unemployment, have been the targets of 'rights' education, including legal and consumer rights, and the rights of women and ethnic minorities. Basic educational and non-vocational study preparation skills are also now being offered. Some Districts are more heavily committed to this type of work with adults than others, but there is no automatic correspondence between the importance attached to such courses and local unemployment levels. In 1980, for example, whereas 58 per cent of the class provision of the North Wales District was categorised as 'education for the disadvantaged', only 6 per cent was so designated in the North West with similar levels of unemployment. Despite such local anomalies in the distribution of WEA provision, initiatives have been launched, either specifically to attract the jobless, or to run programmes where it is known that they will comprise a substantial proportion of class attenders.

Different techniques of approach, but similar philosophies of flexible response, are illustrated in three examples of WEA involvement in education for the unemployed. In Edinburgh, for example, the local WEA tutor-organiser has worked closely with the Edinburgh Centre for the Unemployed to contact small groups of adults, in order to identify through an extensive but informal personal interview some of their learning 'needs', prior to the establishment of a pilot educational course with modular options designed to meet individual requirements. Although designed as a course 'for the unemployed', in that this was to be the qualifying criterion for being offered a place, it was not intended specifically to focus either on unemployment 'issues' or to improve employability, but to offer a supportive environment for a return to structured learning of a personally relevant kind, and to improve self-confidence and communication skills. Options included both 'basic literacy' and the development of 'creative writing' skills. The course now runs for one day per week, for eight to ten weeks, and is free of charge; it offers a referral service for unemployed students wishing to continue their studies thereafter. An enhanced motivation to study has been one of the major benefits for jobless adults, together with the more intangible gain of sharing the experiences of co-learners in similar situations. Student satisfaction with the course appears to be fairly high.[9]

A joint venture of the WEA, the local education authority and the Extra-Mural Department of Exeter University is a 'Use of English' course, designed to attract the unemployed on the assumption that 'the morale-boosting skills of communication' would be valuable in helping them to overcome 'feelings of inferiority and inadequacy' arising from continuous exposure to the work ethic.[10] Extensive local publicity through newspapers, radio, posters and leaflets offered the course as a chance 'to Take a New Direction' and attracted some 60 students initially, about half being unemployed. Teaching input is on a voluntary basis and employed, fee-paying students effectively subsidise the jobless who attend free of charge. Classroom instruction centres on the teaching of basic English, with private counselling opportunities available after the determination of individual student priorities from a prepared checklist of subjects. A route is offered for entry into more conventional courses, such as 'O' levels. The development of self-confidence is considered to be the major benefit of the course to date, but a number of individual difficulties, associated with a return to learning, have been identified which would undoubtedly have defeated many adult students enrolled in more conventional classes.

Perhaps the best known and longest established example of WEA involvement in this area is that of the 'Second Chance to Learn' project in Liverpool. The history of this inner-city adult education exercise[11] illustrates the importance attached to developing a programme of study with a *local* focus through the identification of issues which exercise the minds of residents. The original issue was housing and the locals' status as council or private tenants. 'Second Chance to Learn' is a joint WEA/Liverpool University Institute of Extension Studies initiative, with contributory urban aid funding, which offers a one day per week, 20-week social studies course explicitly aimed 'to stimulate a critical consciousness' through a study of economic, industrial and social issues as they relate to the lives of participants in Merseyside. The course is not offered specifically for the unemployed, but has inevitably evolved from a dockside community development and action research project to include a large number of jobless manual workers. Women in fact form the majority of course applicants, who 'outnumber places available by about three to one'. Participants are involved in writers' workshops, local history and various thematic projects including unemployment and women's issues, and individual tutorials are provided to improve study techniques. The course is academically demanding, yet the organisers are on record as stating that they 'are keen to avoid creating a model of academicism which would deepen the isolation of the course from its roots among the activists'.[12] Drop-out rates have been quite high, but a number of individuals have proceeded to degree-level study.

Whereas the Edinburgh and Exeter courses may be characterised as being 'therapeutic', the Liverpool course emphasises reflection on the experiences of working-class adults and has a more radical pedigree. In their different ways, and for a comparatively small number of unemployed adults, courses such as these are providing some important learning supports for those who have been neglected by more conventional education delivery systems.

(c) Community Education. The theory of community-based educational initiatives is especially relevant to provision for jobless adults where unemployment is concentrated in particular localities, such as inner cities and peripheral housing estates. Social isolation and a lack (or ignorance) of local amenities, the argument goes, can be overcome by an approach which is problem-centred and concentrates on the shared need for association with others and the generation of local resources. Learning is seen as an organic concept and education as a co-operative venture in which the classroom or tutorial is not the prime focus of activity, but rather the many dimensions of neighbourhood life itself. Community education operates an outreach philosophy in which making local contacts, and developing and organising learning resources as far as possible within the community itself, is considered to offer the most meaningful and convenient service to the unemployed. Unlike the mechanical 'provider-consumer' model of adult education, curricula as such may be initially undefined and targets will be identified only gradually; *any* local resource has educational potential to be developed through, for example, advice and drop-in centres, skill-exchanges, voluntary activities or recreational programmes. These may involve not only adults and those without work.

The potential of community education to facilitate an integrated provision of locally-based learning supports would, if realised, help to solve what for many unemployed adults are the most important barriers to educational participation, namely ignorance of conventional providers, institutional formality and inconvenient siting. Crucially, the theory addresses itself to individuals as members of a community and as having a stake and a status therein, *not* as workers or non-workers as such. It is less likely therefore to segregate the unemployed as targets for special provision in the way that some of the initiatives already discussed may do. So much for the theory; how is this being applied locally?

A pilot scheme called 'Connect' was set up in Clydebank in 1981[13] with the goal of bringing together local unemployed people in recreational and learning activities, opening up community resources to them and persuading the local authority to provide free facilities. A lone community education worker had the job of tapping the skills and interests of her area team colleagues, organising publicity and siting an educational and leisure programme in local community centres. Classes were run on two days each week. Limited amounts of trade union and private employer funding were secured to launch the scheme. The technical college agreed to operate an 'open door' policy for the unemployed who wished to attend classes, and offered the use of a film viewing room. The local authority offered free use of recreational facilities and the library service loaned relevant books. An Urban Aid welfare rights project gave its services. As an exercise in inter-agency co-operation the scheme has been judged a success and has helped to widen the horizons of participants, but those involved have tended to be the more active locals whose knowledge of, and willingness to use, community resources is already relatively high. Publicity has not attracted the 'non-joiners', especially women and the older unemployed. The scheme has now been integrated into mainstream local authority provision, and to that extent has been formalised in a way that runs counter to the 'ideal' community education response.

Maryhill is one of Glasgow's 'special initiative areas', an area of high local unemployment, which was selected for Urban Aid funding to develop an outreach adult literacy and basic education programme under the auspices of Strathclyde Regional Council's Community Education Service in 1978. The local organisations contacted were initially suspicious of the presumed need for a literacy service, but posed a variety of questions concerning how to generate voluntary and self-help services, support groups, advice and information facilities. 'What they were asking for could not be categorized as "adult literacy" or "basic education" or "formal FE" [Further Education] or "informal FE" but simply as adult education. The subtle divisions of formal/informal FE are meaningless in an area like Maryhill. Responsiveness and categorization do not mix.'[14] Importantly, local residents were defining the terms in which they wanted a community education service to respond. Learning groups have been established which offer provision at various levels in English and Arithmetic. The gain in confidence of participants has had a multiplier effect in community development terms, with students becoming involved in local housing issues, youth work, play groups, parent-teacher groups, etc. — an involvement that previously they had either not thought themselves capable of or had not even considered. The value of this kind of initiative is to be seen not only in terms of improvements in individual abilities, but also in developing a collective sense of what is desirable and possible by capitalising on the natural sociability of neighbours and friends. The unemployed *as such* have not been the focus of adult educators' concerns, which have centred on the associated and locally experienced conditions in which widespread joblessness plays a major role. Although there are reservations about particularising Maryhill residents in this way, the project recognises the difficulty of attracting the more isolated, longer-term unemployed and their families into programmes — outreach work on the scale required and with limited resources is a frustrating and time-consuming business.

Many other local programmes could be described in which the adult education component of community-based initiatives is undefined; where learning proceeds, as it were, 'by stealth' and may be secondary to the achievement of other objectives such as the development of leisure opportunities, job-creation and job-sharing.[15] These include the community arts and co-operative business ventures which are integral parts of such relatively well-established projects as the Craigmillar Festival Society, Edinburgh and the Easterhouse Festival Society, Glasgow.[16] Craigmillar's 'Communiversity' sees its priority in developing skill exchanges and resource banks, on the basis of indigenous talents, so as to instil a belief in the learning capacity of target groups, rather than leave them dependent upon subject-based, institutional providers of adult education.

In view of the tenuous nature of many community projects in funding terms, achievements to date do seem to support the theory underlying this kind of educational response to adult unemployment, but community educators admit that they have much work to do, especially to increase the participation of the older and longer-term unemployed. This requires extra professional and voluntary supports, and more secure financing.

(d) Unemployed Workers' Centres. The trade union movement is committed to the establishment of centres for the unemployed and their emergence in the 1980s has been rapid, if uneven.[17] There are probably now more than 100 such centres throughout the country which offer some form of adult educational activity, with many others in the planning and early development stages. The quality, staffing and management structure, operating philosophy, financial security and local acceptability of existing centres varies enormously so that a 'typical' one would be difficult to describe. Some have been set up on the model of the oldest and best known, in Newcastle. This offers a wide range of drop-in facilities and campaigning activities, has established a referral service and access for the unemployed to local adult education providers.

Local authorities, trades councils, the MSC and charitable trusts have combined to provide sites and a range of facilities, including the funding of temporary workers in centres where day-to-day operations are controlled by the unemployed themselves. The impetus for educational courses has come from an early recognition of the need for a rights service, including information on welfare and redundancy claims. Some centres emphasise the 'political' dimension of education for the jobless, for example, by setting up discussion groups to explore the causes of mass unemployment and possible solutions. The collective voice of the unemployed has been encouraged through the production of local radio material and video tapes. Other centres concentrate on basic skills training for individuals, job-search and interview techniques. Most existing centres are attempting to gain free or easier access to educational and recreational facilities.[18]

The development of adult learning initiatives by the centres themselves is presently limited because centres are experiencing similar problems of establishing credibility to those faced by community educators. In the case of facilities supported by trade unions or local trades councils there is an additional difficulty. There is some evidence to suggest that the real or imagined association of supporters of unemployed workers' centres sponsored by these bodies with political activism may limit both the clientele and the willingness of agencies to supply funds. Perhaps regrettably, many unemployed adults — especially the unskilled and women — are not former trade unionists and see little or no value in such centres for themselves.[19] In some cases also, the siting and stigmatic designation of centres have limited their appeal.[20]

Prospects

The examples which have been given of existing educational initiatives for the unemployed sketch only some of the main services and supports available. It is not known how much adult education is indirectly available for the unemployed, but to the extent that all existing self and co-operative employment, voluntary work, hobby and recreational schemes have associated elements of learning, then these also represent 'adult education' in its widest sense. Furthermore, techniques of evaluation are undeveloped; we can only speculate on the qualitative effects of this myriad and diverse provision. It has been shown that the mere existence of 'initiatives' of whatever type does not mean that those without jobs will automatically take them up.

The prospects for the unemployed of obtaining an 'effective' service (however that is defined) depend not just upon the level of funds available to adult educators, but on increasing our knowledge of the *nature of the needs of people without work and how these can be translated into learning terms*. It is also necessary to develop comparative indicators of the 'success' or 'failure' of educational programmes by various criteria, so as to answer for different groups of jobless adults some of the questions of principle posed earlier.

The report of the Advisory Council for Adult and Continuing Education[21] has considered how to improve the effectiveness of provision for unemployed adults, concentrating on general educational needs. In addition to promoting the idea (among those in and out of work) of mainstream adult education as a means of personal enrichment, the Council supports the extension of generic skills programmes to equip adults to take advantage of a variety of educational and training opportunities. It considers that adult education can provide the supports for personal adjustment, the framework for realistic self-assessment and the realisation of potentials both within and outside work. Adult education is ideally placed, in theory, to tackle alongside other agencies the social pathology of unemployment by offering a wide range of learning supports and a chance to experiment in styles of delivery.

However, realising the potential of adult education to serve the needs of the unemployed depends upon creating and organising the appropriate means of delivery in which fee concessions, flexible siting and timetabling are the major considerations. According to the ACACE 'the obstacles are severe ... without the release of additional resources ... progress beyond the present local small-scale toes-in-the-water efforts will be unlikely to be made'.[22] Administrators are indicted for the rigidity of existing institutional arrangements in public adult and further education, which effectively discourages the unemployed.[23] There is evidence that local authorities and individual providers are not consistent in their application of the '21 hour' rule, to allow the unemployed part-time study without loss of social security benefit,[24] and the concession is not widely known among the unemployed themselves.

The Council recognises that the educational prospects of the unskilled unemployed, in particular, depend upon increasing public awareness of the need for flexible learning opportunities and the political will to generate the required funds. With typical liberal modesty, it has suggested that £15.6 m. annually could support development programmes of general adult education in which the Council expects ten per cent of the unemployed in any one year to be engaged. Realistically, in the present climate the educational prospects for the majority of men and women who are out of work remain uncertain, if not bleak.

Notes

1. A. Charnley, *et al.*, *Review of Existing Research in Adult and Continuing Education. Vol. IX: Adult Education and Unemployment* (National Institute of Adult Education, Leicester, 1982).
2. MSC Manpower Paper, *Long-Term Unemployment* (HMSO, London, 1982), p. 48.
3. R. Berthoud, *et al.*, *Poverty and the Development of Anti-Poverty Policy in the UK* (Policy Studies Institute, 1981), Table 8.1.
4. A. Sinfield, *What Unemployment Means* (Oxford University Press, 1981), pp. 18-23.
5. MSC Manpower Paper, *Long-Term Unemployment*, p. 48.
6. I. Bryant, *The Educational Needs of Long-Term Unemployed Adults* (A Report for the Scottish Education Department. University of Glasgow Dept. of Adult and Continuing Education, 1982).
7. Workers' Educational Association, *Report of the National Executive Committee, 1979-81*; M. Doyle, 'Reform and Reaction: The Workers' Educational Association Post-Russell' in J.L. Thompson (ed.), *Adult Education for a Change* (Hutchinson, London, 1980), Ch. 6.
8. A. Charnley, *Review of Existing Research*, p. 49.

9. Workers' Educational Association, *Work with the Unemployed*, 1981.

10. T. Tupp, 'Close Encounters with the Unemployed', *Adult Education 55 (2)* (September, 1982), pp. 139-42.

11. M. Yarnit, 'Second Chance to Learn, Liverpool: Class and Adult Education' in J.L. Thompson (ed.), *Adult Education for a Change* (Hutchinson, London, 1980), Ch. 9.

12. Ibid., p. 190.

13. *Scan* (February, 1982), p. 15.

14. H. Munro, 'The Maryhill Project — Basic Education in an Urban Area', *Scottish Journal of Adult Education 5 (1)* (Autumn, 1980), p. 6.

15. For a brief description of community schemes, see, for example, Scottish Community Education Centre — *Unemployment Action: A Selection of Unemployment Initiatives* (Scottish Community Education Centre, Edinburgh, 1982).

16. A. Charnley, *Review of Existing Research*, pp. 69-88.

17. Labour Research Department, 'Unemployed Workers' Centres', *Labour Research 70 (10)* (October, 1981).

18. For example, see Scottish Community Education Centre, *Unemployment Action*, pp. 16-21; A. Charnley, *Review of Existing Research*, pp. 51-3.

19. I. Bryant, *The Educational Needs of Long-Term Unemployed Adults*, p. 111.

20. A. Charnley, *Review of Existing Research*.

21. Advisory Council for Adult and Continuing Education — *Education for Unemployed Adults* (Leicester, 1982).

22. Ibid., para. 56.

23. Ibid., para. 75.

24. I. Bryant, *The Educational Needs of Long-Term Unemployed Adults*, p. 109.

3.3

WOMEN AND ADULT EDUCATION

Jane Thompson

Source: Copyright © The Open University 1983 (specially written for this volume).

Allegations about male sexism and women's oppression in the context of adult education are claims which are usually dismissed as unfounded or tendentious by a profession which considers itself profoundly democratic in its relationships with students, highly responsive to students' needs, and characterised by values and practices which are clearly distinctive when compared with the rest of the education system.

The non-statutory and mainly non-vocational nature of adult education emphasises the voluntary commitment of those who participate. University and Workers' Educational Association (WEA) roots in liberal education assume that students are concerned with the pursuit of knowledge for its own sake rather than for vocational or instrumental purposes, and the local education authority (LEA) curriculum comprised of practical crafts, physical skills, leisure time and recreational activities appears to reflect the notion of education for pleasure rather than purpose. Adult education is described as 'a service for the whole community' concerned with 'self fulfilment', 'personal growth and development' and 'useful citizenship'. The rhetoric of its opinion leaders and enthusiasts is unquestioning in commitment, energetic in the pursuit of reform and expansion and critical only of those — either as funding bodies or reluctant recruits — who do not appear to value the significance of what it has to offer.

Theory and practice in adult education reflect a remarkable complacency and consensus. Its philosophy and provision has been infrequently subjected to the kinds of sociological analysis which has become common in the examination of compulsory schooling, so that the links between education and control, education and capitalism and education and culture, for example, have rarely been developed. The early origins of adult education in independent working class movements and some liberal-democratic commitment to the plight of 'the disadvantaged' has meant that the question of social class has always been of academic interest, but there is little evidence of anything other than technical or pathological explanations being given for working class non-participation in adult education.[1]

But those who have depicted schooling as a training ground for capitalism,[2] and a powerful ideological instrument in the battle for the hearts and minds of dutiful workers[3] have none the less failed to consider the position of women within the education system. The preparation of young women for domesticity and the relationships of reproduction have been generally ignored or treated as subsidiary to the main plot.[4] Only when feminists have entered the debate has discrimination based on gender been taken seriously as a characteristic of all education systems operating within capitalist patriarchy.[5] Indeed, only as a consequence of feminism has the problem of patriarchy — of the power and control which men exercise over women in both private and public relations — been named and exposed as a system of exploitation which is as ubiquitous and as serious in its implications as race and social class.[6]

But this analysis applied to education, especially in circumstances in which co-education seems to be reinforcing the underachievement of girls in comparison to boys rather than reducing it,[7] has yet to penetrate the general consciousness of adult education theory and practice. Despite a number of obvious contradictions and clear indications of oppression and repression, conventional wisdom within adult education continues to protest its innocence and to deny the patriarchal character and significance of its condition.

Adult education is of course the only sector of the education system in which women as students constitute a significant majority. Women outnumber men in LEA provision by approximately 3 to 1 and in university and WEA provision by approximately 2 to 1. Women are also much more likely than men to make up the groups engaged in non-formal community education, outreach programmes and adult basic education initiatives.

Explanations for women's relatively high participation levels in adult education compared to men, and compared to their lower participation in other forms of post school education provision, are usually couched in terms of social-recreational reasons. The views of a publication by the Northern Advisory Council for Further Education in 1963 concerning women's reasons for attending courses, and offering suggestions to part-time teachers of women's subjects, would still go largely unchallenged within contemporary conventional wisdom.

> The desire for the company of others and a change from household duties (sic) . . . this recreational attitude and motive is perhaps even more potent in the country than in the towns for it is in rural districts that the evening class provides women with one of their few chances of meeting their friends and neighbours.[8]

A variation on this theme is the classification of adult education as 'a safe pursuit' which women can go to easily and which provides a female equivalent to the male leisure space of the pub, the golf club or the football game. Given the nature of conventional adult education, it is also seen as an activity which is essentially unthreatening to masculine authority in the home and in the workplace — less threatening, presumably, than if women were to appropriate the pub or the football terraces as their meeting place.

But these explanations are not good enough. They ignore the extent to which the options which women have for cultural and educational expression are seriously restricted compared to men, and more important, the extent to which an essentially feminine pastime is none the less managed and orchestrated by men within a system of female subordination.

The detailed history of adult education for women in the nineteenth and early twentieth century has still to be written[9] but the indications are that women have always been well represented as students in the mechanics institutes and working men's colleges, the university extension movement and the early WEA, although they were not treated equally with men[10] and the curriculum which they were offered reflected serious problems associated with their subordination to patriarchy. Only in the relatively independent and separatist Co-operative Women's Guilds[11] and in the early women's trade unions did women define and control their own education and seek to further their expectation of an existence which was not bound and restricted by the sexual division of labour in the home and in the demands of capital for a cheap, unskilled, secondary labour force.

The participation of women in the past is of course generally ignored by the historians of adult education, as is the significance of women's majority interest as students in contemporary provision. And seen in this light the career structure in adult education is equally revealing. Women constitute the majority of volunteer tutors in

Literacy, Adult Basic Education and English as a Second Language schemes. They are also more likely than men to be part-time tutors in Local Authority provision. As such they have little influence, receive low rates of pay, and enjoy no recognisable career structure except as token women in an essentially male-dominated profession.

Full-time appointments, especially at WEA tutor-organiser and divisional secretary level, university lecturer level and Local Authority centre principal and advisory level, are predominantly held by men. The field-workers and classroom teachers in adult education may well be women but the managers and decision makers, the opinion leaders and rhetoricians, the theorists and philosophers are men — men used to consulting with other men in institutional committees, academic departments, conferences and professional journals. Their assumptions and experience are constructed within a context of male values, male definitions and male authority and are then generalised to represent human assumptions and experience and credited with universal validity and objective truth. Any suggestion that female experience may be different or that women's general exclusion from the power and career structure of adult education seriously distorts the vision and provision of what is offered is rarely conceded by those who monopolise debate. The suggestion made by feminists that male definitions of female need and the patterns of provision that emerge from it are invariably counter-productive in terms of women's *real* needs are all too easily dismissed by men who rarely consult with women on an equal basis and in equal numbers. Most often they ignore the significance of women, thus making us invisible. Just as frequently our significance is assessed in terms of male assumptions about our interests. It's not surprising — given the nature of the society in which we live, in which the sexual division of labour bolsters the economic and the family systems of production — that these are seen as interests restricted to domestic service.

The tendency of the adult education establishment to ignore or to stereotype women in this way is apparent in even the most cursory review of recent literature. In 1973 the Russell Report[12] was welcomed with eagerness and gratitude by fieldworkers at a time when adult education seemed to have lost some of its earlier momentum. The report reminded the service of its origins in working class and independent education and is perhaps best remembered for its encouragement to the WEA particularly to get involved in work with socially and culturally deprived groups, trade union education and political education. Given the close association of adult education in its formative years with social and political movements seeking social change, and given the loyal participation of women in the university extension movement and the WEA, it is perhaps surprising to find the Russell committee making precious little reference to women and no reference whatsoever to one of the most significant, voluntary, independent, political, educational and spontaneous grass-roots movements of recent years — the women's movement.

The re-emergence of feminism in Britain in and around 1968 was accompanied by a proliferation of informal meetings, study groups, conferences, newsletters and publications which, although related to campaigns and the concern to change the subordinate position of women in society, also reflected a serious educational purpose and commitment. Feminists within adult education have seen to it that adult education classes increasingly reflect the interests and concerns of this important popular movement, but five years after its appearance, in the wake of similar developments in Europe and North America, and amidst considerable publicity and public discussion, the Russell Committee, defending more than a century of popular and political education, was apparently oblivious to its significance.

Women are rarely mentioned in the report except to register that they constitute a majority of students, but when they are, it's as mothers — even working mothers — rather than women that they are defined. A single sentence of the report calls for attention to the needs of women in industry, but whilst this is seen as important 'for their own intellectual progress', more significance is attached to 'their influence on their children'.

> The working mother is particularly important, perhaps with a special educational need, and as many more women will be at work in the coming decades, the influence of working mothers on children at the starting point of the whole learning process will spread widely. There will be a need for adult education to ensure that this is a supportive influence.

It is noticeable that 'working fathers' are not charged with the same responsibilities for the pre-school education of their children and that women as political activists, trade unionists, seekers after truth, feminists, full-time workers and major breadwinners in single parent households, among many other possibilities, are still subsumed within the primary concept 'mother'. So far as Russell was concerned women were only visible as mothers and totally invisible in every other respect.

In 1978 Graham Mee and Harold Wiltshire produced a report on local authority adult education entitled Structure and Performance.[13] Their investigation made it clear that, despite claims to the contrary about 'meeting individual needs' and 'responsiveness to local communities and conditions', an amazing consensus exists throughout LEA non-vocational adult education about what kinds of programmes ought to be offered. Wiltshire and Mee do not utilise the classification 'women's interests' which appears in countless institute prospectuses and centre programmes, preferring 'crafts and arts', 'physical activities', 'cognitive skills' and the like. If they had, their findings may have been even more revealing and disturbing for the core curriculum in local authority adult education is little more than an inventory of traditional female skills concerned primarily with domestic management (e.g. hostess cookery, creative embroidery, flower arranging, soft furnishing and machine knitting); personal relationships (e.g. child development, encounter groups and co-counselling); and physical appearance (e.g. make-up and beauty care, home hairdressing and ladies keep fit). Wiltshire and Mee hesitate to explain and indeed claim, 'not to know what the processes are that determine and maintain this consensus and what the channels are through which they operate'. For feminists they are obvious. The common denominator is of course in the definitions of relevance and the assumptions held about students which those responsible for provision reproduce with monotonous regularity and tenacious predictability every year in every corner of the country.

They operate according to a series of social imperatives which conform women to a close allegiance with their traditional roles. They service the 'vocation' of home-maker, wife and mother and despite declarations about students' *self*-fulfilment and *personal* development they exist primarily to reinforce the obligations women are usually assigned to enhance the care and comfort of others.

In 1979 the Advisory Council for Adult and Continuing Education produced a Strategy For The Basic Education of Adults.[14] The report committee was chaired by Henry Arthur Jones — already a considerable influence in adult education circles on the subject of 'disadvantage'. The report has been quite properly criticised for its failure to examine the structural causes of economic and social disadvantage and its presentation of adults who are assumed to be in need of basic education as in some way responsible for their own ineptitude.[15] The analysis is of course consistent with Jones's earlier contributions to the Russell Report and with Peter Clyne's research,[16] and with the proliferation of social policy statements concerned to keep public spending to a minimum and to blame the victims of social inequality and oppression rather than the social and economic arrangements which capitalism promotes to further the interests of dominant groups.

But the report is also disturbing in its implications for women. As usual the fact that women constitute a large proportion of the participants engaged in Adult Basic Education schemes is ignored and women are subsumed within the general categories 'parents', 'adults', 'immigrants' and 'students'. And yet the language and tone of the report, couched in terms of caring and confidence and coping, reflect implicit assumptions about women which need to be examined carefully. The language is certainly not of the variety which would be applied to male industrial workers, students on vocational courses or those engaged in prestigious academic study. And seen in this light the report is very worrying. The 'feminine' nature of the language and the assumptions which it records are not to women's advantage because they rely on constructions of female need in circumstances in which men are the 'authority', the providers and the need-meeters and women are the functionaries and the recipients. The stereotypes which emerge are of feckless, pathetic, unconfident individuals in need of remedial education and behaviour modification, encoded in the kinds of coping and caring courses offered to less able and less amenable pupils in schools. The lifeskills prescribed specifically for women are those which assist in domestic management and health and family relations — a confirmation of women's traditional roles with an insinuation that professional intervention is necessary to ensure that they are performed satisfactorily.

If women really are disadvantaged because of limited opportunities, or poverty, or their social class position, or their subordination to men, learning to cope — to put up with — unsatisfactory circumstances, defined as an essential lifeskill, can hardly be described, as the report claims, to be concerned with the pursuit of personal development and self-confidence.

So long as the opinion leaders and policy makers in adult education continue to describe the world as though women don't exist, or to associate women simply with domesticity and child rearing, adult education will continue to reinforce inequality between the sexes to the long term detriment of both men and women. In the short term, the sexist condition of adult education produces a number of interesting contradictions. We have seen how adult education is presented as a resource for the whole community and is concerned with general educational aims like personal growth and development, responsible citizenship and the creation of self-confidence. And yet the core curriculum of local authority provision is rooted in domestic management, recreational activities and rational skills. As Nell Keddie[17] points out, adult education has made women's work its curriculum and represented it to women as skills in which they are deficient and yet is embarrassed to promote itself as a profession which services domestic labour. The dilemma of the opinion leaders and theoreticians becomes increasingly difficult in the face of criticisms about indulging petit bourgeois consumerism and wasting public money on fripperies and leisure frills.

> The public rhetoric of adult education claims that it is a universalistic service which provides for the whole community and we can see that attacks on cake icing and flower arranging threaten to expose the limitations of this claim. To confront it adequately would expose not only that women are the main users of adult education but that the LEA curriculum is strongly located in the home and in women's activities.[18]

She points out that this dilemma is not made explicit but means that adult education has to justify what is generally regarded as trivial and frivolous whilst, on the other hand, taking care to disguise the extent to which its professional status depends upon servicing women's work. Keddie's contribution[19] to our understanding of the limitations imposed upon the curriculum of local authority provision because of sexist assumptions is invaluable although rarely conceded by those responsible for organising provision. The suggestion that the core curriculum of university and WEA provision is also sexist, albeit in a different way, is equally denied.

The liberal tradition associated with this provision has progressively abandoned any early commitment it might have made to 'really useful knowledge'[20] concerned with social change. Its roots in academic scholarship and the patronage of the leisured and genteel classes in the nineteenth century[21] has contributed to the sense of detachment from contemporary society. Current defenders of this legacy still advocate it in preference to the 'practical instrumentalism' which they associate with recent developments like trade union studies and community education, preferring adult education's

'traditional role of general cultural diffusion and personal development through studies on a broad perspective'.[22] The extent to which
'general cultural diffusion' actually means 'dominant cultural diffusion' has been well argued by those commentators critical of the
cultural exclusivity of so much university and WEA provision. But it
is important to realise that this knowledge — seemingly 'the best that
has been thought and said', the renowned and universally accredited
epitome of our cultural and academic heritage — is, in fact, a form and
variety of knowledge selected, constructed, protected and dis-
seminated within the historical context of male supremacy.

Considerable scholarship by feminists on both sides of the Atlantic
has revealed the extent to which the male academic tradition and the
knowledge which it has created is only a partial definition of reality
which has consistently discounted female experience and erased it
from the records.[23] The criticism made by Otto Rank in 1958[24] about
psychology 'that it is not only man made ... but masculine in its
mentality' has increasingly been applied to all other disciplines
including the so-called neutral sciences. The significance of the
increasing demand for Women's Studies courses in adult and higher
education is a recognition of the extent to which conventional
academic scholarship and the curriculum which it provides is viewed
by feminists as a system celebrating predominantly male knowledge,
values and achievements.[25]

Seen in this context it is not just that women are channelled into
certain kinds of 'female' subject areas but that within certain subject
areas women do not appear to feature at all. The study of history,
philosophy, religion, art, music and the like is very much a consideration of male interests and achievements. The social conditions which
produced such achievements and have accorded them so much value
and prestige are left unquestioned. Through this kind of educational
transmission in extra-mural and WEA classes both men and women
subscribe to the belief in female inferiority and male supremacy. Nor
is it simply a question of reducing a bias which has largely ignored
women's experience and exploits. Women have been, and continue
to be, left out of the discourses which construct the knowledge that is
considered valuable in the first place.

Dorothy Smith[26] puts it like this:

Women have been largely excluded from the work of producing
the forms of thought and the images and symbols in which thought
is expressed and ordered. There is a circle effect. Men attend to

and treat as significant what men say. The circle of men whose writing and talk was significant to each other extends backwards in time as far as our records reach. What men were doing was relevant to men, was written by men about men for men. Men listened and listen to what one another said. This is how a tradition is formed.

The contradiction in this kind of adult education, so far as women are concerned, is that an essentially female student body is engaged in a form of learning, and in the pursuit of knowledge controlled by men, which takes very little account of the social, political, economic and cultural conditions of being female and which, in the guise of liberal studies, operates to confirm illiberal discrimination against women.

A further contradiction lies in the problems and possibilities associated with marginality. Adult education is the poorest and meanest outpost of the education system — a service which Mike Newman has referred to as 'the poor cousin'.[27] In terms of the educational pecking order in further and higher education, adult education enjoys the least prestige. This is one reason presumably why women have been allowed to monopolise its provision. And because women have monopolised its provision and been offered, in educational terms, fairly low-status knowledge, it has been difficult to argue the case for more prestige or more resources. The incidence of women's participation is at the same time ignored and yet held to be responsible for adult education's weak position. Current arguments about adult education as 'the cure' for unemployment, and discussions about paid educational leave, continuing education and retraining are invariably debated in the context of male industrial workers and manpower requirements.[28] If, as the ACACE report, *Continuing Education — From Policies to Practice*[29] recommends, all adults should be entitled to continuing opportunities for education throughout their lives and the education of adults should be given increasing priority in the allocation of resources, the odds against either women as a group or mainstream adult education monopolised by women benefiting from such developments are tremendous. It is no coincidence that the expansion in training and retraining which has taken place has done so under the auspices of the Manpower Services Commission and the further education sector; and that discussions within the universities, for example, about mature students and the opportunities afforded to universities by promoting continuing education programmes have been taken over by internal depart-

ments looking to consolidate their positions in periods of retrenchment, rather than departments of extra-mural studies whose low
esteem and weakness in the intellectual and political pecking order is
only too apparent.

And yet for feminists, the relative accessibility of adult education
and its potentially sympathetic rhetoric about 'student centredness'
and 'student responsiveness' and, in the WEA at least, its proclaimed
commitment to student democracy and accountability, all represent
possibilities in which the preponderance of women could be seen as
strength rather than a weakness. If nothing else it provides the
opportunity for women to meet, to generate their own knowledge
and to become their own teachers. Certainly women's studies courses
organised in the context of adult education are proving to be an
important connecting point between the informal expression of
feminist demands and dissatisfactions and the translation of these
into political and cultural practices which consolidate the growing
rejection of patriarchal authority by increasing numbers of women.

In Southampton, for example, the women's studies programme
has grown from modest beginnings in neighbourhood action groups,
trade union meetings and women's liberation concerns into a thriving
programme which not only provides an alternative curriculum to that
which is consistent with patriarchal provision but which engages a
wide cross-section of women in the exploration of feminism. Strong
roots in Second Chance education, which positively discriminates in
favour of working-class women and women who have received least
from the education system in the past, have ensured that new
developments have remained committed to the needs of all women
rather than to the concerns of those who more easily monopolise
provision. But the energy and preoccupations of feminist women
have also been an important catalyst in the elaboration and development of this work. In 1981 we were able to open the country's first
Women's Education Centre in which the shared resources of the
University, the LEA and the WEA are combined to provide a comprehensive range of courses and activities which take serious account
of women's concerns as they are defined by women themselves. The
Centre is responsible to the women who are its members and
decisions about Centre policies and activities are taken collectively.
Funding from the Equal Opportunities Commission has provided a
measure of independence and there is a growing sense of control
being exercised directly by the participants of the Centre rather than
by external funding bodies.

In other areas women's studies programmes, women's trade union studies, New Opportunities for Women courses, re-entry to education and employment projects and a whole range of short courses, day schools and conferences related to campaigns concerned with, for example, child care, male violence, equal opportunities at work, health issues and the women's peace movement have all provided educational support to women who do not want to be confined by their traditional and domestic roles. And all of these have been argued for and established within the parameters of conventional provision. They are the developments which the men who monopolise decision-making power in adult education must be persuaded to take more seriously.

But encouraging women's access to institutions created and controlled by men, or demanding that the reality of adult education increasingly lives up to the rhetoric, is only half the battle. So long as men continue to control the organisation and provision of adult education, and so long as male-centred knowledge and relevance defined in male terms continues to determine the nature of the curriculum, then women's experience and expectations will continue to be discounted. If male power holders in adult education are genuinely concerned to promote equality of opportunity between the sexes, and to provide the space for women to create and control their own education free from the impositions of vested male interests, then they must equally be prepared to let women get on with it themselves and be prepared to relinquish the authority, and power and influence which their control implies. In the education system generally men control 97 per cent of the government of education.[30] The distribution in adult education is not radically different. Only when this is shared on a 50–50 basis with women, and when the cultural heritage and validity of women's experience is reflected in the curriculum, shall we begin to imagine an education system which serves both sexes equally.

Notes

1. See Jane L. Thompson (ed.), *Adult Education for a Change* (Hutchinson, London, 1980).
2. See, for example, Samuel Bowles and Herb Gintis, *Schooling in Capitalist America* (Routledge and Kegan Paul, London, 1976); Dale, Esland and Macdonald (eds.), *Schooling and Capitalism: A Sociological Reader* (Routledge and Kegan Paul, London, 1976); Geoff Whitty and M.F.D. Young (eds.), *Society,*

State and Schooling (Falmer Press, London, 1977).

3. Louis Althusser, 'Ideology and Ideological State Apparatuses — Notes Towards an Investigation', *Lenin and Other Essays* (New Left Books, London, 1971).

4. Note for example Paul Willis's almost total lack of reference to the cultural, social and educational experience of girls in *Learning to Labour — How Working-class Kids Get Working-class Jobs* (Saxon House, Aldershot, 1979).

5. See, for example, Dale Spender and Elizabeth Sarah (eds.), *Learning to Lose* (The Women's Press, London, 1980); Dale Spender, *Invisible Women — The Schooling Scandal* (Writers and Readers Co-operative, London, 1982); Rosemary Deem, *Women and Schooling* (Routledge and Kegan Paul, London, 1978).

6. See, for example, Jane L. Thompson, *Learning Liberation* (Croom Helm, London, 1983).

7. See Spender, *Invisible Women*.

8. *Suggestions for Part-Time Teachers of Women's Subjects*, 4th edn. (Northern Advisory Council for Further Education, Newcastle, 1963).

9. But see June Purvis, 'Working-class Women and Adult Education in Nineteenth-century Britain', *History of Education*, vol. 9, no. 3 (Taylor and Francis, London, 1980).

10. In the institutes and colleges, for example, women did not pay the same dues as men and were excluded from voting rights on matters concerning institute policy and curriculum.

11. Margaret Llewelyn Davies (ed.), *Life As We Have Known It, by Co-operative Working Women* (Virago, London, 1977).

12. The Russell Report, *Adult Education: A Plan for Development* (HMSO, London, 1973).

13. Harold Wiltshire and Graham Mee, *Structure and Performance in Adult Education* (Longman, London, 1978).

14. *A Strategy for the Basic Education of Adults* (ACACE, Leicester, 1979).

15. By Nell Keddie and Jane Thompson, for example in *Adult Education for a Change*.

16. Jones and Clyne's co-operation on a research project based at the University of Leicester became incorporated into the policy proposals of Russell and is elaborated in Clyne's book, *The Disadvantaged Adult* (Longman, London, 1972).

17. Nell Keddie, unpublished paper, forthcoming.

18. Ibid.

19. Ibid.

20. See Richard Johnson, 'Really Useful Knowledge, Radical Education and Working-Class Culture' in Clarke, Critcher and Johnson (eds.), *Working-Class Culture* (Hutchinson, London, 1979).

21. Raymond Williams in *The Long Revolution* (Penguin, Harmondsworth, 1961) distinguishes four sets of educational philosophies or ideologies which rationalise different emphases in the selection of the content of the curricula, and relates these to the social positions of those who hold them. The liberal position he associates with the nineteenth-century aristocracy and gentry.

22. K.H. Lawson, 'Community Education: A Critical Assessment', *Adult Education*, vol. 50, no. 1 (National Institute of Adult Education, Leicester, 1977).

23. See, for example, Dale Spender (ed.), *Men's Studies Modified* (Pergamon Press, Oxford, 1981) and Adrienne Rich, *On Lies, Secrets and Silence* (Virago, London, 1980).

24. Otto Rank, *Beyond Psychology* (Dover, New York, 1958).

25. Thompson, *Learning Liberation*.

26. Dorothy Smith, 'A Peculiar Eclipsing, Women's Exclusion From Men's Culture', *Women's Studies International Quarterly*, vol. 1, no. 4 (Pergamon Press,

Oxford, 1978).
   27. Mike Newman, *The Poor Cousin: A Study of Adult Education* (Allen and Unwin, London, 1979).
   28. Thompson, *Learning Liberation.*
   29. *Continuing Education: From Policies to Practice* (ACACE, Leicester, 1982).
   30. Eileen Byrne, *Women and Education* (Tavistock, London, 1978).

3.4

RACE RELATIONS AND THE TRADITIONS OF ADULT EDUCATION

John McIlroy

Source: *Studies in Adult Education* (National Institute of Adult Education, Oct. 1981), *13 (2)*, pp. 87-97.

[...] The purpose of this paper is to argue that there is a deep-seated, complex and explosive racial problem in the United Kingdom today and that education and specifically adult education can play a part in attempting its resolution. [...]

The Tradition of Social Relevance

A strong dynamic in adult education from the earliest days has been the demand that such education should be socially relevant. Universities, it was argued, cannot be ivory towers. They are social institutions and have a broad social role, not only to promote the intellectual development of the individual and the growth of scientific research but also to take the knowledge thus generated into society and see that it is applied to the development of social institutions and the resolution of social problems.

The view of early adult educators was that society cannot develop and democracy cannot operate if citizens are ignorant and apathetic. Adult education should therefore provide citizens, who ultimately possess an ability to influence social problems, with a rigorous forum for the discussion of those problems, developing the ability to form rationally grounded views and the intellectual equipment to translate those views into action. 'The dominant ethos of British adult education', says Paul Fordham, 'has been reformist.'[1]

The view of knowledge as a prerequisite for informed action, and of adult education as possessing a specific social relevance, has co-existed with the view that adult education should be simply a process of individual self-fulfilment:

The adult educational movement is inextricably interwoven with the whole of the organised life of the community. Whilst on the one

159

hand it originates in a desire amongst individuals for adequate opportunities for self-expression and the cultivation of their personal powers and interests, it is, on the other hand, rooted in the social aspirations of the democratic movements of the country. In other words, it rests upon the twin principles of personal development and social service. It aims at satisfying the needs of the individual and at the attainment of new standards of citizenship and a better social order. In some cases the personal motive predominates. In perhaps the greater majority of cases the dynamic character of adult education is due to its social motive.[2]

In the post-war years attention has tended to centre on adult education for personal development. But in evidence to the Russell Committee the WEA argued that its purpose was both to enable people to approach a deeper personal development and to stimulate and aid responsible social action. The Russell Report[3] itself restated many of the old conceptions in terms of the problems and necessities of the 1970s and 1980s.

The way of democracy is to submit areas of controversy to debate in the belief that right judgements are built upon knowledge, critical enquiry and rational discussion ... Society needs an educational forum in which controversial issues can be studied and we believe adult education should be free to explore such areas fully.

The Report went on to assert that broad social and political education designed to enable the individual to play a role as citizen, voluntary worker and consumer was an essential need of adult education; universities should be involved in pioneer work in connection with special problems of adult education; and the WEA should undertake priority work in the areas of political and social education and education for the deprived. Russell thus affirmed one of the basic traditions of adult education, that alongside the process of personal development there is also concern for social problems.[4] One of gripping importance which had not existed in the early days of adult education is that of race relations.

The Symptoms of a Social Problem

A cursory glance at history shows that in the past various groups in Britain such as Jewish and Irish immigrants have been the subject of a bitter racist experience.[5] Today the major recipients of racism are *black* immigrants from what is termed the New Commonwealth, largely from the West Indies, India and Pakistan. [...]

Exactly when race relations came to be perceived as a major social problem is doubtful. The Notting Hill Race Riots in 1958 are often regarded as a watershed.[6] Certainly during the 1960s evidence began to accumulate of wholesale discrimination against the new black community.[7] [...] While such studies influenced public policy and led to legislation and the establishment of public bodies (culminating in the Race Relations Act 1976, the Commission for Racial Equality and the Community Relations Councils) they do not appear to have had a significant impact upon the problem. A report from PEP in the mid-1970s disclosed a picture similar to that of the earlier research.[8] Another report from the Department of Employment claimed that blacks were

> concentrated in conurbations where the pressure of demand for labour has usually been relatively high and in semi-skilled and unskilled jobs to which it is difficult to attract other workers because of such features as low earnings, a need to work unsocial hours and/or unpleasant working conditions.[9]

[...] Work is vital as a determinant of social role and blacks, of course, also suffered from extremely high rates of unemployment. Whilst lack of training or language difficulties may tell against an immigrant in the early stages the fact that they *remain* in the worst jobs and that discrimination persists against their children means that we are facing a deeply rooted problem. By the early 1970s it was apparent that the problem was not simply one of immigration.

> Among the incipient ghettos in Britain today, Handsworth, Birmingham, displays the classic symptoms: poor housing, a strained education system, households struggling to make ends meet and few social amenities. It also has the usual hustlers, prostitutes and ponces. *Second generation blacks* are beginning to show a resistance to all authority.[10]

[…] Situations like this do not simply persist: they develop. More and more blacks are progressively losing faith in the structures which they perceive as oppressive, from the police and the legal system to the trade unions and the conventional labour market. It has been authoritatively argued that 'if present injustices are allowed to continue political organisation by the minorities, when it comes, is likely to be extremist and destructive'.[11]

The Role of Adult Educators

My argument is that, as large-scale social problems remain, adult educators have a role to play in their resolution. This role is a limited one and we shall be wise to recognise this. First, we know we can touch our students' lives, but so of course do a myriad of competing and often stronger pressures. This is particularly true when we are dealing with an entrenched and complex social phenomenon such as racism. For example, in talking about racism with a group of managers, a tutor will be aware that he is confronting a lifetime of experience as well as an established work structure to which the student will shortly return. The adult education course is hardly likely to be the determinant of attitudes and behaviour in face of influences such as the structure in which the manager operates his company's policy, the attitudes of his superiors, the views of other managers he works with, the attitudes of those he manages, the responses of their representatives, the policies of their trade union; and above all the values and institutions of the wider society.

Secondly, reference has already been made to the inadequacies of the schools in dealing with race relations. Recent public expenditure cuts are likely to worsen this position. Alan Little was recently quoted as saying, in relation to schools: 'One way of judging the political commitment to eradicating racial disadvantage is by the resources created to eliminate it. On this measure we fail the test and in failing we are responsible for whatever human and social consequences follow.'[12] Bullock[13] also points out that the problem is often of ideas and approach: 'Many schools in multi-cultural areas turn a blind eye to the fact that the community they serve has radically altered over the last ten years and is now one in which new cultures are represented.' The need to grapple with these consequences is a daunting challenge to adult education.

There is a third kind of limitation to meet. Miller[14] carried out research with 1,000 young apprentices on day release at a London College of Further Education in the 1960s. Short sessions on race relations were included as part of a Liberal Studies Course. His tests found that the students were highly prejudiced at the start and more prejudiced by the end of the sessions: 'It seemed that up to three hours' work on the topic produced the most harmful effect. Three hours' work was worse than two hours which was worse than no teaching at all'.[15] Miller concluded that a short time-period plus a weakened form of argument from a teacher might well increase prejudice.

This well publicised study is sometimes used to justify shying away from the problem of race relations. But another report, commenting on Miller's article, took a larger view:

A working hypothesis from this research would be not that race relations teaching is necessarily ineffective but that people are unwilling to admit to the existence of a high level of prejudice; that if you then provide a forum for its existence it may then become overt and articulate, thus giving the impression that it has increased.[16]

The lesson would seem to lie rather in the necessity for more careful planning and preparation and, of course, for more time. Other recent studies have in fact found favourable attitude change.[17]

However, as Verma and Bagley state: '... there is in Britain some anxiety about teaching race relations and considerable reluctance to engage in curriculum experiment and development'.[18] A certain anxiety in this situation may be healthy; but this reluctance appears to stem from a sincerely held belief that the problem has been exaggerated so that to focus on it will simply intensify it, and from the fact that the area is one which can lead to vigorous and perhaps at times unpleasant controversy in the classroom.

Adult educators have never shied away from controversy. Indeed they have often seen in controversy education's opportunity. Surely that is the situation here where the controversy is so often ill informed and obscurantist. Impassioned ignorance has to be replaced by calm dispassionate scrutiny, derived from a mastery of the research and careful planning of the correct approach for the specific group. As in any other area the tutor must prove himself by his command of his subject; though here we will also come up against our own fears and prejudices which we will to some degree share with our students. We may then emerge from the exchanges not merely as better teachers but as more whole and developed human beings.

When all the limitations have been faced, there remains one other clear role for adult education, for we run courses, not only for the general public, but for social workers, teachers, managers, trade unionists, administrators, police — all of them groups who are in a position themselves to influence attitudes.

Approaches and Methods

[...] Racism is a matter of attitudes — in my submission, socially dangerous attitudes — among the white population. What can adult education do here?

First there is the point that courses explicitly dealing with Race Relations will generally attract only those who are enlightened or relatively easily convertible. Such courses are still of value if they lead to a deeper understanding among people who can play a part in influencing others.

Secondly, what of integrating sessions on race relations into courses whose syllabuses are centred elsewhere? Occasionally one finds a reluctance by students to engage in this area but more often, in my experience, they are only too anxious to discuss it. The question can come up at any time. As one WEA tutor put it:

> My general experience with the topic of racism in the classroom is that it usually erupts when you least expect it. In one class, a class next door were having a session on race and trade unions and we could hear them arguing noisily. So my class said 'What's going on in there?' When I told them there were suddenly several voices saying, 'Bloody foreigners ... take our jobs ... ought to be sent back from where they came ...'

In many types of courses it is essential to start from the concrete, not the abstract. A realistic case study related to the practical problems the students face may be the best starting point. Indeed, at times, race relations may be one of the problems involved and the discussion can then naturally evolve. Other ways of organically introducing this subject may be through novels, short stories, films or historical material, according to the particular needs of the class.

Unfortunately, the literature on the teaching of race relations for adults is as yet a sparse one, but a number of different approaches can be discerned already and the tutor needs to be aware of their implications.

The first may be termed 'the technical approach'.[19]

Just as trade union officials or personnel managers need training in matters such as government's role in industrial relations or the Industrial Training or Redundancy Payments Acts, so, it can be argued, there is a need for those engaged in most British industries to receive instruction in the provisions and philosophy of the Race Relations Act and in crucial technical questions concerning matters such as the keeping of racial statistics or personnel policies affecting the recruitment and promotion of immigrant workers.

The sessions are developed by a workbook on the legislation, a series of fact-sheets, bibliographies and case studies on race relations and are intended for use in day-release courses and summer and weekend schools. The problem here, of course, is that one is not dealing with the problem of *race*. Not merely that: can one 'instruct' potential actors in specific knowledge, skills and techniques when they are not convinced of the necessity for the action in the first place nor the desirability of the assumed end? (Cynically, one might point out that a good working knowledge of the Race Relations Act, for example, can be as useful in *evading* the Act's provisions as in implementing them.) [...]

Stephen recognises the problem. 'Generally speaking enthusiasts for liberal education argue that the "technification" of education leaves value questions untouched', but he claims that 'obviously the *assumptions* here are liberal and educational — we would expect people to proceed from knowledge of facts and techniques to analysis and understanding — but in conception and practice we have decided for the moment to keep the operation a largely technical one'.[20]

Somewhat similar is what might be called the 'immigrant approach'. Students are given questionnaires to answer, generally based on a Myth/Fact distinction. The assumption is made that students will hold common misconceptions: that, say, black immigrants are taking over jobs which could be done by whites, that blacks get priority on housing lists, that black immigrants get more than their fair share of social security, that blacks all have large families and so on. These questionnaires form the basis for small-group discussion and the tutors then lead a large-group discussion, feeding in the relevant facts and figures. The assumption is that once students learn that immigration trends are not leading to a crisis of overpopulation, a housing shortage or unemployment, then they will at least reconsider the framework in which they view black immigrants. Nobody would deny the importance of shedding light on some of the myths and distortions which sustain and develop prejudice against Britain's black communities. However, the extent to which in using this approach one is grappling with the real problems is doubtful, for one is dealing with immigration, not with race. The two are not the same. This approach underestimates the depth and complexity of the problem. Someone who is actively prejudiced against black people may be encouraged to know that immigration has slowed to a trickle. It will hardly shake his basic prejudices. If this type of approach does not help in dealing with racism it also has potential disadvantages. For example, some would argue that by focusing on the immigration trends of blacks one is accepting the view that the problem lies simply in the *number* of blacks.

A third alternative is what might be called the Human Relations approach.[21] Variants of this approach are sometimes used on longer courses with groups such as teachers, social workers or managers. The most sophisticated example of this approach that I have come across is the package presented by Katz.[22] Katz argues that white racism is the problem but that white people do not see themselves as white.

> Because United States culture is centred around white norms white people surely have to come to terms with that part of their identity ... This is a way of denying responsibility for perpetuating the racist system and being part of the problem. By seeing oneself solely as an individual one can disown one's racism.[23]

Katz discards inter-racial T-Groups and encounter groups and argues for 'White on White Training Groups' so that white people can explore their own racism. 'The purpose of these groups is to create a positive change in attitudes and move white people to take action to combat racism.'[24]

Katz presents a detailed programme of exercises with goals, materials, instructions, notes to tutors and timings. These develop from exercises in defining and discussing prejudice and racism, through exercises examining aspects of racism in work and education, of cultural racism, of black culture and history, to exercises examining one's own racist attitudes and acting to combat racism.

The programme includes the imaginative use of films, records and tapes as stimulation for discussion, and case studies and role plays to illustrate particular aspects of the problem and stimulate awareness in participants. It has been used, the author states, in a whole range of formats from brief three-hour sessions to forty-five-hour term-long University courses.

Many of Katz's materials and exercises are excellent and could well be developed or adapted by those involved in adult education in the United Kingdom. However, I would argue that as a *total* educational approach her conception is deficient. Katz is aware of the complexity of the racist problem in the USA. She points out that, from the time of formalised slavery to the present, 'whites have oppressed Third World people through the perpetuation of racism at every level of life. It is present in our institutions, our culture and our individual actions'.[25] She does discuss *racism* but to my mind her documentation and exercises are too skewed in the direction of cultural racism and the feelings of whites. More seriously there is no discussion of the various arguable explanations of why racism exists, how it developed and what function it performs. Without any explanatory underpinning, racism becomes a big misunderstanding, a failure of communication. A large part of the problem will then be solved if white people sort themselves out through group therapy. As with the Human Relations school generally, economic social and political forces and their role in generating racism are severely underestimated.

I wish therefore to offer tentatively a fourth approach which I feel would be more educationally effective and more within the traditions of adult education. What is suggested is a content and framework which might be adapted to different forms — discussion groups, questionnaires, films and so on. In a developed form it will require fairly intensive reading. However, my experience is that even in short courses one is pressed into discussing history and the explanations of racism, albeit in a brief and condensed form, rather than immigration trends and government institutions; that is, if one wants to discuss racism, and my experience is that classes invariably do.

This approach would start from the specific attitudes and experience of the students involved but would lead through this to the area of definition. What is racism; ethnocentrism; prejudice; discrimination; bigotry; stereotyping; nationalism; and fascism? This would develop into a discussion of *explanations* which would necessitate a historical exploration of the roots of racism.[26] A discussion of social and economic developments will be required as well as an examination of the development of racist ideas. Is racism specific to particular societies; why does it develop; what are its functions? Then, rather than looking at myths and facts about immigration, one can look at myths and facts about race.[27] Is it correct to talk about different races? What does this then imply? What is the scientific evidence for differences between blacks and whites? Is it useful to talk of the inheritance of characteristics by groups? Are cultural and national characteristics biologically determined? Have we anything to learn from the recent IQ controversy? Is there a relationship between race and levels of civilisation? A context has then been established in which to analyse race relations in the UK. Again the approach will be a rounded one. The literature on theories of immigration can then be discussed as well as the controversy as to its economic and social effects:[28] whatever the approach, unless the discussion remains at a superficial level, the students will force the discussion into these areas. We must start where the students are, then lead them in a search for explanatory frameworks that can draw insights from history, economics, sociology, psychology and politics as requisite. From that point an examination of the contemporary situation — the position of whites and blacks today, immigration, racism in education, housing, employment and trade unions, the role of legislation and the institutions created to combat racism — is likely to be sharper and more effective in leading to attitude-change.

In this framework the most useful aspects of the approaches outlined above can all be integrated. We shall have established a critical method, examining basic forces at work in society in a probing and analytical fashion, but without attempting to impose one particular analysis or explanation on the students. But by involving the students themselves in both the interpretation of the information and the construction of the arguments we shall be working within the twin traditions outlined earlier, helping individuals to develop as whole men and making a contribution to a pressing social problem. We shall be practising, in the fullest sense of the term, liberal adult education.

Notes

1. P. Fordham, 'The Political Context of Adult Education' in *Studies in Adult Education*, vol. 8, no. 1 (April 1976) p. 61.

2. *Final Report* of the Adult Education Committee (Ministry of Reconstruction, 1919). Cmnd 321, para. 330.

3. *Adult Education: A Plan for Development* (HMSO, London, 1973), pp. 12-13.

4. Ibid., p. 19; pp. 72-3; pp. 77-81. See also p. 94 on immigrants.

5. See for example J. Garrard, *The English and Immigration 1880-1910* (Oxford University Press, Oxford, 1971); B. Gainer, *The Alien Invasion* (Heinemann, London, 1971).

6. See however the evidence in J.A. Griffith *et al.*, *Coloured Immigrants in Britain* (Oxford University Press, Oxford, 1960).

7. See for example M. Banton, *White and Coloured* (Cape, London, 1959); S. Patterson, *Dark Strangers* (Tavistock, London, 1963); S. Patterson, *Immigrants in Industry* (Oxford University Press, Oxford, 1968); J. Rex and R. Moore, *Race, Community and Conflict* (Oxford University Press, Oxford, 1967); E.J.B. Rose, *Colour and Citizenship* (Oxford University Press, Oxford, 1969).

8. D.J. Smith, *The Facts of Racial Disadvantage* (PEP, 1976); D.J. Smith, *Racial Disadvantage in Britain* (Penguin, Harmondsworth, 1977).

9. Unit for Manpower Studies, *The Role of Immigrants in the Labour Market* (Department of Employment, 1976).

10. *Sunday Times*, 4 January 1970 quoted in S. Hall *et al.*, *Policing the Crisis* (Macmillan, London, 1978).

11. D. Smith, *The Facts of Racial Disadvantage*, p. 188.

12. Quoted in D. Kuya, 'The Black Child in Britain' in D. Rubenstein (ed.), *Education and Equality* (Penguin, Harmondsworth, 1979).

13. A. Bullock, *A Language for Life* (HMSO, London, 1975).

14. H. Miller, 'The Effectiveness of Teaching Techniques for Reducing Colour Prejudice', *Liberal Education*, 16 July 1969, pp. 25-31.

15. Miller, 'The Effectiveness of Teaching Techniques', p. 27.

16. *Race Relations and the Curriculum* (Schools Council, 1972), p. 10.

17. See for example the research findings by Verma and Bagley, 'Measured Changes in Racial Attitudes' in G.K. Verma and C. Bagley (eds.), *Race, Education and Identity* (Macmillan, London, 1979). pp. 132-43.

18. G.K. Verma and C. Bagley, *Race, Education and Identity*, p. 134.

19. D. Stephen, 'Teaching Racial Understanding in Industry', *The Industrial Tutor*, vol. 3 (September 1970), pp. 12-17.

20. Stephen, 'Teaching Racial Understanding', p. 13.

21. For some of the educational problems within this approach see John Shaw, 'Attitude Change Among the Police', *Race Today* (August, 1971). For broad criticisms of the Human Relations School see C. Wright Mills, *The Sociological Imagination* (Penguin, Harmondsworth, 1970); P. Blumenberg, *Industrial Democracy: The Sociology of Participation* (Constable, London, 1968).

22. J.H. Katz, *White Awareness — Handbook for Anti-Racist Training* (University of Oklahoma Press, 1978).

23. Katz, ibid., p. 13.

24. Katz, ibid., p. 19.

25. Katz, ibid., p. 9.

26. See, for example, O.C. Cox, *Caste, Class and Race* (Monthly Review Press, 1970); E. Williams, *Capitalism and Slavery* (Andre Deutsch, London, 1964); E. Genovese, *In Red and Black* (Vintage Books, New York, 1972); J. Gabriel, G. Ben Tovim, 'Marxism and the Concept of Race', *Economy and Society*, vol. 7, no. 2 (May 1978), pp. 118-54; R. Miles, 'Class, Race and Ethnicity — a critique of Cox's Theory', *Ethnic and Racial Studies*, vol. 3, no. 2 (April 1980), pp. 169-87.

27. See, for example, L. Kuper (ed.), *Race, Science and Society* (Allen and Unwin, London, 1975); A. Montague (ed.), *The Concept of Race* (Collier Macmillan, London, 1969); K. Richardson and D. Spears (eds.), *Race, Culture and Intelligence* (Penguin, Harmondsworth, 1972).

28. See, for example, M. Nikolinakos, 'Notes Towards a General Theory of Migration in Late Capitalism', *Race and Class*, vol. XVII, no. 1 (July 1975); A. Gorz, 'Immigrant Labour', *New Left Review*, no. 61 (May 1970); S. Castles and G. Kosack, *Immigrant Workers and the Class Structure in Western Europe* (Oxford University Press, Oxford, 1973).

Part 4

DISTANCE EDUCATION

The three chapters in this section comprise two case studies (see also the chapter by Cepeda in the first Reader) and one general, analytical study.

Judith Calder describes the Open University's Community Education programme, part of its continuing education provision made in addition to the undergraduate and associate student degree-level programmes. The community education programme offers a range of formal and informal study opportunities based on materials developed in relation to different life stages and roles. Careful planning and preparation of the materials is involved, a range of media are used in their delivery, and national, regional and local networks of helpers have been established to support learners before and during study.

Similarly detailed preparation has gone into producing the educational opportunities offered by the National Extension College, the subject of the second chapter by Richard Freeman. Freeman discusses the origins of the National Extension College in the 1960s as a prototype 'open university', and charts its changing role as it absorbed a traditionally orientated correspondence college, was rebuffed at the time of the establishment of the Open University, and developed 'flexistudy' schemes in association with local colleges of further education. There are many interesting comparisons to be drawn between the National Extension College and the Open University as a whole, not least in terms of their cost-effectiveness.

Len Masterman's chapter concentrates on the understanding and use of one powerful medium, television, for the education of adults. He indicates the considerable importance of television as a source for much informal learning amongst the adult population, and as a means for deliberately transmitting more formal programmes of education. Many of Masterman's points — about interpretation, selectivity and presentation, for example — may be related equally well to other popular media, such as the press, radio and paperbacks.

4.1

THE OPEN UNIVERSITY COMMUNITY EDUCATION PROGRAMME

Judith Calder

Source: Copyright © The Open University 1983 (an earlier version of this paper, by Judith Calder and Nick Farnes, appeared in A.R. Kaye and K. Harry (eds.), *Using the Media for Adult Basic Education* (London, Croom Helm, 1982)).

The Community Education programme at the Open University started in 1977. It is specifically concerned with promoting 'the educational well-being of the community generally'[1] within the University's Continuing Education programme, and has the following objectives:

1. To meet the learning needs of individuals at various stages in their lives: in their roles as parents, consumers, employees and citizens, in the context of their family, workplace and community by ...
(i) encouraging learners to value their own experience and the experience of others and to facilitate dialogue between learners and others;
(ii) providing information to assist personal and collective decision making;
(iii) helping learners make personal and collective decisions based on their own experience, values, resources and on information provided; and to implement changes;
(iv) enabling learners to take action individually and collectively to improve the services and facilities in their community and workplaces.
2. To reach as wide a range of learners as possible regardless of prior educational achievement, through appropriate learning materials and support for their learning.
3. To collaborate with national and local organisations in defining needs, developing learning materials, sharing resources, publicising and promoting learning opportunities, organising support for learners and in evaluating the provision.
4. To finance this work, within the rules laid down by the University, from student fees, external grants and other sources of income.

173

There are three particularly important ideas within the objectives. First the term *learner* is used rather than student. This makes explicit the aim of the Community Education programme to reach people in a variety of ways in their everyday lives. Thus in addition to those prepared to formally register as students, the programme aims to involve people who do not formally register — who indeed would never consider that 'formal' education had anything to offer them. Second, *learning materials* are referred to rather than 'courses' in order to open up our views of appropriate provision. The term 'learning materials' imposes no restrictions about media, length, format or structure, nor about usage or potential for adaptation. Third, the incorporation of *collaboration with national and local organisations* into the objectives highlights the importance placed on working with other bodies in using existing local and national networks already rooted in the community, both as a means of identifying needs and for dissemination of materials and support for learners.

So who is the Community Education programme for? The target group is somewhat wide, encompassing all adults aged 16 years or more. The aim is therefore to provide learning opportunities for adults not only regardless of social or economic circumstances but also for all ability levels. The programme aims to meet the learning needs of the educational 'failures' as well as of the educational elite.

In order to meet relatively specific 'role' related needs, courses and learning packages have to be designed and developed with well defined target groups (i.e. subgroups within the community) in mind. Even if these target groups are not, however, comprised of homogeneous groups of individuals. So if a group of adults at a similar stage with similar roles (e.g. new parents) is identified as having a particular learning need, the degree of learning experience and educational attainment, and the level of motivation to learn will all differ substantially between individuals. Thus the problem of defining the many different target groups is relatively complex.

The two main dimensions within which target groups are located are the 'learning' needs of adults at particular stages in their lives, and the 'materials and support' needs of adults accruing from their prior learning experiences, level of motivation, level of study skills, etc. Within the Community Education programme learning needs are dichotomised into (a) stages and (b) roles, for example:

(a) Illustrative stages of adult life:

Being single
Getting married
Planning families[a]
Pregnancy and birth[a]
Babies
Pre-school child[a]
Childhood 5-10[a]
Adolescence[a]
Marriage problems
Middle age
Planning retirement[a]
Retirement
Old age

(b) Illustrative concerns for each role:

Parent role:
  Child development
  Happy families
  Adoption and fostering
  Schools
Employee role:
  Starting work
  Women returning to work[b]
  Job change[b]
  Unemployment[b]
  Retirement
Consumer role:
  Consumer decisions[a]
  Energy in the home[a]
  Health choices[a]
  Food
  Money
  Housing
  Transport
Citizen/Community role:
  Governing schools[a]
  Magistrates
  Community advisers[b]
  Local councillors
  Race relations[a]

Notes: a. Courses in these areas are currently available within the OU Community Education Programme; b. Projects for developing materials in these areas are either approved or are actually under way.

The materials and support needs of the target audiences are similarly complex. Learners are handicapped by problems such as lack of motivation to study, access to appropriate provision, lack of confidence and non-ability to 'study', variation in familiarity with learning skills, and by external commitments and pressures, including lack of money to pay for learning materials or courses. Thus any given learning materials and student support system may be ideal for one group of learners with a particular learning need, and entirely inappropriate for another group with the same learning need.

The strategy adopted by the Community Education programme at the Open University has therefore been one of sequential definition and redefinition. The target audience is initially determined *as a whole* by the stage and role the learning materials relate to. The formal course is then designed with the aim of reaching as wide a range as possible of learners within the target group. Groups of learners which are found to be missing from the formal student body then become 'target groups' themselves for both formal and non-formal provision. Learning materials from the course are further developed or adapted to meet special needs, while further support services, or special forms of support, are organised where possible. In this way learning materials can, with varying degrees of adaptation, successfully reach audiences ranging from semi-illiterates to university graduates.

What is Provided Within the Programme

There are three broad production phases within the programme:

(i)   the identification of learning needs;
(ii) the development of appropriate learning materials;
(iii) the dissemination of these materials.

In higher education, especially at the undergraduate level, the contents of courses are determined largely by the requirements of the subject disciplines and the need to provide students with coherent programmes of study. In the Community Education programme our materials must be based on the needs of the learners and on the problems they face in their everyday lives. The staff at the University do not know what the needs are, what problems should be tackled, nor do they possess expertise in all the possible areas of knowledge that might be brought to bear on an everyday problem. They do however, have expertise in designing integrated multi-media learning materials.

It is in the area of needs and problems identification that national agencies, particularly those which have been built up from the grass roots, are particularly well qualified to help. They can also facilitate access to a wide range of national and international subject experts, whose knowledge relates to the 'everyday' problems a course may try to grapple with.

The learning materials development phase follows on from the identification of a particular area of need. Although course production was initially the main vehicle through which learning materials were developed, course materials are specifically designed so that they lend themselves to multiple uses and adaptations for 'informal' use.

In general terms, the materials are designed so that learners are able to examine issues and make decisions over a range of situations. The material is developed in such a way that individual issues can stand alone and be studied in isolation (e.g. as leaflets), *and* the same material can be put together with other material on interrelated issues (e.g. as a booklet). The cumulative impact of a highly structured and interrelated series of materials (i.e. the course) on the learner is greater than the sum of the individual and independent parts.

While course production will continue to be an important means of building up a resource of learning materials, materials development projects are in existence which take a more developmental approach which involves discussing, transcribing, editing, testing and adapting. This process of dialogue leads to the production of items of material which may then be linked with others as packages or booklets and eventually courses. Adaptations from the early courses can also be fed back into updated and revised courses.

The Process of Materials Development and Redevelopment

Thus the development of materials is a cyclical process involving a variety of formats and a range of learners. Figure 1 shows the main print formats, learners and inputs. A similar process applies to audio-visual materials.

The materials development process has two main phases:

1. The *dissemination* phase (the first half of the cycle) where course material is adapted for various delivery and support systems and for different target audiences.
2. The *assimilation* phase (the second half of the cycle) starting with dialogue with local people, which is captured in some form and then transformed into leaflets. These can be grouped and used by other learners. The common core of a group of leaflets can also be extracted

Figure 1: The Materials Development Cycle

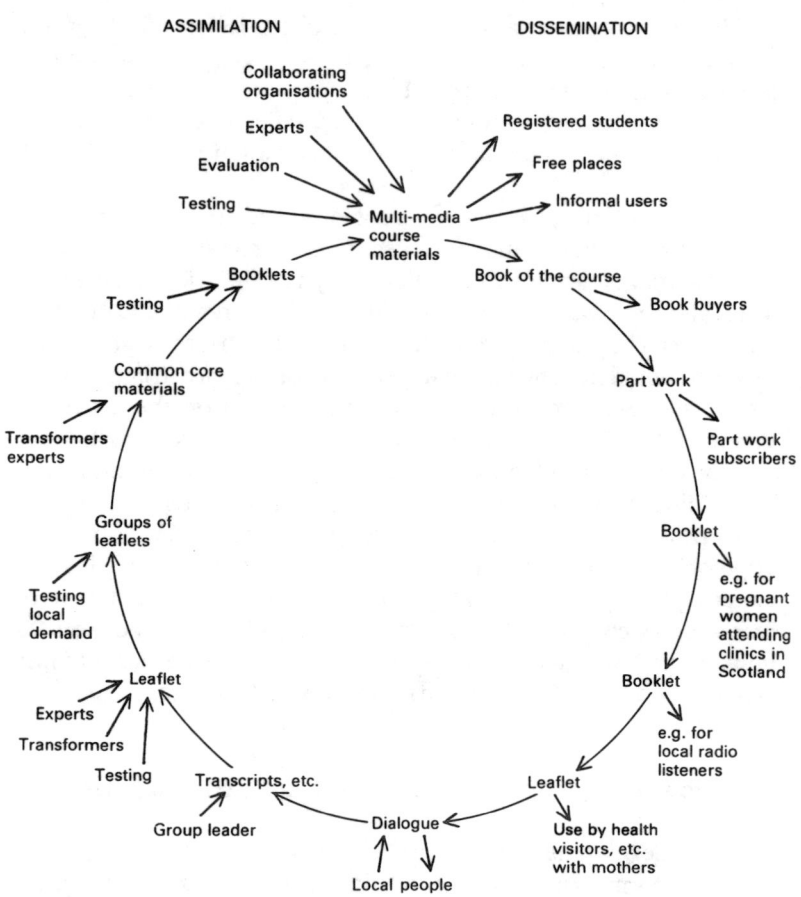

Source: Farnes (1979)[2]

and produced as a booklet, which may form the basis for a new or revised multi-media course.

Two major grants have funded materials development. The first, from the Health Education Council, has funded course development for parent and health education. These courses are then exploited to produce booklets and leaflets for use by non-registered students. Thus, this activity is in the dissemination phase of the materials development cycle. The second major grant has come from the

Bernard Van Leer Foundation, which funded a collaborative research project involving the University and local community education projects in four areas of acute economic and social need within the United Kingdom. This work involves local dialogue to produce the source material for the development of leaflets and booklets based on the experience of local people. Materials developed through this process will feed into the creation of new courses and are in the assimilation phase of the cycle.

The Support of Central Production at the Local and Regional Level

The development and production of materials at the centre is underpinned by local and regional support. This takes two main forms: (1) extension of access to the learning materials; (2) support for individual learners. With the wide range of both media and methods used within the programme, support for learners needs to be very flexible.

First, there are various kinds of support that affect whether or not a learner will come into contact with and take up the provision. If the opportunity is mediated by someone who is trusted, or if barriers such as the fee are removed, the provision becomes more accessible to the individual. Support at the local level is provided right from the outset with volunteer 'enthusers' or 'animateurs' assisting the University to extend and widen access to the learning materials by placing and delivering publicity and promotional materials. These volunteer co-ordinators may be professionals in the content area involved (e.g. health education officers for the course 'The First Years of Life') or committed activists (e.g. women involved in the running of the local pre-school playgroups for the course 'The Pre-School Child'). They are recruited after agreement with the appropriate agency is reached at the national level.

Barriers to access are often more complex than simple lack of awareness. Special schemes have therefore been set up whereby it is possible to make available free places on certain courses, organise group discounts, or arrange for learning materials to be shared, thus bypassing economic barriers. Where lack of confidence is a major disincentive to participate, individual personal support for study within a group can often be organised.

Initial support is also provided through local radio stations and an 'in-house' newspaper, 'Routes'. Local radio disc jockeys and other professionals known in the area encourage and support their listeners to become 'informal' learners, not only by listening to the local radio programmes related to the learning materials, but also in encouraging them to write in for associated print material which is provided free of charge. 'Routes' is sent two or three times a year to all students and former students. Former students are now recognised as providing an extremely valuable service in supporting prospective students (data suggests that around a quarter of the students first heard of their course from a friend or colleague at work). The newspaper keeps past students up-to-date with new developments and courses, and seeks to introduce prospective students to the aims and ethos of community education provision at the OU.

Once the learner has made the decision to become 'active', the support given to him can vary considerably. In some local initiatives, one-to-one tutoring/counselling is carried out, whilst others have organised group discussions structured and led by a 'professional'. Distance support from TV, radio and print is given to all learners. Clearly, more support can be provided by direct contact on an individual basis, where it is adapted to the needs of the learner. Less support can be given where contact is limited to groups of learners through a distance medium, where it cannot be adapted to individual needs.

Just as important as the support provided by professionals and para-professionals, however, is the support provided by other learners. Self-help groups, set up by volunteer co-ordinators, can provide 'moral support' for anxious learners and boost their self-confidence in a way which would be impossible 'at a distance'. The contact between these groups and local professionals or para-professionals can vary: some groups operate totally independently while others have a professional in attendance who can provide additional local resources, organise audio-visual aids, and who may help guide and advise the group.

The self-help group system was set up to enable students to share their experiences and resources and to enable them to help each other. Those who wish to study alone or with a friend or neighbour are perfectly free to do so. Those who wish to participate in a self-help group (about half the students) normally have to take the initiative by contacting the local co-ordinator for their course. If there are any other students in the area studying that course who have also signified an interest in joining a self-help group, the co-ordinator will then put them in touch with each other.

There are, however, many problems in setting up groups in this way, and the proportion of students who want to join a group who actually do so is, unfortunately, smaller than we would wish. Problems in making contact with a co-ordinator, in contacting other students, and distances between students, all hinder students and co-ordinators in trying to set up groups. Many of these problems do not apply, of course, to sponsored students, who consequently have a much higher participation rate in self-help groups (one in four) than fee-paying students (one in eight).

Students appear to receive such great benefits from self-help groups that considerable efforts are being made to overcome the problems identified. The typical self-help group has about five or six members and meets at the house of one of its members about once every two weeks. The role the group appears to play is that of a forum for airing problems, and giving and receiving of advice between members; in effect, acting as a 'counterbalance' to the course 'proper'. The group provides the participants with a non-threatening environment in which their own attitudes and behaviour can be challenged and either modified or reinforced. The reassurance that each participant provides for the other students in terms of shared problems is essential within this process.

Support for the volunteer co-ordinator network itself has changed considerably since its inception. During the first five years of the Community Education programme, separate networks were set up for each course. The increase in the number of courses, the resultant growth in the number of volunteer co-ordinators (almost 500 in 1981), and the expressed desire of many volunteers to take on a wider non-course specific role led to their reorganisation into a general student support network. Within this reorganised network, which is currently being introduced, volunteer co-ordinators take responsibility for a defined geographical area and support students across the full range of Community Education courses. In this way the patchiness of geographical coverage will be 'smoothed', while professional support at the regional level will facilitate local dissemination and outreach activity.

The volunteer co-ordinators are supported by Open University regional staff as well. These staff also have a dual role as back-up to the volunteer co-ordinators and in undertaking a professional 'enthusing' function. Back-up is provided by recruiting additional volunteer co-ordinators to fill gaps or replace those who leave, by organising briefings for volunteer co-ordinators, and by providing specialist information and advice as and when needed.

To What Extent have the Aims and Objectives been met?

During the five years since the first two courses were offered to the public, over 85,000 students have formally registered for Open University Community Education courses; translations of course materials have been made into Spanish, Hebrew and Portuguese; 'book' versions of the course materials have been produced in hard and soft-backed form for sale in retail bookshops and by mail order (one book sold over 57,000 copies in its first year of sale); booklets have been developed from the course materials (325,000 copies of a special booklet of adapted course materials were distributed in Scotland); and projects with local radio and local newspapers featuring extracts of course materials have provided other dissemination outlets for offprints from the learning materials. None of this includes the 'normal' informal use of Community Education materials. Such use has, with encouragement and support from co-ordinators and OU staff, grown astonishingly over the past five years.

Accepting then that the dissemination of the learning materials has been successful in terms of numbers, the question remains as to whether the aims and objectives for the overall programme have been met. Let us consider the list of objectives with which this paper started.

The first objective (1 (i)) aimed to meet the learning needs of the individuals by encouraging them to value their own experience, and the experience of others, and by facilitating dialogue between learners and others.

Findings from evaluation studies indicate that this objective was achieved for many learners, in the sense that they felt greater self-confidence in themselves in a particular role. What is particularly important about this objective is that it is not one held initially by the learners themselves. Only a small minority of learners (around 6%) started off their studies with this as a main aim. Subsequent to their studies however, particularly among the more disadvantaged learners, a significantly greater proportion (20%) see this as the main benefit from their studies. This perception appears also to have been shared by those co-ordinators involved in organising and administrating the 'sponsored places' scheme for disadvantaged learners. A third of them, totally unprompted, identified signs of increased self-confidence on the part of the sponsored students as one of the most common ways in which they benefited. The same co-ordinators also reported that sponsored students gained from discussions with other parents on the course and from sharing experiences and learning together (22% of co-ordinators).

'Valuing the experience of others' and 'facilitating dialogue between learners and others' are objectives which are implicit rather than explicit in the learning materials. Nevertheless a follow-up study of registered students of 'The Pre-School Child' three years after discovered evidence of the achievement of both these objectives for at least some of the students. The main support for achieving these objectives came from self-help groups. Sponsored students in particular felt that their groups had been 'very useful' in enabling them to talk with people with the same problems (49%). Self-help groups were not the only way of achieving these objectives however. The follow-up study discovered that 88 per cent of students discussed the course with others — at home (75%), with friends (50%), with relatives (16%), with neighbours (12%), and so on. Even after the end of the course, 54 per cent of students loaned the learning materials to others.

The next objective (1 (ii)) related to the provision of information to assist personal and collective decision-making. This objective appears to be relatively most successful, in that it matches with the main benefits of study as perceived both by learners and volunteer co-ordinators. For example, the most common way in which sponsored students were seen as benefiting from 'The First Years of Life' course was in 'gaining a greater understanding of children's needs and behaviour or developments' (59% of co-ordinators). The students themselves were also clear that the *main* benefit of the course had been 'adding to my knowledge of children' (70%). The importance of this benefit to learners does however appear to have diminished somewhat over time, as three years after study, only 49 per cent reported 'knowledge' as a main benefit from the course, with other benefits having become relatively more important over the period.

Helping learners to make personal and collective decisions was the focus of the third objective (1 (iii)). Clearly this objective is a particularly difficult one to which to attribute causality. Although most of the research and evaluation findings relate to the courses for parents, which were the first courses to be offered in the Community Education programme, some data is available from other courses such as 'Consumer Decisions' and 'Energy in the Home'. Both courses are clearly 'change' oriented. For 'Energy in the Home', for example, 40 per cent of the students reported installing one or more energy-saving measures as a direct result of doing the course. Similarly, for 'Consumer Decisions', 40 per cent reported that they had changed the way they decided to spend money, at least with the occasional 'big' decisions involving large sums of money. It would appear that the subject matter of the courses affects the confidence with which the achievement of this particular objective can be identified.

The fourth objective was concerned with enabling learners to take action both individually and collectively, particularly with regard to the services and facilities in their communities and work places (1 (iv)). Those courses and packs within the programme relating to the 'citizen/community' role are clearly the ones most likely to achieve this particular objective. Unfortunately, no evaluation data is yet available for the two courses in this area. For learners using materials from courses concerned with other roles, such as parent or consumer, the evidence is at best inconclusive.

In spite of this caveat, a three-year follow-up of students found that membership of community groups and voluntary organisations was all up following their studies (those who belonged to none at all dropped from 21% before the courses to 9% during the period after). No causality can be proven, but it is interesting to note that half the students had gone on to further study, with a quarter of these taking courses connected with running playgroups or mother and toddler groups. One phenomenon related to this which is frequently reported is the 'seeding' effect which can emerge from group work based around a course:

> four individuals in the group wished to go further. The eighteen year old intends to study for the PPA certificate and run a playgroup of her own, while two other women are busy preparing to run other groups on the estate using P912 and the 'Consumer Decisions' course materials.[3]

The fifth objective (2) was rather different from the previous ones in that it was an objective for the providers rather than the learners. It defines the target audience for the learning materials as being as wide as possible 'regardless of prior educational achievement'. Data from the early courses suggested that fee-paying students were, on the whole, very similar in terms of prior educational achievement to those who registered for the OU undergraduate programme; i.e. between 5-13 per cent had no formal qualifications at all. Since approximately 50 per cent of the population between 16-50 years have no qualifications at all, it was clear that there was a significant imbalance in the student population. A series of experiments subsequently identified a range of ways of reaching the educationally 'disadvantaged'. Between 38 and 51 per cent of the women in the 'sponsored places' scheme had no educational qualifications. The 'Local Radio' scheme was similarly successful; at least 25 per cent of the learners had no formal qualifications.

The most successful schemes, however, have been those initiated and carried out by community based professionals and para-professionals. The use by health professionals of four page offprints of selected topics from the courses with their clients, in particular, appears to have been a useful and successful way of reaching people who had specific learning needs but who would never of their own accord have dreamt of turning to a 'course' to help them work out a solution.

What has become quite clear from the work undertaken within the Community Education programme is that although the target audience encompasses the full spectrum of learners, it must be seen as two separate and distinct groups for the purpose of facilitating access to the programme. The one group is already motivated, already has a formal educational qualification, and if the course materials appear to meet a need, is relatively likely to register for a course. The other group comprise people whose previous experience of education and whose immediate social circle is such that they are totally unlikely to consider that 'education' has any relevance for them personally. These learners will not be reached by conventional means, but may be reached by the carefully targeted dissemination of structured learning materials through non-formal community educators.

The last two objectives (3 and 4) are rather different in kind, being more a 'means to an end' rather than an end in themselves. Collaboration has worked extremely well at both national and regional levels. Access to local networks has been facilitated and collaborators have proved to be both generous and imaginative in promoting learning opportunities for a wide range of learners. At the local level, a number of experiments are currently in progress, but at present no coherent 'model' has emerged.

Financial objectives are included as the programme, as part of the Open University's Centre for Continuing Education, has to be self-financing. In practice, the programme has been relatively successful in meeting its financial obligations through fee income (approximately 70% of total income) and through specific grants from collaborating agencies. In addition, the University has sympathetically supported new ventures by the programme.

Finally, attention should be drawn to two important types of unanticipated outcomes. Both types of outcome related to the use of Community Education materials by people other than those in the target audience, i.e. by professionals. They are:

(i) the use of Community Education materials for training purposes (both initial and in-service training); and

(ii) the use of Community Education material as resource material by professionals.

What does the Future hold?

Developments in four main areas will determine the future direction of the Community Education programme: materials development, learner support, extension of access to the programme, range of provision.

More of the materials development and redevelopment in the future is likely to be located on the left hand side of the Materials Development Cycle, involving a sequential form of development, whereby an overall framework is established during dialogue with potential users and learners, and individual topic leaflets are developed, tested and grouped together within main themes ·as 'mini packs' and across themes as the print component of a course. There is also likely to be more materials redevelopment, aimed at both extending the use of existing materials by extending the target audience, and at meeting the needs of specific subsections of the target audience more precisely.

Material developments will not be restricted to Community Education originated material. Linkages with materials and courses developed by other sectors of Continuing Education are increasingly likely as common concerns are identified. For example, an 'Education for Family Life' pack for teachers is being developed which it is hoped teachers who have used the 'Parenting' courses as resource materials for their students will benefit from. A course for both parents of, and professionals working with, mentally handicapped children could have a common core of material which identified the issues, with different structured activities for the two audiences. Similarly, material developed by other bodies could be made available through the Community Education Catalogue, where they contributed to the aims of the overall programme.

Community Education originated materials would continue to be highly developed, in that, as well as appropriately presenting information, they would contain devices for sensitising the learner, for analysing and evaluating his experience, organising this to make decisions and taking action to implement those decisions. In other words, the learning materials will be designed so that learners of relatively average ability can use them to achieve learning objectives without support. However, many of the materials which originate outside Community Education are less highly developed. Thus the support needed by learners using this type of material is likely to be greater.

While much of this support could be developed and enhanced by the new network structure described earlier, support for some areas of provision could well be provided entirely separately by the collaborating body. This would, in a sense, be a more formal version of the various local developments which have sprung up in the past, and which the 'outreach' work by the new network would continue to extend.

Finally, there is the continuing aim to meet a wider range of learning needs of a wider range of learners. The emphasis to date has been on reaching a wider range of learners with a relatively limited range of learning materials in role terms. This emphasis is likely to continue, in that alternatives for the disadvantaged learners are still extremely limited. Nevertheless the range of provision will also be extended to deal with a wider range of learning needs in the context of the roles and stages discussed at the beginning of the paper. The unemployed, for example, are a clear priority, and as people become familiar with Community Education materials, externally generated proposals are likely to point the way to other priorities in the longer term future.

Notes

1. Open University Charter (April 1969).
2. Farnes, N., 'The Open University's Role in Community Education', in N. Farnes (ed.) (1979), *Community Education with the Open University.*
3. Calder, J. 'Informal Use and Learning Needs', *Teaching at a Distance No. 19* (The Open University, Summer 1981).

4.2

THE NATIONAL EXTENSION COLLEGE

Richard Freeman

Source: Copyright © The Open University 1983 (specially written for this volume).

Origins and Development

The National Extension College (NEC) was founded by Michael Young and Brian Jackson in 1963. Perhaps its major asset at birth was its grand sounding name, but in reality it was modest in the extreme. NEC was one room, nine feet square, in the back of 57 Russell Street, Cambridge — a condemned artisan's cottage housing the head-quarters of the Advisory Centre for Education (ACE). ACE had been founded by Michael Young one year earlier as an advice and information centre for parents. ACE was not a provider of education, nor had it plans to become so, but nevertheless it spawned NEC which was to become much larger than its own parent body.

At the start NEC's total staff stood at one. However the founders of this upstart college intended nothing less than a major transformation of adult learning in the UK. Four years later, in its first major report,[1] the college described itself as having four aims:

1. A Second Chance College

From the start, NEC saw itself as providing education both for adults who had missed something in their initial education and for adults who could not make use of existing facilities.

> Even in a highly-developed educational system like ours, there are still huge numbers of people who do not get as much as they ideally should out of our schools, colleges, and universities, or the work of independent bodies such as the Workers' Educational Association (WEA). These are men and women who might have failed in the past, or who were early leavers, or unsuccessful university applicants. They may be adults who, through all the accidents and vicissitudes of life, find themselves in the wrong jobs or discover the excitement of learning only after schooldays are over. They may be women, who, after the second class educational oppor-

tunities too frequently offered to girls ... find themselves married with growing children, and the possibility of 20 or 30 working years still ahead of them. They may be handicapped, blind or in hospital ...

2. *Correspondence and Broadcasting*

The report started this section with a distinct lack of confidence in the new college's proposed methods: 'Like everyone else we prefer to teach students face-to-face, in one day or weekend residential schools, or by means of study circles centred on a local tutor.' But this faltering attitude did not seem to inhibit the college from fostering major innovations or pressing the case for such innovations.

> Our second aim in launching the College was to pilot the way for a University of the Air. This meant advocating the notion as widely as possible, helping to keep the idea alive during lean economic years ... But more than this it meant mounting practical experiments in which broadcasting, correspondence, and face-to-face teaching were combined so as to amass the kind of social, educational and technical data which must precede any University of the Air ...

That showed very clearly the special role that NEC had set itself: experimenting with new methods of distance teaching not just for NEC's benefit but as demonstrations to the community at large. And, to prove that it meant business, the report included a list of eleven experiments that the college had carried out ranging from 'After School English' (NEC/Anglia Television) to 'Mathematics in Action — Logic and the Computer' (NEC/BBC Television).

3. *Projects*

The report stated:

> Our third aim has been to use the centre we have established for a series of projects aimed at discovering what other needs in education might possibly be met by the kind of teaching techniques and media evolved at the National Extension College.

A number of completed projects in this category were listed.

4. *Developing Countries Overseas*

The report drew attention to the problems that developing countries would have in providing enough education for their populations and then suggested that experiments in the UK would have valuable results for developing countries.

We now have the benefit of hindsight and can look at the intentions of the founders of NEC and at the college's activities in practice. Two things seem striking. First, the percipience of people such as Michael Young and Brian Jackson. Michael Young was a lawyer turned sociologist who spurned traditional university research departments and established his own research body, the Institute of Community Studies. Brian Jackson was a young English graduate who, through teaching, had become aware of the need to attack the deep inequalities in educational provision and opportunity in the UK. It is probably no accident that these two people in NEC's origins worked *outside* the statutory system. They saw that system as being in need of urgent reform but chose to provoke such reform through demonstrations outside the state system. Their foresight was remarkable: they rightly forecast that new technology had a lot to offer home students and they were also right that the push had to come from NEC — it was not going to come from the established institutions. There was a need to help adult students at home even though few adult educationists agreed and most were hostile to distance education.

Second, the structure of the college and its methods was quite unlike that of any other educational institution. Here was a college prepared to tackle things which at the time were risky like training social workers at a distance or teaching people to build radios in their own homes. Yet it had virtually no staff or resources and it could only suceed if it could persuade other institutions to change. *All* its major experiments were collaborative — with ITV, with BBC, with the WEA and so on. By itself, NEC could provide very little but, acting as a catalyst, it triggered a major extension to education for adults. Equally, it aimed to make some of its provision through very indirect means, i.e. through persuading others to provide. This was how the Open University came about: NEC showed it could be done, but others were to do it.

Consolidation

Innovation is easier when one has few continuing commitments. So, at the start, everything was new. Then came an unexpected change.

The Trustees of the University Correspondence College (UCC) asked NEC to take UCC over. UCC was an old established non-commercial college, much run down but with 3,000 students. NEC agreed to the proposal and, overnight, changed from an experimental body to one with a duty to provide education for 3,000 students. For better or worse, that amalgamation decidedly shifted the balance in NEC. The major effort, and what little money NEC possessed, had to go into trying to keep a range of GCE 'O' and 'A' level courses up to date.

NEC was in distinct danger of slipping into being yet another British correspondence college. For those who were aware of the danger, it reminded them of the continuing question 'What does NEC exist for?'. Reaching a clear answer to this question was postponed by another outside event when the Government announced its intention of setting up a 'University of the Air'. How that proposition transformed itself into the Open University need not concern us here. What does concern us is how that decision and its consequences affected NEC. It was clear from the outset that the Government had no part for NEC in this new university. Perhaps NEC should not have objected: its declared aim was to experiment and pilot and here was one of its pilots being transformed into the real thing. But it is one thing to declare yourself to be experimental and another to accept that others will benefit more than you from the results. If there were to be a 'University of the Air' without NEC involvement, did NEC have any reason to continue?

Once again, reaching an answer was postponed by a request from the Open University Planning Committee to NEC, the BBC and the Associated Examining Board (AEB) to set up 'Gateway' courses for intending Open University students. These courses were prepared during 1969 and run for the first time in 1970 when 4,181 students enrolled for them. NEC's turnover went up from £95,301 in 1969 to £149,394 in 1970. NEC seemed set to have a role in life even under the shadow of this big brother. Then came two major catastrophes. First the Open University withdrew the support that the Planning Committee had given to the Gateway courses, because it thought at the time that its students would be sufficiently well-prepared without formal study (subsequent experience showed, however, that many students without experience of post-secondary education failed to complete their first year at the Open University). Second, early 1971 saw an eight week national postal strike. Income for 1971 fell to £87,895.

It looked as though, rejected by the OU, NEC had no further role and no chance of surviving. It was time to re-examine what NEC was for.

Developing New Models of Learning

There was no sudden insight. Indeed NEC staggered through 1972 to 1976 trying to run a high quality correspondence college. Enrolments gradually rose from 5,748 in 1972 to 10,433 in 1975. Then they fell to 7,869 in 1976. Clearly NEC was not firmly based and was in no position to feel secure about its place in national educational provision.

The problem was simple: NEC had set out to be a catalytic, innovative organisation which inevitably implied a high risk type of existence. But whatever the risks, it had a clear role. In accepting UCC into itself, NEC had acquired a commitment to be a service organisation, a role requiring a low risk existence and a sense of stability. NEC was a contradiction.

What was required was that NEC should be needed on a continuing basis by someone. If that someone was to be the education system, then NEC had to move from being a catalyst to having a role in the system. Only in 1976 had this become completely clear to the college. Finding that role was not easy but it crystallised between 1976 and 1981 and has now placed NEC fairly firmly within the state system yet not quite part of it. An explanation of how that has been achieved is best done through looking at the new developments that were instituted in 1976-7 and how they have worked out.

FlexiStudy

FlexiStudy is a collaborative method of provision involving NEC and local colleges. It provides students with a distance learning course tutored by their *local* college but based on NEC's centrally produced course material. FlexiStudy grew from an analysis of the weakness of NEC's position as a provider of correspondence courses. As NEC had made clear from the start, distance students needed a variety of kinds of support: good texts, a reliable administrative system, good distance tutors, face-to-face tutorials, lab work, broadcasting and so on. The Open University provided this by the simple expedient of having enough money to pay for all the desirable elements: it relied on no one's favours. But NEC courses were unsubsidised so NEC could only spend about one thirtieth per student of what the Open

University could afford. (The Open University budget for 1983 is approximately £60 m. for 60,000 undergraduates, i.e. around £1,000 per student. NEC's 1983 budget is £36 per student.) Increasingly it became clear that NEC was getting less and less able to provide the 'extras' such as weekend courses, audio tapes, science kits and Saturday seminars. Inflation was making such items too expensive whilst at the same time, restrictions on local expenditure were making it more difficult for local colleges to provide support for NEC students.

The solution to this problem came from recognising a fact of life that NEC had tried to ignore for 14 years. From the start, NEC had mounted experiments involving many organisations but invariably what NEC wanted was for other organisations to support NEC students. The other organisations *gave*, the NEC students *received*. Much can be done by trading on such goodwill but only for limited periods. There comes a time, or a scale of activity is reached, when the other organisations feel that they are being asked to give too much. By 1977 it was clear to NEC that it was asking too much of local colleges in expecting them to provide long-term face-to-face support for NEC students. Colleges had to place their own students first.

There was a solution to the problem if a way could be found of making NEC students into local authority students. If that could be done, the colleges would want to provide support for the students. Out of this idea the notion of FlexiStudy was born. What is important to this account is the role that FlexiStudy casts NEC in. NEC had looked at what makes for a successful distance learning course and had identified the ingredients, amongst others, as:

Distance learning materials
Distance tutoring
Counselling
Face-to-face tutorials
Facilities for practical work (e.g. labs, computers)
Examination facilities
Library facilities
Access to multi-media resources

What was significant about this list was that, apart from the first item (distance learning materials), a *local* college was better placed to provide all the resources than was NEC. Why then did correspondence colleges exist at all? This analysis led to the concept of Flexi-

Study which was jointly worked out by NEC and Barnet College of Further Education. In FlexiStudy, the student enrols on a distance learning course with the local college (they may only live 100 yards from it). That college provides:

A distance learning text for his/her chosen subject and objectives

A tutor to mark and comment on his/her written assignments

Face-to-face tutorials

Access to labs, computers, etc.

Examination facilities

Counselling

Students can then study at home, posting off assignments to the college just as if they were NEC or Open University students. The local college becomes a local distance learning centre.

However, this is only possible because NEC can provide the local college with the distance learning texts. Few local colleges have enough students in any one subject to justify the costs of writing, editing, designing and printing their own material. On the other hand, with hundreds of colleges running FlexiStudy, it does make economic sense for NEC to develop FlexiStudy texts. In the process, a symbiotic relationship has been established between NEC and the Flexi-Study colleges. The colleges need NEC in order to have a supply of texts to sustain their FlexiStudy enrolments and NEC needs the colleges in order to have customers for its texts. And, whilst NEC and the colleges are locked together in this way, the local student is getting a type of distance learning course that neither NEC nor the local college could provide alone. Although it now operates in 130 colleges and has about 10,000 students, the NEC correspondence student body continues to grow as well. FlexiStudy appears, therefore, to have found new students and not to have diverted old students from other modes of study.

This role is characteristic of NEC at the present time. It is neither catalytic/experimental (and therefore of a short life expectancy) nor is it NEC trying to go it alone. Instead, NEC has found a job that needs doing more or less indefinitely and in which the state sector is pleased to see NEC doing the job. What is also characteristic for NEC is that FlexiStudy would not be possible without the local colleges. It contrasts strongly with the Open University model where the Open University provides all that the student needs, buying in whatever can't be directly provided. Each is a viable model of distance education.

Resources for Other Institutions

In its narrowest conception, NEC came into existence to serve the home student. From the start this was taken to include students of other institutions with, for example, weekend courses being run for London University degree students regardless of who they were studying with. This line did not prove fruitful, possibly because few institutions wished to promote such services to their students. So for many years NEC turned back to supporting its own students and no one else's. More recently though it has become clear that the notion of NEC serving a mixed body of students could be interpreted in another way (FlexiStudy is, of course, an example) — the learning materials of NEC could be used to improve or extend the courses offered by many other institutions.

Such a notion brings a genuinely new element into some of the courses offered by local colleges and it can do this in two ways. First, there are subject areas where no learning material exists, or at least none for the adult age group. Second, there are many courses which are 'over-taught', leaving the student with little to do. Both types of course can be transformed by the use of good learning materials and both types of development have been pursued with success by NEC.

In the first category (subjects where no learning material exists), NEC has been able to make significant contributions in several areas including adult numeracy ('Make it Count' and 'Numbers at Work') and in small business education ('The Small Business Kit'). The NEC course material gives content to the course, brings to each course the successful experience of other centres and does so in a way which encourages self-study alongside the taught course.

Using Broadcast Television

From the very start of NEC, broadcasting, and particularly television, had been seen as important to NEC.[2] All these projects shared one characteristic. The object from NEC's point of view was to find a broadcasting organisation that was willing to make and transmit a series of programmes that would be of direct benefit to NEC correspondence students. Such series make little sense to broadcasters who are increasingly having to produce good audience ratings in order to hold on to their budgets and air time. So, NEC has had to rethink what it can achieve when working with broadcasting organisations. The parallel with the development of FlexiStudy is of interest for the same underlying problem was there: to find a role in which all participants need each other.

That role has come about by ceasing to look for television series which are related to NEC's correspondence courses and instead to look at less formal and extensive forms of education. Much if not most of adult learning takes place outside both educational institutions and the structure of a formal course. It is a recognition of this fact that has led broadcasters away from formal sequentially organised educational series to less formal formats. These formats have less to offer the committed viewer so it becomes more important that something beyond the series is offered to him/her. Broadcasters have therefore had to find more and more ways of stimulating follow-up to their series. The word 'stimulating' is important: the broadcasters do not want to have to provide follow-up themselves, but do wish to see it provided by organisations which are sympathetic to the aims the broadcasters have set themselves.

This type of follow-up service is one which NEC seems to be particularly suited to providing. One can only hypothesise as to why. Possibly it is because NEC has never quite lost the atmosphere which it had before it took over the UCC. The very qualities that do not promote the smooth running of a correspondence college may be just the ones needed for efficient television back-up. The *lack* of a rigid system, the *lack* of a bureaucracy dedicated to doing things in a particular way and the *lack* of any formal ties with the state system may be essential for television back-up work.

Why essential? First, no projects are alike. In television back-up, the staff concerned may one week be dealing with a counselling service for unemployed young people and the next week be providing a different type of service for well-educated people wanting to learn computer programming. Second, broadcast television works on very short schedules. It is by no means unusual for the last few programmes of an educational series only to be in outline when the first programme goes out. Any organisation providing the back-up does therefore have to be able to work quickly and informally — there is no time to wait for approvals through committees.

Those qualities are not enough to guarantee that a job will be done. After all, there is very little experience of how to provide education of this type. There is a tendency for the adults attracted to follow an educational series on television to be less well educated and less experienced in organising their study. Equally, the experience and methods of established adult education are not necessarily a good model for television back-up. So, new models have had to be developed. Looking for common aspects of these new models is not easy but perhaps the following is not an unreasonable list:

Easy-to-use Referral Services. Perhaps the most significant development in this type of education is the telephone referral service. NEC cannot claim any credit for this — the crucial work was done by Broadcasting Support Services Fund in connection with 'On the Move'.[3] The existence of such services is very important to NEC's work since many of NEC's projects would not be possible if no efficient referral services existed.

Non-formal Materials. Most of the series that are likely to attract large numbers of learners attract people with limited study skills. Traditional adult study materials assume a high level of study skills and are not therefore a suitable model for this type of work. NEC has therefore had to develop new formats for educational print materials. Probably the most successful examples to date have been the 'Jobhunter Kit'[4] and the 'Make it Count Workbook'.[5]

Easy Feedback Systems. One particular characteristic of traditional distance education is quite unsuitable for the new audiences attracted by television — that is the tutor marked assignment. Nothing encapsulates the formality of education more than the process of formally sitting down to write answers to a problem which exists only for that purpose. What is more, the school system seems to leave adults not only frightened of such work but unable to learn from it. They see assignments as something for the tutor to mark, not for the student to learn from. These problems demonstrate the need for something new to match the less formal learning of adults. From 1983, NEC will be using a computer feedback system, MAIL, which produces 1 to 3 page A4 letters in response to the student answering multiple choice questions. Whilst it is too early to say what effect this will have in the UK, similar systems in Sweden (CADE) and the USA (RSVP) have been very successful. We hope that MAIL will enable large numbers of adults to get more involved in education than they would previously have dared to do.

Better Distribution. The final important advance under this heading has been the distribution of learning material. Traditional education has largely involved the teacher giving out knowledge in the classroom. The textbook was (and in many cases still is) a teacher aid, not a means of self-instruction for the pupil. Distance education and programmed learning greatly improved the learning text so that the typical Open University or NEC text is an excellent learning aid for a well motivated student with good study skills. But such texts are not easy to come by — the student has to know about them and write off for them or enrol into a formal system. Such systems are not very accessible to the average adult. It has therefore been important to NEC to find more effective ways of distributing adult learning material using bookshops, libraries and other outlets. NEC has now reached the point where more NEC course material is distributed through bookshops than through all other systems put together.

None of the mechanisms described is of itself unique to NEC or unique to television back-up. But it is the combination (and the existence of trained staff to whom such ideas are natural) that counts.

Structure

To some extent what NEC has done and what it is able to do is a product of its legal status. The College is a company limited by guarantee and, because of the nature of its work, is registered as a charity. In effect that gives NEC all the benefits of being a limited company (which are many under British law) whilst the company itself has no shareholders. Because it has no shareholders — and is not permitted to have any — any surplus made by the college must, by law, be put back into the company for the purposes of the company, i.e. for more educational work. Apart from financial benefits, charitable status opens up relationships in a way which perhaps no other status could do. It smooths the way to grants and financial concessions in many quarters.

NEC has no formal or legal ties with the state sector, nor is it legal for any other company to hold a share in NEC. This independence has undoubtedly shaped NEC. On the debit side, it has made it hard for NEC to be accepted as a formal provider in the way that the Open University or the local education authorities (LEAs) are. On the credit side, it has meant that NEC can innovate without permission or consent. That has led to many NEC experiments which could not have been mounted so quickly or so easily within the state sector.

As NEC grows, its independence becomes more and more of an

anomaly. Despite its now wide range of work and links with state providers, it is no more part of the state sector than it was on the day it was founded. Yet, in practical terms, more and more parts of state provision come to rely in some way on an NEC activity. (And, conversely, NEC becomes more and more reliant on the continuation of its links with the state sector.) At this time there is no indication that these relationships will lead to a formal change in NEC's status but that is presumably not unthinkable in the long run. Meanwhile, NEC becomes more and more a specialist agency enabling the state sector to make certain types of provision that it could not otherwise make.

The Staff and the Trust

The guardians of the Trust and the directors of the company are individual trustees who together form the Council of Trustees. The Council is a self-appointing body, electing its members at an Annual General Meeting. Most of the Trust's members are academics with leading positions in other educational bodies: that is, the Trust would seem to see itself as needing to guard its educational objectives and standards first and foremost. Naturally the day-to-day work is done by the employees of the Trust of whom there are currently 58 full-time together with about 350 part-time correspondence tutors. The staff are distributed as follows:

Direction and finance	8
Correspondence services	17
Media services unit	2
Marketing and despatch	5
Printing	3
Grant aided research and development	23

Two major activities are *not* carried out by full-time staff: assignment marking and writing courses and publications. Assignment marking is carried out by part-time correspondence tutors, many of whom have full-time jobs in other educational institutions. They are paid a fee for each assignment marked. Courses and publications are written by freelance authors who are paid a fee or royalties for their work. Almost everything else is done by NEC's full-time staff. That includes: commissioning new courses and publications, editing, design, typesetting, printing, stocking and distribution; student and tutorial records, student advice and counselling; research and development. The resulting system is complex with many connections between different departments and activities. It functions because the whole process is tied together by an IBM computer that holds the records of 25,000 students, 400 tutors and 4,000 customers' accounts, and performs stock control, invoicing, direct mail selling and all the internal administration of NEC.

As a broad description that sounds much like the OU. There are however two structural differences of some importance. First, the fact that courses are written by freelance authors, and second the fact that NEC has no regional structure. When courses are written by freelance writers, most of whom will only write occasionally for NEC, the role of the full-time staff changes. They are not subject experts but they are experts in the design of distance learning texts. Our experience shows that commissioning an NEC course author is not like commissioning in publishing. The editor is a major contributor to the course from a very early stage. Each course goes through a set of well-defined stages: course proposal, specimen unit, first draft, second draft (and then more drafts if needed). In some cases there will also be a pilot edition around first draft stage. The total process requires a rare mixture of skills in NEC editors and it is near to impossible to recruit ready-trained editors: they are all NEC trained.

The lack of a regional structure (and hence any equivalent of the OU's full-time staff tutors or counsellors) has implications for NEC. It is probably fair to say that they are largely negative implications: NEC needs a regional structure but can't afford it. It leaves more tasks to be done at the centre but it would be foolish to claim that NEC can do those tasks as well as the Open University with its regional structure. On the other hand, one could say that the lack of a regional structure spurred NEC to make one of its most original creations — FlexiStudy.

Finance

NEC receives no general grant or subsidy. Its correspondence courses and publishing are self-financing and must generate surpluses if they are to grow and improve. Thus these two areas of NEC must market courses and publications at fees and prices that the purchaser is willing to pay. The broad financial picture for these two activities for 1982 was:

Correspondence fee income	£372,183
Number of enrolments in the year	11,800
Average fee	£31.54
Publications income	£457,448
Total trading income	£868,863

In addition, NEC receives grants for specific projects, mostly of a research or developmental nature.

Grant income:	
Basic Skills Unit	£156,856
Jobmate	£116,496
Media Services Unit	£36,379
Training in Race and Health	£42,453
Other Projects	£33,021
Total grant income	£385,205

Perhaps the most interesting material to draw out of these figures is the comparison of the Open University budget with that of NEC's correspondence services sector.

OU[a]	(£)	NEC	(£)
Fees and grant	£65,748,000	Fees	£372,183
Students	63,959	Students	11,800
Cost per student	£1,028	Cost per student	£31.54

Note: a. excluding Continuing Education.

Conclusion

NEC set out to be an innovative, catalytic body. Its founders expected its good ideas to be rapidly assimilated into other educational institutions. They did not see themselves as running a major educational institution in its own right and did not therefore have any clear idea as to how NEC would relate to the state sector. This has had major implications for how NEC has been able to work in practice.

The innovating side of NEC has been a qualified success. Certainly NEC's structure is right for enabling innovation and many original and interesting projects have been mounted. But NEC's structure is not necessarily right for turning those innovations into established practice. People don't have to take notice. More to the point, it is hard to prevent people pinching the good ideas but rejecting NEC (which is what the Wilson Government did when it set up the OU). It may be that no structure is right for both promoting innovation and consolidating it and that NEC is a good compromise.

The other side of NEC — acting as a direct and continuing provider — has not been without its problems either. With no grant aid and no official status, NEC has not necessarily been used to its best advantage by the state sector. It had become clear by 1976 that NEC either had to find a way into that sector or to lapse into being just another correspondence college. That change has now been achieved. Today NEC remains unique but with a special relationship with the state sector. Its future must be to build on that relationship whilst always remaining distinct.

Notes

1. Brian Jackson, *National Extension College 1967. Four Years' Work and the Future* (National Extension College, 1967).
2. Hilary Perraton, *Broadcasting and Correspondence* (National Extension College, 1973).
3. Barbara Derkow, David Hargreaves and Catherine Moorhouse, *On the Move* (BBC, London, 1975).
4. *Jobhunter Kit* (National Extension College, 1977).
5. Bob Laxton and Graham Rawlinson, *Make it Count* (National Extension College, 1977).

4.3

TELEVISION LITERACY AND ADULT EDUCATION

Len Masterman

Source: Copyright © Len Masterman 1983 (specially written for this volume).

Most adult education classes will have recourse, at some point, to videotape, radio, newspaper and magazine materials. Frequently, such materials will be used illustratively, though there will probably be few occasions when the nature of the evidence presented from these sources will be accepted as entirely unproblematic. In most groups, questions of bias, selectivity, and typicality are likely to be raised quite spontaneously. In others, media treatment of the subject under consideration might itself be considered as a sub-topic worthy of serious investigation in its own right (as in courses which have as a component 'images of ...' such groups as women, trade unionists, welfare claimants, ethnic minorities, etc.). There also exist, here and there, fully-fledged courses on the mass media which might typically involve the analysis of specific television programmes or newspaper articles, explore questions of media economics and patterns of ownership and control, and look at problems of audience response. They are likely, too, to involve a practical element, in which participants have the opportunity to make video and audio-tapes, produce their own newspapers, and perhaps even use and influence the media which are available to them locally.[1]

In addition to these situations, there are adult education contexts, some formal, some less so, in which radio and television may be significant, and, in some cases, even primary modes of communication, as in Open University courses and much traditional adult educational broadcasting. Very little of this material is self-reflective in its use of the media. Indeed many avowedly educational programmes may actively contribute to media mystification through their failure to encourage audiences to think about how they go about the business of constructing their meanings.

Finally, and perhaps most importantly of all, there is the enormously powerful 'informal' educational role of the mass media in clarifying for any society those issues which are important and those

203

which are less so. They provide for their audiences handy frames of reference, a ready-made vocabulary, and a stock of common-sense assumptions for the discussion of a wide range of issues, problems and deviances. It is worth stressing in the case of television that this function is not confined to 'serious' programmes, but applies with equal force to the values, attitudes, and linguistic assumptions underscoring such areas as sport and Light Entertainment programmes. There is very little evidence that the media's informal educational role is much considered within mainstream adult education, though it is its evident significance which has provided the impetus for those specialist media courses which do exist.

As we move rapidly into the Information Society, a world of proliferating video-cassette, video-disc and home computer markets, and multi-channelled cable and satellite television, the significant penetration of the media into formal adult educational structures will almost certainly increase. If the case for encouraging a critical understanding of the media is already formidable — as I believe it is — then in the very near future it may well be unanswerable. In every sphere of life, knowledge of the mediated and constructed nature of media messages will need to be part of the common stock of knowledge of everyone who is a citizen in a democratic society. And within every academic discipline the sophisticated assessment of televisual evidence — tele-literacy if you like — will be an ability which all students will need to acquire.

What, then, constitutes tele-literacy? What is the basic level of competence in understanding televisual material which all adult educators will need to develop in their clients? The remainder of this paper will attempt to answer these questions, and to draw from specialist developments in media and cultural studies over the past decade those findings which deserve to have a wider and more general currency.

The first step towards tele-literacy lies in the ability to recognise some of the problems implicit in assessing visual evidence. Television, for example, is considered by most people to be the most reliable source of information available to them[2] because it deals primarily in visual images, which are widely felt to be open, transparent, 'innocent', and authentic, and which establish a consciousness of what Barthes called the subject's 'having-been-there'.[3] They present us, it is felt, with evidence which we can to some extent judge for ourselves on its own merits. How valid is this view?

Consider the three photographs (Figures 1 to 3). The first is taken from a soccer match between England and Holland at Wembley in 1977 (the two players are Madeley of England and Cruyff of Holland). The second is of Labour MPs Tony Benn and Dennis Skinner at the Labour Party Conference at Blackpool in 1982. The third is of a woman (her precise identity is unknown) and some children, and was taken in the early 1970s at a demonstration of London teachers who were protesting against what they considered a derisory increase in their special London allowance. Look carefully at each image. Does it have a pretty clear and unambiguous meaning? If so, what is it? It should be emphasised that the first two images are newspaper photographs, and that they were specifically chosen from many available alternatives, presumably because they lent visual support to the angle from which the event was covered by the paper. Their meanings were taken to be quite clear. Look again at the images. Could each of the images be given quite contradictory captions? If so, what could they be? The first image is particularly interesting since it was used to demonstrate that one team's superiority over the other was directly deducible from the visual evidence presented here. Which team do you think was adjudged to be the superior? (See the note at the end of the chapter for comments on all of these images.)

It should also be borne in mind, of course, that these images have been chosen by *me*, hopefully to exemplify my own point that visual images are *polysemic*. That is, that they are rich in information, and contain many possible 'free-floating' meanings and interpretations, which are available to their potential users. A caption or commentary performs the function of *anchoring* (another term from Barthes[4]) or pinning down one preferred meaning to the image from the many potentially available. Anchorage has two additionally important consequences. It *suppresses*, and makes less easily available to the viewer, the image's alternative, and perhaps contradictory, meanings. And, secondly, through a curious process of what I call caption-image *reversal*, the image comes to *authenticate* and justify the meaning imposed upon it by the caption. The caption (or commentary), we are assured, must have some validity because *there* is the visual evidence which supports it.

The first steps towards tele-literacy then will involve an understanding of the problematic nature of visual evidence, and an ability to 'shred' the meanings implicit in visual images from the preferred position occupied by the commentary and offered to the audience.

Figure 1

Source: *Sunday Times*, 12 Feb. 1977.

Figure 2

Source: *Guardian,* 28 Sept. 1982.

This ability can quickly be developed by viewing silent television news and documentary film, and exploring a range of possible anchorages before the commentary actually used is revealed. What is principally involved in tele-literacy is the *deconstruction* of television texts by breaking through their surface to reveal the techniques through which the medium produces its meanings. It will entail, that is, a reversal of the process through which television selects and edits material into a polished, plausible, continuous and seamlessly 'natural' flow. The project is analogous to that undertaken by Brecht in his attack upon the 'illusionism' of bourgeois theatre, a theatre in which the audience is encouraged to identify with, and accept as real, the play's representations, rather than to reflect critically upon them. The necessity for deconstruction in television analysis is, of course, even more imperative than it is in the theatre. For however much we may be sucked into the realism of a particular play, we are always finally aware that we are watching representations — performances which have been scripted, rehearsed and acted — and not reality. This is far from the case with television, however, where even the most alert viewer must constantly be on guard against the apparent authenticity of what is seen.

Figure 3

Source: The English Centre, Ebury Teachers Centre, Sutherland Street, London.

The earlier captioning exercise, whilst deconstructing the image/
text relationship, takes the process of image production very much on
trust. How can television images themselves be deconstructed, and
the mechanisms through which filmed 'reality' is manufactured be
laid bare? The first steps are straightforward enough. Every television
image is, of course, a selected one. Why have these images been
'preferred'? Can we guess at the kind of images which may be lying on
the cutting-room floor? What is the story's 'angle'? What needs to be
stressed here is the extent to which a reporter's task is not necessarily
to seek out the truth of a particular situation, but to seek evidence
which supports an angle which, as likely as not, will have been pretty
well set (perhaps determined by the angle which newspapers have
taken in covering the same story) before the reporter even leaves the
office.

And what of the effect of the cameras and a camera crew, of, say,
between six and thirteen people, on the events represented? Television continually purports to present what can never be shown — the

event which would have taken place if cameras had not been present. Then there are the constraints implicit in producing images and sounds of 'acceptable' quality and the necessity of 'setting up' situations specifically for the camera. 'Television is the only profession', in the words of former TV producer Philip Whitehead, 'in which the word "cheat" is an inseparable part of the vocabulary. I think it's alarming that so often, in order to preserve a smooth visual flow and in order to re-create an assumed sequence of events ... you do dishonest things.'[5] The existence of this kind of rigging ought to be part of every adult's common stock of knowledge about visual communication. And such routine practices in film making are often inevitable, and certainly acceptable within limits since their intention is to clarify rather than mislead. The problem arises through the continual tendency of broadcasters themselves to posit a more innocent view of the medium. It is precisely this which gives force to Whitehead's use of the words 'cheat' and 'dishonest'. Whitehead is also drawing attention to the inevitable *fictionalising* involved in the editing process — the creation of meaning through the smooth juxtaposing of originally fragmented and unrelated images and events. Documentaries, for example, as Frederick Wiseman has suggested,

> are fictional forms ... Editing is the assessment and evaluation of individual sequences and the assembling of these disparate, originally unrelated fragments, into a dramatic form. This process has an internal and external aspect: internal in the need to compress a sequence down to a usable form, external in the way individual edited sequences are joined so as to impose a thematic and dramatic unity on otherwise chaotic material.[6]

Television does not simply construct events however. It attaches significance to them, gives them meaning. How is this achieved? First of all it is evident that the act of selection itself marks out some events, issues or people as being more important or significant than others. Television tells us what is important, and what is trivial by what it takes note of and what it ignores, by what is amplified and what is muted or omitted. This is sometimes known as the medium's agenda-setting function. But, as I have already suggested, television also defines the *way* in which these events should be discussed and the interpretative frameworks which should be brought to bear upon them. The question of *why* some interpretative frameworks and angles rather than others should become familiar and well-established should lead to a consideration of such crucial ideological questions as the ownership and control of the media by the wealthy and powerful, the essentially conservative and hierarchical nature of media institutions, their susceptibility to overt and indirect political and financial pressures, the middle-class biases of their personnel, the philosophic commitment within broadcasting towards 'balance' and consensus, the extent to which journalists are reliant upon established institutions (the Police, the Army, the Law Courts, big business, football clubs, etc.) as news sources, and the ability of such sources to manage news and set events within their own interpretative contexts, and the over-accessibility of the media to those in powerful and privileged positions in society. This in turn should lead on to a consideration of those voices *not* heard in the media, and to those which *are* heard, but which form part of a 'secondary' discourse which it is the privilege and function of the medium's dominant discourse to place and evaluate for us. It should lead us on, that is, to problems of *representation*, and to a consideration of the images presented of those subordinate groups who have little or no control of the media (blacks, trade unionists, women, the elderly, etc.) and for whom, indeed, the media may constitute a major problem.

How are these images realised? Brunsdon and Morley in their study of *Nationwide* have shown that the anchorpersons convey through the programme's dominant discourse — linking, framing, commenting upon and placing each item — how the programme's other discourses should be read.[7] And it remains true in television programmes of all kinds — even given the inevitable slanting and selectivity inherent in every image — that we are still rarely allowed to judge such images, people and events on their own merits. As the audience, we are habitually nudged in the direction of this or that preferred meaning. This is generally established even before an item begins. Here are two conventional and unremarkable examples:

> Changing the subject completely, over the last few months quite a few musicals have come and gone on the London stage with themes so varied that it seems song-writers will try anything in their search for success. Well, yet another new formula is being tried at Her Majesty's Theatre. It's called *Fire Angel* and it's based on the unlikely combination of a New York Mafia setting and the story of Shakespeare's *Merchant of Venice*. Well, while the Bard may be revolving in his grave, let's meet the co-writers ...

There is no end to the questions that MPs put to Ministers. The most frequent recipient of hard questions is the Foreign Secretary. The most unexpected question, surely, is one he has received from a Birmingham MP. It's all about the clothes the Queen is wearing on her tour of the Middle East. The questioner wants Her Majesty to stop pandering to what he calls 'the customs of religious bigots' by wearing long covering dresses. Now this, he claims, is insulting to the Queen's own sex. The questioner is Mr John Lee, Handsworth's Labour MP. He talks now to Peter Colbourne.

After the interview with Mr Lee the item was 'wrapped up' by the linkperson with the final comment: 'I think that people will agree that, despite problems, the Queen is doing a great job.'[8]

The impressions conveyed here — of desperate exploitation by the writers of the musical, or of quirky eccentricity by the MP — were not at all reinforced by the interviewees themselves who seemed bemused by the angle taken. But they *were* reinforced by the interviewers who far from being 'humble seekers after truth' (in Robin Day's phrase) continually signposted to us, the viewers — by their tone, reactions, interruptions and gestures — how the words of the subjects were to be interpreted. Here are two further examples taken from television coverage of the 'winter of discontent' (termed by one writer a 'winter of industrial mis-reporting')[9] in early 1979:

> Isn't the strike by ambulancemen potentially one of the most disastrous things that could happen to society? (John Stapleton, *Nationwide*, BBC 1, 16 Jan. 1979)

> How do you justify putting lives at risk? If somebody dies will it be on your conscience? Is more money worth a life? (BBC News, 19 Jan. 1979)[10]

It takes extremely confident and accomplished interviewees to challenge such signposting, and construct their own alternative meanings. Arthur Scargill demonstrates the technique:

Interviewer:	The Coal Board does seem to be having some trouble selling all the coal it can at the moment. Presumably that will limit its ability to pay when you do come round to presenting this claim.
Arthur Scargill:	Well, if we'd have listened to that sort of argu-

ment of course we would never have had the increase in 1972, nor the increase in 1974. The fact that we're not able to sell the coal which we are producing at the moment is due to a number of factors, not least of which is the importation of foreign coal by certain industrialists.

Interviewer: So overall you're accepting only a partial defeat today.

Arthur Scargill: Overall I'm accepting a total victory today.[11]

Such reversals are exceptional. For the most part presenters remain firmly in control, their status as guarantors of truth reinforced by the medium's visual codings. For example they, like station announcers, newsreaders, and weather forecasters are amongst the small band of people who are allowed to talk direct to camera. Stuart Hood elaborates:

All these persons have one thing in common. They are there to give us information which we are asked to assume is accurate (as indeed some of it is), unbiased and authoritative (which it is less likely to be). They have authority vested in them by the television organisations and can be deemed in a useful phrase as 'bearers of truth'. But there is another and more interesting category. It includes the monarch, the prime minister, cabinet ministers when they make official broadcasts (what are called ministerial broadcasts) and the leader of the parliamentary opposition front bench, who is allowed in certain circumstances to reply to a ministerial broadcast if the broadcasting authorities judge that it was controversial. All these persons — and one or two others including the Archbishop of Canterbury as head of the Church of England — are allowed to address the television audience ('the public' or 'the nation' as the broadcasters call it on such occasions) directly. They do so by reason of their constitutional or political authority. On other occasions (for instance when the Chancellor of the Exchequer is interviewed about the Budget) they are all (with the exception of the Queen) treated like ordinary people; that is to say, they are shown in profile or in such a way that their gaze is not fixed directly on the viewers but on the interviewer who is with them in the studio. In other words their statements have to pass through someone else, as it were — they have to be mediated. If they attempt to take on the role of a person of authority and address an audience directly, the director will cut away from them and go back to a shot of the interviewer … There are, however, certain politically unimportant persons who *are* allowed to address the camera directly — people like comedians, who are the equivalent of medieval jesters and, like the jesters, are allowed to act as if they had the same privileges as the men and women of power in our society. For that is what the full face picture means: that the man or woman on the screen has power and authority.[12]

The whole area of visual coding deserves specific attention in any consideration of how the medium constructs its meaning, for authority is reinforced or undermined not simply by eye-contact patterns, but by appearance, dress and the way in which the image is framed. Similarly, there are codes of geography within a studio which tell us who is important and who less so, or which indicate the relationship which exists between the subjects on the screen. The positioning of an interviewer between proponents of two conflicting views is a powerful visual reinforcement of the broadcaster's 'neutrality'. On the other hand, in 'chat' shows, interviewees sit together in comfortable chairs in keeping with their roles as 'guests'. The Glasgow University Media Group have drawn attention to the dominant codings in the reporting of industrial relations news:

> … all those things which enhance a speaker's status and authority are denied to the mass of working people. This means that the quiet of studios, the plain backing, the full use of names and status are often absent. The people who transcribed our material here pointed out to us that the only time they had difficulty making out what was said was in interviews with working people. Not because of 'accent' but because they were often shot in group situations, outside, and thus any individual response was difficult to hear. The danger here is that news coverage is often offering up what amounts to stereotypical images of working people.[13]

One of the most interesting features of visual codes is that they can be played around with and isolated by using the simplest video camera. For those adult educators who have access to this kind of equipment, code-breaking exercises are very simple to devise and they do genuinely illuminate what the taken-for-granted codes of television actually signify.

A conventional visual coding within recorded interviews is worthy of particular attention. This is the use of the 'cutaway' from the interviewee either to the interviewer or to a piece of silent film. The purpose of cutaways is to make an edited, constructed event appear 'natural' and unedited by covering over cuts in the original film. The 'jump' cut in which the editing is generally fully exposed to the audience is a more honest device, but it is somewhat infrequently used since it deliberately reveals the illusion behind the 'continuity' of an interview. Silent film will often be used within interviews where it is necessary to cover a large number of edits in a short period of time.

Finally, mention must be made of one of television's dominant techniques for shaping the events it handles: the use of narrative. Television tells stories. News, current affairs programmes, documentaries, and sports programmes all create little dramas with their own heroes, villains, conflicts, reversals, rewards and resolutions. Dramatic shaping is endemic to most forms of editing for television, and, as we have seen, the medium, even when dealing with avowedly factual material, is primarily involved in the production of fictional forms. But the dominant fiction which underpins the medium's penchant for narrative is that there does indeed exist an unproblematic and disinterested 'position' from which the story may be told. In the deathless words of the President of CBS News, 'Our reporters do not cover stories from their own point of view. They are presenting them from nobody's point of view.'[14] Hence the strength of Christopher Williams' assertion that 'narrative is an element that militates against knowledge ... because it attempts to conceal itself, to imply that this is how the world is.'[15] But as we have seen 'how the world is' contains the positions fed to the viewer by editing, framing, commentary, visual codings, etc. This militates against knowledge not because of 'bias' or the suppression or demotion of alternative viewpoints, but because what is concealed is the notion of the text as a construction which needs to be considered and analysed in relation to the position, interests and intentions of its producers. You might wish to reflect upon the extent to which printed texts might be similarly susceptible to the kind of analysis suggested here. Could reading become more scientific through the analysis not of a 'finished text' but of the 'position' of its writer, those offered to its readers, and of the ways in which its meanings are produced?

These, then, are some of the ways in which any group might go about the business of interrogating how television texts produce meaning. Matters cannot be left there, however. Emphasis upon television as a mode of signification, and on the television text as a construction inevitably leads to further questions:

(a) *Who* is responsible for these constructions? Who owns the text? Who has financed the production, and why? Who has planned the text and under what conditions?

(b) *What* kind of world is presented to us by the text? What values are implicit within it? And what does it explicitly endorse? What is its ideological thrust?

(c) *How* is the text likely to be read or understood by its audience? What notions of audience are inscribed within it, or within its positioning in the schedules?

It is necessary to explore each of these areas a little further.

(a) Ownership, Control and Production

As one writer has suggested, 'It is often said that the media are on the side of big business. This is not so. The media are big business.'[16] Owned by the rich and the powerful, controlled by 'the great and the good', it is not surprising that the media do not adequately reflect the rich diversity of views and opinions which exist in society. It would be very difficult, for example, to find a single instance of any of the established media's supporting a domestic strike in defence of workers' rights and livelihoods[17] (though sympathetic coverage of the strikes of the Solidarity movement in Poland, for example, did bring out a quite unfamiliar rhetoric). In the case of newspapers, the relationship between media product and economic base is often simple and direct enough (in the words of Victor Matthews, when his company, Trafalgar House, purchased Express Newspapers in 1977: 'The editors will have complete freedom as long as they agree with the policy I have laid down.'[18]). In television that relationship is more likely to be complex, mediated and indirect, and any simple 'reading off' of the text from its economic determinants will need to be resisted. Space can sometimes be created within broadcasting institutions for the expression of alternative and even oppositional views (though such offerings are generally quite carefully contextualised and distanced from mainstream broadcasting). In addition, it has been argued (in relation to such programmes as *Coronation Street*, for example) that since the media *are* businesses, programmes which express in a lively way the values, attitudes and aspirations of the majority of the audience who occupy subordinate positions in society can attain a high institutional status and legitimacy because of their value in the market-place.

Whilst it may be tempting, therefore, and perhaps *as a general-*

isation even justifiable, to assert that, across a whole range of television's output, the values presented and reinforced are not on the whole likely to be greatly at variance with the values of capitalism and consumerism, nevertheless in studying *particular* programmes one needs to be wary of this kind of economic reductionism and give due weight to the specificity of the text, and to the particular conditions of its production.

In this respect the economic parameters within which television is produced should receive a good deal of emphasis. Unfortunately much basic information in this field tends to be difficult to access. With a little leg-work up-to-date advertising rates can be obtained from commercial television companies, and the annual reports and accounts of the major media institutions are also available to members of the public. Still, it is not easy for the layperson to discover precise details of production costs, though writers such as Alvarado and Buscombe, and Richard Collins[19] have provided some useful guidelines. Much more accessible, and by now quite widely known thanks to the work of the Glasgow Media Group, Cohen and Young, Schlesinger, Burns, Alvarado and Buscombe and others,[20] are analyses of media institutions, and the routine working practices of media professionals. Adult educators will need to be aware of the general thrust of this work if they are to encourage their groups to consider the ways in which television functions as a consciousness *industry*.

(b) Television and Ideology

It is necessary for adult educators who use mass media materials to engage with the notion of ideology, since the media have been seen by many writers as being of central significance to the process by which the ideas of a ruling group in society become the dominant ideas for society as a whole. They are crucial, that is, to the process through which the sense which is made of the world by those with power and privilege is transmuted into, precisely, *common* sense, the sense of us all, and crucially, of course, the sense of those who are dominated and oppressed. Now television's stock-in-trade is precisely what Barthes termed 'the decorative display of *what-goes-without-saying*',[21] and adult groups will begin to understand ideological operations the moment they challenge 'what-goes-without-saying', the moment they begin to see alternatives to dominant explanations, the moment they can put the history and the struggle and the politics back into the process of signification. Tutor and group alike will need to challenge the apparent innocence, spontaneity and naturalness of media representations, and tutors will continually need to stress the *general idea* that powerful and contentious ideas lie behind the world depicted by TV, that those ideas have emerged out of concrete historical situations and struggles, that those ideas have important *functions*, that they have *work* to do, and that they produce, as a result, powerful material consequences. If adult groups can grasp those kinds of relationships between ideas and material situations in studying media materials then they will possess a very powerful conceptual tool for understanding not simply one of the media's most important functions, but some of the political realities which lie behind the taken-for-granted world in which we all live.

(c) The Television Audience

It is a matter of bleak fact that as educationalists we know very little about how students decode the media messages they receive. We are not alone in this. A number of studies have indicated that television broadcasters, too, are quite ignorant about their audiences. 'We would say that we've been broadcasting to the people along the corridor (i.e. to editorial and managerial superiors) not to the people who are listening', as one BBC newsman expressed it.[22] Or, in the words of another 'I'm really writing for myself and the wife ... the wife's my hardest critic.'[23] A worthwhile media education is scarcely conceivable, however, without some insight into problems of decoding, and without some understanding of the issues which arise when audiences make sense of particular programmes. This is beginning to be understood within media criticism, and it is indicative of an important change of emphasis that two of the most recent books written about television (David Morley's *The Nationwide Audience* and Dorothy Hobson's *Crossroads: The Drama of a Soap Opera*[24]) are centrally concerned to examine problems of audience response.

To understand problems of audience decoding it is necessary to examine more closely the nature of the television message itself. As we have seen, it cannot be regarded as an unproblematic, unilateral sign. In an important sense, when a group of people watch a television programme they are having quite different individual perceptions of it, a fact of obvious significance when the medium is being used in any educational context. This is not to say, however, that audience response amounts to no more than a mass of random, differential readings. For in an equally important sense, that group will, at some points, be having the same or at least very similar experiences. And whilst a tutor with a proper desire to encourage the development of mature and autonomous judgement in students will give due weight to the validity of individual perceptions (particularly given their implicit denial within many educational contexts), the mechanisms through which different individuals reach the same conclusions about television messages will need just as much attention by groups wishing to explore the medium's ideological operations.

There are two principal reasons why television images are not simply open to any kind of reading which will gratify the needs of decoders. The first has to do with the nature of the television message itself, and the way in which it is, in David Morley's phrase, 'structured in dominance.'

> The TV message is ... a complex sign, in which a preferred reading has been inscribed, but which retains the potential, if decoded in a manner different from the way in which it has been encoded, of communicating a different meaning. The message is thus a structured polysemy. It is central to the argument that all meanings do not exist 'equally' in the message: it has been structured in dominance, although its meaning can never be totally fixed or 'closed'. Further, the 'preferred reading' is itself part of the message, and can be identified within its linguistic and communicative structure ... The moment of 'encoding' thus exerts from the production end an 'over-determining' effect (though not a fully determined closure) in the succeeding moments in the communicative chain.[25]

The second reason why audience responses tend not to be simply atomised and individually idiosyncratic relates to the way they may be systematically linked to different sub-cultural codes, and socio-economic positions.

Of course, there will always be individual, private readings, but we need to investigate the extent to which these individual readings are patterned into cultural structures and clusters. What is needed here is an approach which links differential interpretations back to the socio-economic structure of society, showing how members of different groups and classes, sharing different 'culture codes', will interpret a given message differently, not just at the personal, idiosyncratic level, but in a way 'systematically related' to their socio-economic position. In short we need to see how the different sub-cultural structures and formations within the audience, and the sharing of different cultural codes and competencies amongst different groups and classes, 'determine' the decoding of the message for different sections of the audience.[26]

Morley himself has provided the only direct evidence we have in the literature on the responses of different groups of students to the same television programmes (*Nationwide*). His report makes salutary reading. Particularly striking is the degree of hostility and alienation expressed by black students towards a programme whose very hallmark is its confident assumption and expression of consensual values.[27] We need to engage much more with sub-cultural readings of television than we ever have in the past. Crucially we must seek to encourage an understanding of the location of individual responses within the patterns of beliefs, values, ideas, and practices which constitute the learner's sub-culture. The aim here is not to move towards supposedly 'objective' evaluations or descriptions of television messages but towards a recognition that any textual reading is the *use* of a text for particular purposes. And, as Terry Eagleton has suggested, judgements about a text, and valuations of it will be very much dependent upon what those purposes are.[28]

Dorothy Hobson's study of audience responses to one of the most cataclysmic events in the history of British television — the decision by a single executive, Charles Denton, to dispose of Meg Mortimore, the central character in the soap opera, *Crossroads*, by writing the actress, Noele Gordon, out of the series — is really a case-study in sub-cultural decodings. The outcry against Denton's decision was enormous. The company was inundated with mail; its switchboards were jammed for days. Noele Gordon sold her story for a lucrative sum to a Sunday newspaper, and the whole saga remained in the headlines for weeks. Overwhelmingly those who telephoned and wrote letters were those whose views do not count for very much with television companies and advertisers; middle-aged to elderly women, and an enormous number of old age pensioners. What Dorothy Hobson did was to read all of their letters, and then seek out some of those who had written in, and watch the show with them in their own homes. What she writes about what those people — mainly women, and principally elderly women — got out of the programme is very moving and affirmative. It is a rare glimpse of the human reality of how people, and particularly the elderly, relate to the media, and it gives the lie to the kind of condescending generalisations too often made by critics whenever they think of audiences as undiscriminating 'masses'. Dorothy Hobson concludes her story:

> Television is a new form of contemporary art and communication; the possibilities for its expansion appear to be endless. If it is to progress and communicate with its audience it should free itself of the forms of criticism which are rooted in other forms of communication. Broadcasters should recognise that when they do attract a large audience they should not despise that audience nor the programmes which most appeal. A soap opera which appeals to and connects with the experiences of fifteen million people is as valid and valuable as a work of art as a single play or documentary which may attract four million viewers. Neither is better nor worse than the other. They are simply different programmes and each is dependent on the understanding which the audience brings to it for its ultimate worth.[29]

Adult educators will need to ponder the radical implications of these words for their own practice. They underscore the inappropriateness of hierarchical modes of transmission, and of the role of the tutor as accredited expert and point to the irrelevance of much of the cultural capital acquired in other disciplines in responding to television material. They suggest the importance of collaborative investigation and group dialogue in clarifying and 'placing' particular responses, and a proper tentativeness in drawing conclusions, and call for the kind of proper humility and sensitivity in handling those responses which is finely exemplified by Dorothy Hobson in her own study.

Note on Images

Figure One. One of the following is the caption actually supplied with the photograph, the other is one which might have been. Which is which?

(a) Our picture embodies the gulf between the two players. Look at their faces: Cruyff's (dark shirt) aware, urgent, looking to create; Madeley (white shirt) gaunt and stressed, being hauled he knows not where.

(b) Our picture graphically demonstrates the gulf between the two teams on the night. Look at the players' faces: super-star Cruyff (dark shirt) curiously anxious and out-of-touch, haunted by the spectre of English confidence at his shoulder in the tall commanding presence of Madeley (white shirt).

Figure Two. Choose between:

(a) The Beast of Bolsover (Dennis Skinner) lends a comradely ear to the words of Tony Benn at Blackpool yesterday,
or
(b) A conspiratorial Dennis Skinner and Tony Benn.

Figure Three. This photograph has been given the following captions by groups of children and adults I have worked with:

A teacher finds time to help children across the road.

The public managed to stay cool.

A penniless teacher looks for cigarette-ends in the gutter.

Onlookers watched the march with interest.

Support for the march grows.

Children came along to support their teacher.

The people on the streets laughed at the demonstrators.

Many children roamed the streets as a result of the protest. Incidents of vandalism were later reported.

Solutions

Figure One: (a) was the caption used by the *Sunday Times.* Figure Two: (b) was the caption used by the *Guardian.*

Notes

1. See D. MacShane, *Using the Media* (Pluto Press, London, 1979).
2. *News Broadcasting and the Public in 1970* (BBC, London, 1971).
3. See L. Masterman, *Teaching About Television* (Macmillan, London, 1980), p. 77.
4. R. Barthes, 'The Rhetoric of the Image' in *Working Papers in Cultural Studies*, No. 1, Spring 1971 (University of Birmingham).

5. J. Bakewell and N. Garnham, *The New Priesthood* (Allen Lane, London, 1970), p. 173.

6. F. Wiseman, 'Pride, Patience and Prejudice', the *Guardian*, 17 March 1981.

7. C. Brunsdon and D. Morley, *Everyday Television: Nationwide*, Television Monograph No. 10 (The British Film Institute, London, 1978), p. 61.

8. The first extract is from *Pebble Mill at One*, BBC 1, April 1979; the second from *Midlands Today*, BBC 1, 20 February 1979.

9. D. MacShane, 'There's a new bitterness ...', *The Media Reporter*, vol. 3, no. 3, 1979 (Brennan Publications, Sale, Cheshire).

10. Quoted in TUC, *A Cause for Concern* (TUC, London, 1979), p. 30.

11. *News At One*, ITN, 12 October 1978.

12. S. Hood, *On Television* (Pluto Press, London, 1981), pp. 3-4.

13. Glasgow University Media Group, *Bad News* (1976), p. 26.

14. D.L. Altheide, *Creating Reality: How TV News Distorts Events* (Sage, London, 1976), p. 17.

15. C. Williams (ed.), *Realism and the Cinema* (Routledge & Kegan Paul, and The British Film Institute, London, 1980), p. 152.

16. H. McQueen, *Australia's Media Monopolies* (Widescope, Melbourne, 1977), p. 39.

17. Ibid., p. 51.

18. Cited by T. Baistow, 'An Express that is Running into the Sidings', the *Guardian*, 13 November 1982.

19. M. Alvarado and E. Buscombe, *Hazell: The Making of a TV Series*, BFI/ Latimer, 1978; R. Collins, *Television News*, BFI Monograph No. 5 (British Film Institute, London, 1976).

20. Glasgow University Media Group, *Bad News*; *More Bad News* (Routledge & Kegan Paul, London, 1980); *Really Bad News* (Readers and Writers Press, London, 1982); S. Cohen and J. Young, *The Manufacture of News* (Constable, London, 1973); P. Schlesinger, *Putting 'Reality' Together* (Constable, London, 1978); T. Burns, *The BBC: Public Institution and Private World* (Macmillan, London, 1977); M. Alvarado and E. Buscombe, *Hazell: The Making of a TV Series*.

21. R. Barthes, *Mythologies* (Granada (Paladin), London, 1973). The quotations are from pp. 151, 142 and 11.

22. T. Burns, *The BBC*, p. 200.

23. Schlesinger, *Putting 'Reality' Together*, p. 119.

24. D. Morley, *The 'Nationwide' Audience*, Television Monograph No. 11 (British Film Institute, London, 1980), and D. Hobson, *Crossroads: The Drama of a Soap Opera* (Methuen, London, 1982).

25. Morley, *The 'Nationwide' Audience*, pp. 10-12.

26. Ibid., pp. 14-15.

27. Ibid., pp. 71-4; 78-9; 87-8; 130-2.

28. In an unpublished paper on *Marxism and Structuralism*, given at a seminar at Nottingham University's School of Education, June 1982.

29. D. Hobson, *Crossroads*, p. 171.

Part 5

FACE-TO-FACE EDUCATION

This part of the Reader concentrates on the form of provision most typical of traditional adult education, the face-to-face encounter between teacher and learner or learners. Each of the three articles included here illustrates, however, less traditional adaptations of the form.

Nick Small and Malcolm Tight describe the organisation and operation of one local centre for the education of adults in the north of England. Many aspects of this centre — the scant resources of finance, manpower and facilities available, the broad curriculum and range of educational opportunities offered — are reasonably representative of similar centres in other parts of the country. The relatively less important role now being accorded at this centre to 'normal' provision (though it is still of considerable absolute importance), with a notable growth in provision for those with literacy problems, the old, the unemployed, the physically and mentally handicapped, ethnic minorities and other 'disadvantaged' groups, is also significant, though probably less typical of local education authority initiatives as a whole. These developments are, however, in accordance with many of the concerns advanced by the authors in Part 3 of this Reader.

Paul Fordham and his colleagues describe some of the conclusions of a collaborative project dealing with local educational provision for adults in another part of the country. This involved staff from the local education authority, the Workers' Educational Association, the local university's extra-mural department, supported by the Department of Education and Science. Their work aimed to extend provision to adults living on a predominantly workiing-class housing estate outside Portsmouth, adults who were largely not participating in existing provision. In attempting this, it was discovered that changes in the nature of the educational opportunities offered were necessary to encourage participation. In particular, non-formal rather than formal kinds of provision were required, and this had many implications for organisation and many parallels with Third World practice (see also the article by Lalage Bown in the accompanying Reader). It also has to be recognised that non-formal work is more demanding and time-consuming than formal provision.

Linda Butler's concern is with another developing area of provision: educational guidance for adults, involving information and advice giving, and counselling. Butler stresses that, if educational opportunities for adults are to be expanded, with a greater emphasis placed on self-directedness amongst learners, the development of more widely available and professional guidance services is one essential support. Given the newness of this area of provision, there remain many difficulties of definition and operation, which Butler discusses in the context of existing examples of provision.

5.1

A LOCAL CENTRE FOR THE EDUCATION OF ADULTS

Nick Small and Malcolm Tight

Source: Copyright © The Open University 1983 (specially written for this volume).

Introduction

The centre for the education of adults which is described in this article serves an area containing some tens of thousands of inhabitants in a large northern English city. It forms part of the local education authority's 'community education' service. The term 'community education' is used partly as an administrative convenience, serving to encompass the authority's adult and youth work separately from their schools, but partly also as a reflection of a philosophy, held by the city's politicians and practitioners alike, of what can and ought to be achieved in this field of provision. The local authority is by no means the only provider of educational opportunities for adults in the city, though it is one of the more important. The city's university and polytechnic, the local branch of the Workers' Educational Association, and many other local associations provide opportunities of different kinds at different levels, sometimes in co-ordination with the local education authority.

The centre is sited in the inner suburbs of the city, an area which largely comprises a mixture of council housing and relatively cheap, privately rented or owner-occupied terraced houses. Traditionally a working-class area, the social composition has now become more mixed, and includes both middle-class elements and a variety of ethnic minority groups, mainly originating from the West Indies and the Indian subcontinent. Unemployment in the area is at present higher than in the city as a whole, and was recorded at 15.7 per cent for the local ward in the 1981 Census.

Though neither the area nor the centre can be regarded as 'typical' of conditions and practice in England or the United Kingdom as a whole (in fact, nowhere is), many aspects of the organisation and provision of this particular centre are reflected to a greater or lesser extent in other parts of the country, and in other centres which aim to offer educational opportunities to adults.

Organisation

The organisation of educational provision for adults in the city has been the subject of considerable changes over the last few years, a consequence of moves towards the development of a community education system. Further restructuring is under way. At present the organisation in the area of the city with which we are concerned (one of 13 areas into which the city is divided for this purpose), seen in terms of staff commitments and responsibilities, can be summarised as in Figure 1. This represents a pragmatic as well as a transitory arrangement of resources, since it is dependent upon the abilities, interests and availability of the relatively small number of staff involved.

From a brief glance at Figure 1 it appears that, for an operation which employs few full-time staff, the organisation is fairly complex. This complexity is largely a result of a split in staff responsibilities between different sites. The centre under consideration operates partly through a number of satellite centres within the area of the city which it covers. These satellite centres tend to offer educational opportunities for adults for only part of the day, however, functioning as schools, sports centres, youth or community centres for the remainder of the time, and often specialise in certain kinds of provision. Their operations can, where necessary, be overseen on a part-time basis by subsidiary heads of centre, under the general supervision and control of the overall head of centre. The main centre itself, though it operates full-time from its own building, is sited within the grounds of a local primary school, and can only offer its fullest range of opportunities in the evenings.

The overall head of centre has a full-time responsibility for educational provision for adults within the area, working directly to the Area Community Education Officer (ACEO), and through the ACEO to city education office and the councillors who direct its policy. There is a parallel full-time post in youth work in the area. There is also a full-time Community Education Worker with special responsibility for ethnic minority groups, assisted by a part-time community worker. The overall head of centre oversees the work of a small number of part-time clerical and secretarial staff, of nearly 100

Figure 1: Staff Organisation in the Area

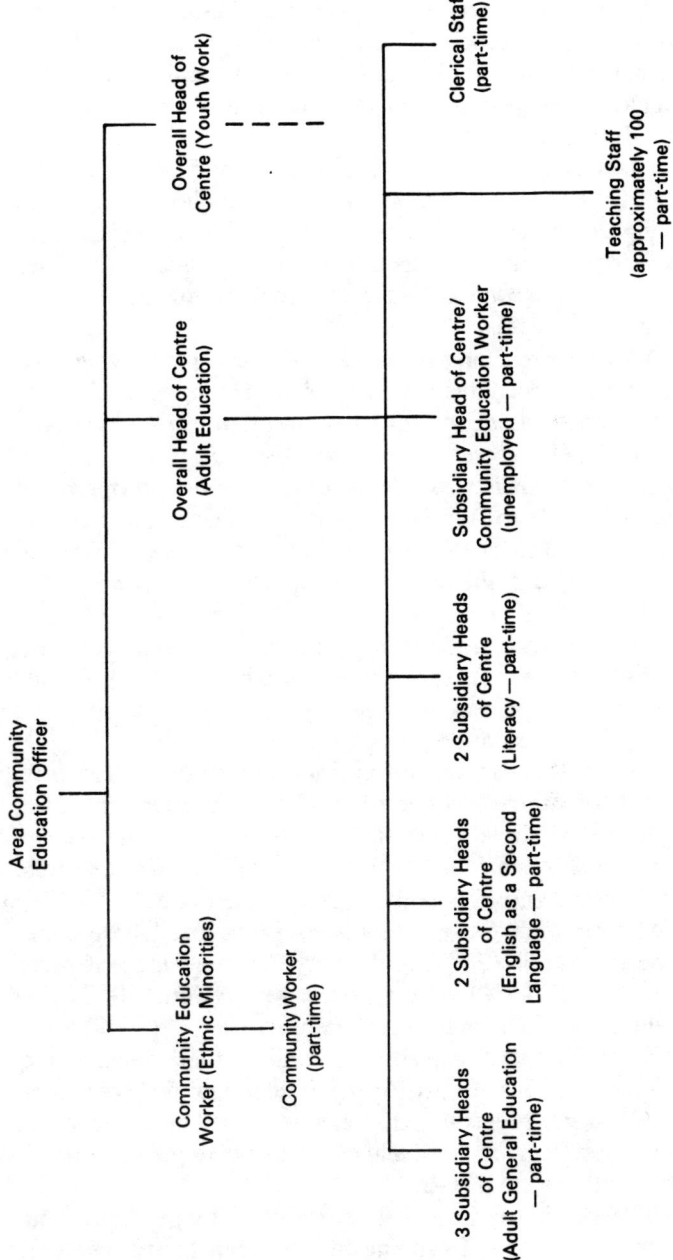

part-time teaching staff, and of eight further part-time members of staff, the subsidiary heads of centre. Among this last group, two have general responsibilities; one has a responsibility for over-seeing English, mathematics and examination classes, two for English-as-a-second-language classes, two for literacy and one for provision for the unemployed.

Most of the clerical and secretarial staff are based at the main centre, but only some of them work throughout the year, the others being employed on a short-term basis when registration and fee enquiries from students mount up at the beginning of each term. They are assisted to some extent in this work by voluntary help from both staff and students.

Part-time teaching staff have commitments varying between two and eight hours of teaching a week during terms, and are paid at the Burnham Further Education Lecturer II rate of £7.21 per hour (1982 rate). They are recruited directly by the head of centre, or in consulta-tion with specialists amongst the staff where appropriate. Problems are only occasionally encountered in filling posts, even though a commitment to the education of adults in the area above and beyond that specified in the contract is expected. This might involve parti-cipation in staff meetings, helping students outside teaching hours and dealing with more general queries. For certain courses, or kinds of provision, visiting speakers will also be used — e.g. health visitors, doctors, interpreters, the community police constable — and paid where necessary and appropriate.

The centre head's encouragement of staff to participate fully in the life of the centre is reflected in a bias in recruitment towards local residents. Complete statistics are not available, but out of 87 part-time teaching staff for whom the information has been collected, 39 (45%) were known to be living in the immediate area — i.e. within the area for which the centre makes provision. These statistics also indicate that 68 (78%) of the part-time teaching staff were female, and that 43 (49%) were aged between 31 and 40. Twenty (23%) were known to be in full-time employment, 14 (16%) as teachers of children. The vast majority had some formal educational qualifica-tion, with at least 40 (46%) being fully qualified school teachers. It would seem, therefore, that at this centre unemployed or under-employed female school teachers make up a good proportion of the part-time teaching staff.

The subsidiary heads of centre work longer hours than do the purely teaching staff, ranging up to a formal limit of twelve and a half hours per week. With one exception, none of them is in full-time employment elsewhere: they are all experienced educators who readily make a commitment beyond that specified in their contracts. They work on annual contracts allowing for one week's notice on either side, but there has been little turnover of staff at this level in the last few years, with jobs so far remaining relatively secure from cuts.

Training and Professionalism

The supervision and training of so many part-time staff presents the centre head with considerable problems. Though most staff do have educational qualifications, only 15 (17%) of the 87 part-time teaching staff already referred to were known to have some qualification specifically in the field of education for adults. The centre head has insufficient resources to fund attendance at local training courses on a regular basis, where such courses are available. Nevertheless, some progress in training has been made. The first two stages of the national three stage training scheme for adult tutors are offered by the Regional Advisory Council for the area, and a small number of staff have taken these courses, though usually only to stage I level. An induction course for English as a Second Language tutors throughout the city was recently run at the centre by the centre staff. Payment for some staff to attend staff meetings or staff days at the centre has been made possible, though only about one third of the total teaching staff attend the termly staff meetings, which are inevitably mainly concerned with administrative matters.

Consequently, most teaching staff employed by the centre have to learn the particular skills involved in the education of adults by practising them. The centre head and the subsidiary heads of centre will visit particular classes where and when they consider this to be necessary (e.g. in the case of newly recruited staff, or when, as occasionally happens, a report on a class which gives cause for concern is received), and will endeavour to get the teaching staff concerned thinking about what they are doing and why, even to the extent of requesting weekly summaries of progress from some teachers. Some guidance and advice is also provided in the form of duplicated handouts given to new staff, stressing, amongst other things, a need to allow flexibility in the syllabus. Such supervision is limited, however, and it is not possible directly and continuously to supervise all classes and all teachers. Hence, while poor teachers and poor teaching may

Figure 2: A Week in the Life of the Head of Centre

	Morning	Afternoon	Evening
MONDAY	Administrative tasks. Meeting with university extra-mural department regarding response to unemployment	Visit day centre for elderly. Start up new community newspaper group. Meeting with part-time tutor regarding methodology. Visit to warehouse to purchase stock	Visit to adult education classes
TUESDAY	Draft job description and advert for literacy organiser post. Meeting at hostel for physically handicapped regarding educational provision	Check on playgroup staffing. Sort out problems regarding self-programming pottery. Sign and check pay claims. Receive visit from Health and Safety Officer	Interview prospective teacher. On duty at main centre. Deal with queries. Visit classes. Chat to students in coffee bar. Meeting with Advisory Committee Treasurer
WEDNESDAY	Arrange for repairs to broken windows. Meeting with clerical staff. Meeting with colleague regarding new courses. Visit Education Office and pick up mail. Meeting with literacy organisers	Induct new teacher. Draft paper on new initiatives with elderly. Respond to discussion paper on English provision	

THURSDAY	Publicise Saturday's fund-raising event and purchase raffle prizes. Meet local Asian self-help group. Draft publicity for new short course	Meeting with Education Officer. Meeting with basic education tutors to discuss progress and problems	On duty at main centre. Visit language classes. Introduce new volunteer into handicapped group. 'Repair' broken cassette
FRIDAY	Meeting with part-time head of centre. Administrative tasks. Union meeting	Visit class at satellite centre. Take mail and material for reprographics	
SATURDAY	Spend most of day at the Centre's annual publicity/fund-raising event		
SUNDAY		Start self-programming Asian music group	

be exposed by students 'voting with their feet' (i.e. dropping out of the classes concerned), it may also be the case that some moderate to mediocre teaching in popular subjects passes unnoticed.

Clearly, a great deal of the responsibility for the successful running of the centre rests on the shoulders of the centre head. Figure 2 illustrates the number and variety of tasks involved in a selected week's work. In this week, as well as completing a full morning's and afternoon's workload from Monday to Friday, the centre head spent three evenings on duty, most of Saturday at the centre's annual fund-raising event, and Sunday afternoon in getting a self-programming group off the ground. The tasks undertaken ranged from 'routine' administration, through meetings with clerical staff, organisers, teachers and self-help groups, to visiting classes and repairing cassette recorders. It seems extremely unlikely that such a workload could be seen through with any success by someone who was not wholly committed to the job.

It is possible that the centre head will be assisted to some extent in the management aspect of this work in the future by the centre's advisory committee, which was set up in 1977. At present the committee includes about 20 members, representing staff, students and the local community (e.g. the local police constable, and representatives from appropriate neighbourhood and community associations). Up to now, however, it has mainly confined its work to fund-raising and social activities.

Finance

The centre's operations are run on a tight budget. For the current year, 1982/3, a total allocation of £90,726 has been made, though this does not include the salaries of the full-time staff (the centre head and the community education worker). The bulk of the sum, £81,776 (90%) is allocated to the direct costs of making classes and other educational opportunities available: i.e. hiring the necessary part-time teaching staff. £5,570, or 6 per cent of the total, is allocated to paying for part-time clerical and technical support. The balance, £3,380 or 4 per cent, is allocated for expenditure on necessary apparatus and equipment (£1,510 — for repair and replacement only), stationery and materials (£1,320), books (£300) and publicity (£250). In addition, it is hoped that some £6,500 might be granted from a special fund for encouraging new initiatives with the unemployed. The overall size and breakdown of the centre's financial allocation is determined centrally by the city's education authority, which receives from the centre the fees collected for class enrolments. The centre head has a limited discretion within this framework, and may influence the breakdown of the allocation before it is finally decided upon, or transfer funds between given budgets after allocation with the agreement of the senior officer. Though the fees charged by this authority for different kinds of course, and to students with different financial circumstances, vary, the centre head is under no entrepreneurial pressure to maximise fee income, and particular courses and kinds of provision are not judged in terms of their ability to generate fee income.

This relative freedom to arrange and operate a programme (within certain constraints) is counterbalanced, however, by the severe shortage of funds for improving the centre's facilities. The fund-raising activities of the advisory committee, most notably through an annual 'October market' at which many local voluntary organisations have stalls, only generated an income of £218 in 1981.

Provision

For planning and organisational purposes, the provision made by the centre is divided into four categories:

1. 'Normal' Provision

This category includes what has traditionally been the mainstay of the educational provision made for adults by local authorities, and by other organisations, namely subject- or discipline-based vocational and non-vocational courses spread over a term or longer, sometimes involving examinations. Examples of such courses include 'Improve Your Chess', 'Hairdressing', 'Psychology', 'Contemporary Dance' and (a recent addition) 'Becoming Self-Employed'. 'O' level courses in subjects such as English, Mathematics and History are offered, as well as Urdu (separate classes for men and women), Punjabi and Gujerati, City and Guilds qualifications in Communications Skills, and Royal Society of Arts Stage I Typing. The standard fee charged to students in 1982/3 is 60p an hour, or £12 for a ten-week term of two-hour classes once a week. A lower rate, 25p an hour, is charged for examination classes. This category of provision received £29,853, or 37 per cent of the allocation of £81,776 made for class provision in the current year.

2.   'Basic' Education

This category is defined by two criteria. First, a basic education course (for this local authority) must intend to teach a skill regarded by society at large as necessary for normal living. These skills will vary with the roles an adult is called upon to play in the home or the community, and through the different stages of life. Second, such a course will only continue to a level that enables the student to cope with ordinary everyday requirements, though the subject may be studied further to more advanced levels under other categories of provision. Examples of such courses are 'Basic Woodwork', 'Family Dressmaking', 'Economical Cookery', 'Money Matters', 'Look After Yourself' and 'Welfare Rights'. Fees for these courses are charged at the reduced rate of 15p an hour. Basic education received £4,962, or 6 per cent, of the 1982 allocation for class provision.

3.   Literacy Provision

This is a specific area of basic education provision which is treated separately for charging purposes and the allocation of funds. Classes are free, and this area received £9,281, or 11 per cent, of the 1982 class budget.

4.   'Other Free' Provision

This final category, which covers provision for the mentally and physically handicapped, English as a second language courses and other basic skills provision for local ethnic minority groups, received the greatest share of the 1982 class budget, £37,680 or 46 per cent. Courses in English as a second language and provision for the handicapped are free. Others are charged for at the standard rate. The most notable provision for the handicapped adult made in the area involves provision for the deaf. This is based at one of the satellite centres, and includes courses in literacy, manual language (for both those with hearing difficulties and those who came into regular contact with them), handicrafts and lip reading.

The fees position is complicated to some extent by the availability of reductions to certain kinds of student. Social security claimants may attend classes free, senior citizens pay a quarter of the going rate (or half in the case of examination classes), and those between the ages of 13 and 18 pay half-price.

The overall breadth of provision, and the split of available resources between different kinds of provision, reflects the characteristics of the area and its inhabitants, the policy priorities of the local authority, and the legacy of past practice. The response which has been made to the calls made at the beginning of the 1970s for provision for 'disadvantaged' groups, to the adult literacy campaign and its later broadening into basic education and skills, and to the needs of ethnic minorities, is very evident. On the other hand, there is an absence of provision in sports and other physical activities (such as ballroom dancing) as a consequence of the transfer of such courses from education to leisure services in an earlier restructuring of the local authority's responsibilities. These are popular areas of provision at many centres for adults in other areas.

A good indication of how the provision made appears to the prospective student is given by Figure 3, which is an extract from the 1982-3 prospectus for the area detailing courses offered at the main centre on one day of the week. This is to some extent atypical of the range of opportunities provided throughout the area, since some of the satellite centres specialise in particular kinds of courses. One of these, as already mentioned, is exclusively concerned with provision for the deaf, and others offer continuing help with literacy and basic skills to handicapped groups. A lot of non-formal provision is also made at satellite centres: one, in a local community centre, runs 'activity nights' without teachers, operating on the basis of a general sharing of skills, knowledge and interests amongst participants in activities such as sewing, dressmaking, cookery, health, diet and keeping fit. Provision at weekends is limited, with only youth groups and woodwork for the deaf classes operating at present, though rooms are hired to community groups as well. More classes were offered on Saturdays in the recent past, but these have been discontinued on grounds of cost.

Twenty classes are recorded in Figure 3, slightly more than half of them being put on during the evening. All of them are timed to last an hour and a half or two hours. Short descriptions of some of the classes draw attention to their aims and the flexibility possible. One interesting feature is the timetabling of two classes in Mathematics at different levels together in the afternoon. This is deliberate, and is intended both to enable students to transfer easily between the different courses to find their own level, and to encourage the staff involved to meet on a regular basis. On a different day of the week, a group of English classes are similarly timetabled together in the

Figure 3: One Day's Provision at the Centre, Autumn 1982

9.30 — 11.30:	English as a Second Language
9.45 — 11.45:	Pottery
	Brush Up Your English[a]
	Family Dressmaking[a] — make clothes for yourself and your children. Useful money saving ideas. For people with little or no experience
10.00 — 11.30:	Mums and Toddlers Group
10.00 — 12.00:	Urdu[b]
1.00 — 3.00:	Brush Up Your Maths[a] — individual help with Maths for everyday use
	'O' Level Maths[b]
1.30 — 3.30:	'Spare Time Group' — free advice on education, welfare, retraining, job creation. Visiting speakers, social activities, a co-operative allotment — a varied programme built around the interests of the group. You're welcome to drop into this informal group at any time
6.00 — 8.00:	Urdu — for speakers of Urdu who wish to improve their basic reading and writing skills
7.00 — 8.30:	Contemporary Dance
7.00 — 9.00:	Woodwork — make articles of your choice in a well-equipped workshop. Appropriate advice on DIY
	Pottery
	Indian Cookery
	English as a Second Language
	'O' Level Sociology[b] — a very relevant course covering the family, education, class, social change, etc.
	Punjabi[b] — for speakers of Punjabi who wish to study for the 'O' level examination
	Lacemaking
	German (2nd year) — for people who have a basic knowledge of the language. The emphasis of the course will be on giving students the confidence to communicate more effectively in the spoken language
8.30 — 10.00:	Keep Fit (Leisure Services Department)
Fees:	Basic Education Classes (marked [a]) 15p per hour
	'O' Level Classes (marked [b]) 25p per hour
	Other Classes 60p per hour

evening — 'O' level English in one year; 'O' level English in two years; Communication Skills (City & Guilds); Basic English; Reading, Writing and Spelling (free individual help in a very friendly group); and English as a Second Language. English as a Second Language courses are available at a variety of levels, including examination classes, and short topic-based courses are also offered, for example a 'Maternity Language' course is available at a local health centre. An attempt has also been made to avoid possible clashes of student interest in organising the timetable. Thus, English and Maths classes are separately timetabled, with the basic education courses in 'Brush Up Your English' and 'Brush Up Your Maths' offered successively in the morning and afternoon. The remainder of the timetable is largely related to staff availability and convenience for known interest or target groups.

The 'Spare Time Group' timetabled for the afternoon makes use of visiting speakers in an informal drop-in group, and reflects both the realities of local unemployment and a direct community orientation. On other days of the week, related classes are offered on 'New Ways to Work' and 'Practical Household Maintenance'. A full day course on contemporary British society is offered as well. This is given by two tutors from the extra-mural department of the local university, and is indicative of an increased desire on their part to become involved in educational activities in local centres in the city outside of the university.

Figure 3 shows the provision planned at the beginning of the autumn 1982 term. A slightly different range of classes will be offered at other times of the year, particularly in the summer term, with some classes (e.g. the examination classes) continuing and other new groups starting up. Some may also disappear as, in this local authority as in most others, a certain minimum level of recruitment is required to justify provision and expenditure. In this area, the level and its interpretation is perhaps more generous than in many others. Numbers of active students per class are expected to average 12 overall, with a minimum of 9 permitted in any one class. These numbers were reduced recently from 16 and 12 respectively in recognition of the effects of the transfer of relatively popular sports classes out of the educational programme. Some discretion is allowed to the head of centre, who is able to put on classes with numbers below the minimum with the permission of the senior officer where a good case can be made. In practice, it is difficult to assess 'active' student numbers accurately, since some classes are arranged on a drop-in basis, and in others numbers of students may drop out after registration.

Constraints and Development

The main constraints on the programme offered at this centre do not relate, therefore, to a need to draw in large numbers of fee-paying students, but to the resources available for provision — facilities and staff — and their quality. The lack of a dark room, for example, severely limits the development of photography classes, and the lack of a computer means that computing courses cannot be offered. Duplicating and reprographics facilities, and a limited amount of audio-visual equipment, are available. The shortage of ground floor accommodation during the daytime, when only the upper floor of the adjacent school building is available in addition to the centre's small building, is a major constraint, particularly given the age or infirmity of many of the clientele. They may also be put off by the appearance of the buildings, with the centre appearing as a rather drab adjunct in a playground dominated by a three storey, fortress-like Victorian school building, and by the necessity to make use on occasion of equipment or furniture intended for five- to nine-year-olds. On the whole, the relationship between the centre and the school remains rather formal, and full dual use of facilities is far from being a reality. The school piano, for example, is kept locked up, whilst the centre's pottery and woodwork facilities have yet to be used by the school (though the woodwork room is used by the local Youth Opportunities Programme).

The centre head and staff are attempting to overcome these disadvantages by adopting an increasingly outward-looking approach to the local community. At present, volunteers help to run a coffee bar, playgroup and crèche, and it is hoped to expand provision of refreshments linked to the home economics unit. Some courses encourage people to drop-in or to sample activities, especially when they are timetabled alongside social events such as the Wednesday Second Hand Stall. A luncheon group for senior citizens meets on Mondays. Some self-programming work has been introduced, in pottery in the first instance, but this may soon be available in woodwork and cookery as well. Here, the intending user is interviewed regarding experience and safety aspects, and is then given the run of the facilities available (though all pottery firing is done by staff) at a fee of 15p per hour, provided that a member of staff is always present. Work in parent education for those with pre-school children has also been started, and there are a number of youth groups (e.g. the Asian girls group) in operation.

The corollary of these efforts to introduce a less formal and more relaxed atmosphere within the centre is the outreach work being carried out, primarily aimed at helping ethnic minorities, the unemployed, those with literacy problems, and other 'disadvantaged' groups in the local community. The two part-time staff who are most involved in this aspect of the centre's work are allocated specifically to the ethnic minority and unemployed groups (see Figure 1). The former tends to deal mainly with women and children. The outreach staff pursue their work by developing contacts with local groups, calling in on people, leafleting, and by arranging to be available at local centres to give advice at given times. As well as directly educational work, a good deal of more general, non-educational help and advice is given. Individuals are encouraged, where appropriate, to take up the opportunities offered by the centre or by other organisations. Outreach work has been helped by the development of links with the staff of other central and local government organisations in the area, most notably health workers and a recently appointed part-time social services information worker.

The influence of this outreach work on the provision made by the centre is very evident. Most influences on the centre's work are structured through staff or local councillors, with little direct influence being exercised by members of the community. Occasionally, pressures are felt, however, as was recently the case with English as a second language provision, when it became apparent that temporary residents, often the spouses of overseas students studying at the city's university or polytechnic, were taking up facilities intended for permanent residents. These demands, when realised, were redirected. Pressure from local politicians led to the expansion of examination classes, which had been concentrated in further education colleges, at the centre a couple of years ago. A course aimed at helping potential self-employed businessmen get under way was also recently started in this way.

Participation and Publicity

In total, there were over 3,000 enrolments for courses run by the centre, either at the main centre or one of its satellites, in 1981-2. About 2,000 of these were at the beginning of the autumn term, and were duly recorded in the statistics submitted annually to the Department of Education and Science, whilst the remainder came in during the summer term. The majority attend classes at the main centre. Participation has increased over the last few years, but its pattern has also changed, with a considerable increase in daytime enrolments, related to the development of adult basic education and ethnic minority provision. Casual use of facilities is not recorded and is difficult to estimate, but drop-in is increasing and numbers of local community groups meet in rooms at the centre or in the school. Females out-number males in classes by a factor of nearly 4 to 1 in daytime provision and nearly 2 to 1 in the evening. This disparity appears to be decreasing, however, probably as a result of unemployment and the changing nature of the opportunities offered. A survey of those enrolling in fee-paying classes in the autumn of 1981 indicated that about half of the respondents were new to the centre or had not attended any classes in the previous three years, and that three-quarters attended in part because of the proximity of the centre to their homes. Most students were in the 18-35 age range, but with a further important group over 55, and were divided equally between tenants and home owners.

Publicity for the opportunities provided by the centre is produced and distributed in early autumn. Printing of prospectuses is arranged centrally by the local authority, and this limits the influence of the centre head. Local press and radio outlets are used for citywide publicity where possible, posters are placed in libraries and elsewhere, and a minibus is hired to visit local meeting points, such as shopping centres, cinemas and pubs, for three days before the beginning of term. A considerable number of students, about one third of those responding to the survey mentioned earlier, nevertheless enrol on word-of-mouth recommendation. Further and continuing publicity is provided throughout the year through outreach work, which may be better geared to recruiting from specific groups within the community.

On enrolment at the beginning of term, traditionally a hectic time for staff, some attempt is made to counsel and advise students over the suitability to them of the different opportunities available. This is inevitably a rather haphazard and inadequate process, however, and classes may start with an awkward or unsuitable balance of participants of widely differing ages and backgrounds. Special arrangements are made at enrolment time for those entering English and mathematics classes. Counselling may also be provided on an *ad hoc* basis throughout the year, largely dependent on the good will and interest of specific members of staff, and some opportunities exist for transferring between courses at different levels where this becomes desirable. As a consequence, drop-out does not feature as a major problem. Perhaps 100 students will enrol but never turn up to their classes (and thus not pay a fee) at the beginning of the autumn term, and small numbers will leave, for a wide variety of reasons, at different times later in the year. Little follow-up of drop-outs has been carried out. Clearly, it is a difficult phenomenon to assess and respond to when classes may be free or open access, and when many participants are temporarily or permanently unemployed.

The head of centre and staff have little time to consider in more abstract terms questions of demand and needs identification, or to monitor and evaluate the effectiveness of existing provision. At the present time, the position is that demand for the opportunities provided is satisfactory, whilst too much publicity or encouragement of participation might create demands on the centre which it lacks the resources to cope with.

Future Developments

Further development of the provision made by the centre is largely dependent upon an increase in funding, either from the local education authority itself or from other sources. A bid has been made for funds from the national inner city programme to upgrade and extend the present centre building, but the response to this was not known at the time of writing.

Nevertheless, a number of trends may be identified which appear likely to influence the future development of the centre. These are all apparent in the ways in which the centre's organisation and provision is changing at present, in accordance with the objectives of the centre head and the education authority, and in response to the changing nature of the local community. First, the centre will become increasingly open and accessible to the community, perhaps with greater local control, with more drop-in and informal classes added to the more formal offerings, and increased social facilities and outreach work. Indeed, it is planned to rename the centre a 'community centre' as a reflection and substantiation of these changes. Second, the target groups within the community at whom different aspects of provision are aimed will become better and more closely identified — for example, the elderly, the handicapped, parents of pre-school children, adult and youth unemployed, etc. Third, closer co-opera-

tion with other local organisations and groups, and with other providers of educational opportunities for adults in other parts of the
city, will become evident. There is, for instance, a plan currently
under discussion for co-operation with a local residential college
regarding short residential courses for local students. All of these
trends represent a commitment to an ideal of what a community
centre ought to be about. Such a responsive and relatively unstruc-
tured programme will, however, be more time-consuming and
demanding to operate.

NON-FORMAL WORK: A NEW KIND OF PROVISION

Paul Fordham, Geoff Poulton and Lawrence Randle

Source: P. Fordham, G. Poulton and L. Randle, *Learning Networks in Adult Education: Non-Formal Education on a Housing Estate* (Routledge and Kegan Paul, London, 1979), pp. 207-21.

By themselves attempts to increase working-class participation in the kind of education we already provide are likely, at best, to have only marginal success. Certainly in both the WEA and the universities we have lived for too long with the myth that a commitment to working-class education publicly asserted, plus the experience of the past, can somehow make recruitment to our classes more representative. If we are really serious in wanting to achieve this as one of our long-term aims, then we have to develop a new kind of provision alongside the existing programmes of classes.

We do not see this as totally distinct and certainly not just 'for the disadvantaged'; rather it is something that should influence much of what we now do. Initially, it may need to be seen as rather separate because it has to be encouraged to grow in new ways and probably in the main outside existing institutional structures and traditions. Unless it is recognised as a different *kind* of activity from much of what has gone before, we fear that the attempts of adult educators to reach and work with working-class groups are likely to remain small-scale and dependent on the enthusiasm and initiative of isolated individuals.

We say this for a number of reasons. First, the Project team found itself working across the boundaries between education and 'community work', where the educational activities that were generated could hardly have occurred inside the framework accepted as appropriate by the existing providers. Second, initial attempts to bend the programmes of local adult educators in the direction of needs as perceived by the team were unsuccessful. It was only in the Project's final stages that the development of new work — as with the street-based groups organised by Havant Further Education Centre — showed that we were at last beginning to influence local providers. Our own department, which had, after all, created the Project, took three years to begin to take account of Project activities in its own programme planning. And that was largely as a result of a new staff appointment in 'community education'. Finally, our work with the people of Leigh Park has been with those for whom formal education meant either failure or irrelevance to life's major and immediate problems. As one of them put it, she did not 'set out to have a learning experience in the first place',[1] but wanted to achieve better organisation for her family.

Work in areas like Leigh Park, where formal education does not seem to relate closely to the major and immediate needs of adult life, provides distinct parallels with the much larger educational problems of some Third World countries. Because of these parallels, and because of recent efforts to move their educational policies away from an exclusive concentration on formal education, there is also a refreshing opportunity to learn from Third World achievements. It is for this reason we use the term 'non-formal' to describe much of our work in Leigh Park. The term now has wide currency in the developing world and is the subject of a growing literature.[2]

The concept of non-formal education stems largely from recent experience in the Third World, where formal educational systems appear more clearly dysfunctional in relation to development goals than they do in a country like Britain. High costs, the unequal distribution of educational resources, 'failure' for those who are not selected for secondary school, unemployment for many who do succeed and the inflexibility characteristic of most formal systems all point to the misuse of scarce resources on a truly massive scale. Only in a few countries like Tanzania, where there has been a major shift of emphasis towards the non-formal education of adults,[3] has any serious attempt been made to reorientate educational policy towards the development goals of the 1970s and 1980s. And, as the World Bank recently stated, there have been[4]

> changes in the definition of development itself during recent years. Questions of employment, environment, social equity and, above all, participation in development by the less 'privileged' now share with simple 'growth' in the definition of the objectives (and hence the model) of development toward which the effort of all parties is to be directed. These changes have their counterpart in the education sector.

Of course, many of these objectives are echoed by educational and social reformers in developed countries. The work of Jackson, Lovett, Halsey, Midwinter and others led directly to our own initiatives. But their work has been directed in the main towards the reform of curricula and institutions within existing formal systems. They have given less attention than Third World thinkers like Freire or political idealists like Nyerere to the growth of non-formal alternatives. It is in the literature of and about the developing world from which many of our own ideas have been drawn.

In Tanzania and India, for example, non-formal education has been used to bring about dramatic improvements in rural hygiene; the quality of rural life has thus been enhanced without the necessity of prolonged and expensive development of sophisticated medical services.[5] Again, and building on the experience of radio learning campaigns in Tanzania, Botswana has been able to mount a large-scale exercise in public education which sought to explain and consult about a new grazing policy.[6] These, and similar projects elsewhere, have shown an ability to respond rapidly to new and urgent needs, partly because formal educational systems were clearly too slow to change and too undeveloped to be able to cope. Without the constraints imposed by existing structures of further or adult education, it has been possible to answer directly the question of how education can help overcome pressing social or economic problems.

Plunkett has argued that in this respect the Third World has a head start on countries like Britain. He asserts that 'with its settled bureaucracies and silent majorities', the West is now far outpaced in the experience and understanding of social and economic change by people in the developing world. As a result, 'coping with change may now be a skill that is better developed outside the West'.[7]

The World Bank's objectives quoted above certainly seem relevant to areas like Leigh Park; this shows the same failures of formal education and the same kind if not degree of deprivation in terms of resource distribution as do inner city areas and the rural Third World poor. Leigh Park's population also has to concern itself with employment, environment, social equity and participation — and the non-formal education of adults can and should make its contribution. Urban Britain and the rural Third World have more to learn from each other than is often supposed. Indeed, in some respects we have been slow to learn. For example, in Leigh Park we made little use of local radio. The use of radio as a learning resource in non-formal education has now received much attention elsewhere and could form the starting-point for similar efforts here.[8]

Because of the bewildering variety of non-formal programmes it is tempting to resort to definition when asked the question 'What is non-formal adult education?' The following widely quoted definitions are taken from P.H. Coombs *et al., New Paths to Learning,* prepared for UNICEF by the International Council for Educational Development, New York, 1973.

Formal education: the hierarchically structured, chronologically graded 'educational system', running from primary school through the university and including, in addition to general academic studies, a variety of specialised programmes and institutions for full-time technical and professional training.

Informal education: the truly lifelong process whereby every individual acquires attitudes, values, skills and knowledge from daily experience and the educative influences and resources in his or her environment — from family and neighbours, from work and play, from the market place, the library and the mass media.

Non-formal education: any organised educational activity outside the established formal system — whether operating separately or as an important feature of some broader activity — that is intended to serve identifiable learning clienteles and learning objectives.

But definition by itself often takes us no further than a debate as to whether this or that programme can properly be labelled as 'non-formal'. Tim Simkins[9] offers a more useful method of analysis by listing the characteristics of non-formal and formal programmes as an alternative to precise definition and categorisation. He argues that formal education is criticised mainly for its costliness, irrelevance and inflexibility, and that non-formal alternatives have attempted to achieve lower costs, greater relevance and greater flexibility.

We believe it would be misleading to assume lower costs as a general characteristic of non-formal education. This was certainly not true of our own Project. The attempt at lower costs is not necessarily met in practice either here or in developing countries. However, we agree that[10]

Perhaps, the greatest potential advantage of non-formal over formal education ... is its flexibility. Programmes are heterogeneous, and are the responsibility of a variety of agencies, often non-governmental and voluntary. Central direction and control is minimised and substantial autonomy exists at programme and local levels. It is therefore possible to vary programmes to meet the specific needs of different areas and different client groups and to respond quickly as these needs change. Local initiative, self-help and innovation is encouraged. The importance of these factors becomes apparent when the enormous diversity of non-formal programmes both within and between societies is compared with the high degree of uniformity of school systems across a range of societies whose social and political characteristics differ enormously. In essence, whereas non-formal programmes arise to meet particular learner and community needs, formal education expects students to conform to its own rigidly structured requirements concerning the timing of study, standards of entry, progression, and so on.

King has examined the range of formal and non-formal characteristics that is possible.[11] Modifications to the formal schooling model are seen as movements along a number of bands, with traditional, formal schools at one side and non-formal centres at the other (Table 1). And, as Simkins points out, although this analysis takes the traditional school as the starting point, 'all kinds of educational programmes, whether modifications of schooling or not, can be fruitfully analysed using this approach'.[12]

Simkins takes the analysis further, listing 15 polarised characteristics of formal and non-formal education under the general headings of purposes, timing, content, delivery system and control (Table 2).

Table 1: Movement from Formal to Non-formal

Traditional schools	from teachers towards animateurs	Non-formal centres
	from academic subjects to developing areas	
	from single-use buildings to shared use	
	from diffuse fields of knowledge to modular units	
	from centralised control towards devolved	
	from paid personnel towards community control of resources	

Source: Adapted from K. King (ed.), *Education and Community in Africa*, 1976, p. 13.

Table 2: Ideal Type Models of Formal and Non-formal Education

Formal		Non-formal
	Purposes	
Long-term and general		Short-term and specific
Credential-based		Non-credential-based
	Timing	
Long cycle		Short cycle
Preparatory		Recurrent
Full-time		Part-time
	Content	
Input-centred and standardised		Output-centred and individualised
Academic		Practical
Clientele determined by entry requirements		Entry requirements determined by clientele
	Delivery system	
Institution-based		Environment-based
Isolated (from the socioeconomic environment and from social action)		Community-related
Rigidly structured		Flexibly structured
Teacher-centred		Learner-centred
Resource-intensive		Resource-saving
	Control	
External		Self-governing
Hierarchical		Democratic

Now much traditional adult education — at least in theory — tends to non-formal polarity; this is true of purposes and timing; there are many other respects where it would make a mockery of the truth to assert that the formal model applies throughout. There are no formal entry requirements; much of the class programme is 'environment-based' and held outside institutions; there has never been a *standardised* content (though much is academic); delivery systems can be flexible (and sometimes are); and the WEA (and some LEAs) are democratic and self-governing as far as the participants are concerned. Mo 'eover, as presently constituted, although some adult education might be described as 'resource-intensive', much of the non-formal work with disadvantaged groups is labour-intensive and, where paid staff are used, can be much more expensive per student hour than the traditional work; it is only with the use of trained volunteers that non-formal programmes can hope to be adequately financed.

But if traditional adult education does tend towards the non-formal in some respects, in others it does not. Adult education is constrained by registration requirements, set fees, pre-determined curricula and the whole panoply of organisation around our class programmes, which can be comforting to participants and professional organisers but is inhibiting to those not already in tune with the education business. As one colleague recently expressed it,[13]

> We have to change our style of operation. We have to meet people on their own terms in settings where they feel comfortable and discussing issues about which they feel a need to know. Initially this means that university buildings, lecture rooms, didactic teaching, long reading lists, academic terminology and the whole hidden curriculum of our way of operation, are out.

Non-formal work has to eschew this hidden curriculum while at the same time building on the strengths of the traditional work.

Our non-formal methods of intervention in the area did succeed in recruiting new types of student. Some came because they wanted better to carry forward a particular piece of social action (like the campaign for better nursery school facilities), while others were often motivated by personal problems rather than a conscious search for knowledge; commonly, this second type of new student would be referred by friends or agencies as in need of some kind of 'help'. Indeed, 'A Chance to Chat' and similar non-formal discussion groups were seen by many outsiders as the provision of social therapy, opportunities for rewarding group experience or a convenient child-minding service — but were they something more as well?

As in many traditional adult education classes (e.g. those of the WEA) the social interaction was certainly an important feature, but could these non-formal groups also be legitimised as adult education? What was it that replaced the carefully prepared syllabus, guided reading and written work and rigorous class discussion of the best kind of tutorial class? And if there was some doubt as to the educational quality of group life, should adult educators (as distinct from social workers or political activists) really be involved? Even if they were to take part, was this merely a better or slicker form of recruitment or an education worth developing in its own right? If the latter turned out to be true, how could non-formal work link up with more traditional class provision?

Now there is always an element of learning in any social group work — and this is not at issue — but any judge of educational quality must also have regard to whether there is present both an intention to learn in some systematic way and an organisation that enables this to happen. For the educator, it is not enough merely to bring people together because they 'just want a quiet afternoon to themselves with the children off their hands',[14] or as a cure for loneliness, or to provide a meeting place to discuss how to achieve better social facilities. These may all be worthwhile in themselves and may even provide good starting points for organised learning; but they do not necessarily lead to such learning, and when they do it is usually the skill and experience of the tutor or group leader that enables this to happen.

In discussing the educational quality of this work, we take as our starting point the definition of education accepted by the *1919 Report*[15] — which itself formed the basis of much traditional adult education in the inter-war years:

> By 'education' we mean all the deliberate efforts by which men and women attempt to satisfy their search for knowledge, to equip themselves for their responsibilities as citizens and members of society, or to find opportunities for self-expression.

The key words here for our purposes are 'deliberate efforts' and the 'search for knowledge'. The dilemma for the professional adult educators we used as tutors was that for many of our working-class participants the initial motivation was certainly not 'educational' in any 'deliberate' sense. Perhaps informal learning was expected, or a facility to enable the creation and organisation of a pressure group (nursery schools), or a particular kind of social organisation (one-parent family group); but it was the job of the tutor both to help demonstrate the usefulness of systematic learning to serve whatever purposes motivated the students *and* to enable this to happen. Tutors in traditional classes ought to be able to assume a desire for systematic learning; methods of recruitment and publicity assume this to be the case. Tutors of non-formal groups must be sensitive to a much wider spectrum of concerns and, at the same time be able to help to concentrate attention on the way education can play its part in this whole process of student growth and development. The social group worker can legitimately be satisfied with effective group interaction and informal learning, or the political activist with organisation and effective action. But the adult educator, while at the least conscious and at the most a participant in all of these, must concentrate above all on the quality of the learning process — and on ensuring that the image of 'education' as either alien or irrelevant is eroded. In other words, he has to be both a teacher and a propagandist for the value of education as a problem-posing or problem-solving activity.

The route from initial motivation to systematic learning can be tough going for the tutor. [...]

Sharing ideas and the beginnings of an analytical approach to evidence need careful nurturing. [...] Such teaching demands carefully trained skills which are not common at present. In traditional classes it has been usual for the tutor to move out from the security of competence in a particular discipline, and although[16]

> aware of his subject as an organized body of knowledge shaped by generations of scholars ... the understanding teacher of adults will ... quickly discover that his students are not primarily interested in the formal divisions of academic knowledge, but in seeking the solution of problems which affect their own lives and the life of the society in which they live.

Moreover, in the normal university or WEA class the tutor must also be concerned about the integrity of his subject and the coherence of the work of the group as a whole:[17]

> It is no easy task for the scholar to transmute the sometimes arid products of academic learning into terms of living meaning, without at the same time breaking through the bounds of his own specialism and perhaps losing himself and his class in a pursuit that has no end. Yet he must attempt some compromise if his teaching is to be adapted to the needs of his students and of the society of which they are a living and active part.

Such a compromise takes on a different character in non-formal work. Systematic learning will usually be both multi-disciplinary and inter-disciplinary and there will be many occasions when the tutor needs to call in as consultant someone with a more specific or different knowledge base. The tutor must become skilled as the organiser of learning processes rather than more and more expert in particular academic disciplines. This is, of course, partly true of all adult education; in non-formal work the academic approach through particular subjects becomes totally irrelevant. What must remain, however, is a consciousness of the processes that inform the study of subjects — the use of concepts, the proper evaluation of evidence, logical steps in argument, the search for hidden assumptions.

We have argued that Project experience shows that the skill, experience and determination of the group leader or tutor is a major

Figure 1: Non-formal Adult Education and Social Change

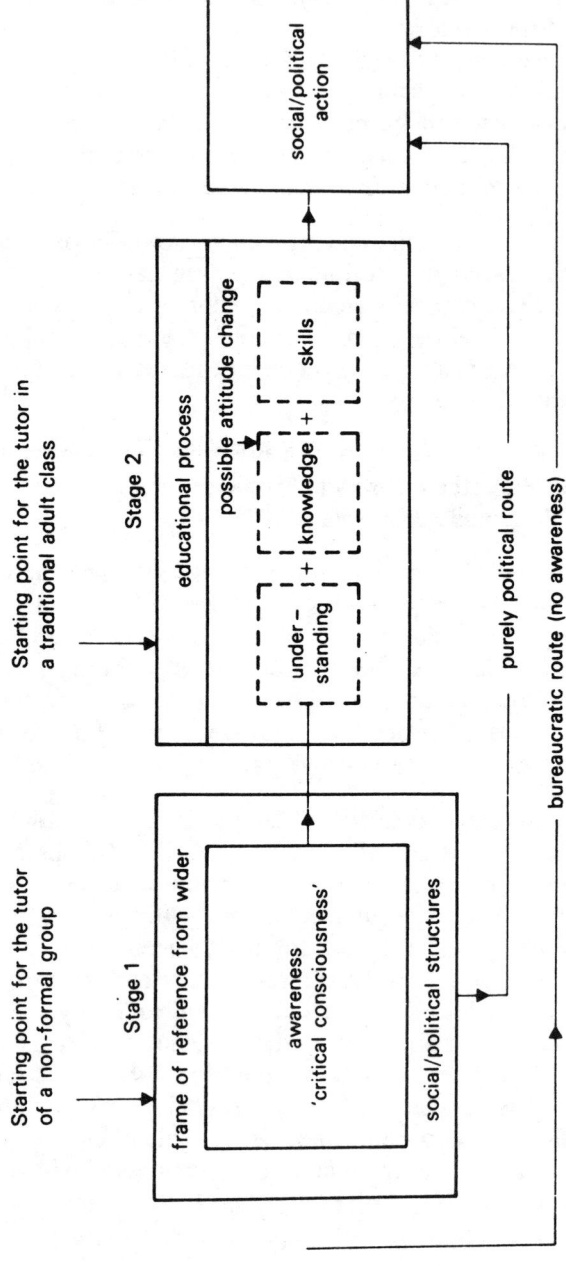

determinant of whether or not the group that does not start as a class and is often not consciously 'educational' nevertheless comes to achieve systematic and sustained study. This is the 'professional' element in non-formal learning whether undertaken by paid staff or trained volunteers.

For the agency or individual wishing to promote non-formal education it is crucial to recognise that the preparatory stages are all-important. Whereas the tutor in most existing adult education enters the field at Stage 2 in the processes indicated in Figure 1, the non-formal teacher must engage himself at Stage 1.

This can be bewildering for some existing staff. They must be more conscious than ever before both of the political/social/economic frame of reference and of the state of mind of participants who, at this stage, may not yet be ready for the learning experiences the professionals have to offer. Before he can organise learning groups the non-formal educator must first of all engage with and support the potential learning networks.

The legitimisation of non-formal work as 'adult education' will depend on the quality of work done in the first stage. The way this happens will depend to some extent on the response of existing providers to the challenge of non-formal work.

Notes

1. In an interview with A. Halsey quoted in P. Fordham (ed.), *Access to Continuing Education* (Open University, 1976), p. 22.

2. Lyra Srinavasan, *Perspectives on Nonformal Adult Learning* (World Education, New York, 1977), gives examples from both developed and developing countries.

3. See B. Hall, *Adult Education and the Development of Socialism in Tanzania* (East African Literature Bureau, Dar-es-Salaam, 1975); A.L. Gillette, *Beyond the Non-formal Fashion: Towards Educational Revolution in Tanzania* (Center for International Education, University of Massachusetts, Amherst, 1977).

4. World Bank, *Education: Sector Working Paper*, Washington, December 1974.

5. See: *The Mabubnagar Experiment: Non-formal Education for Rural Women*, Council for Social Development (Delhi), 1976; and *Mtu ni afya: An Evaluation of the 1973 Mass Health Education Campaign*, Institute of Adult Education (Dar-es-Salaam), 1974.

6. *Lefatshe la Rona — Our Land*, Republic of Botswana, 1977.

7. H. Dudley Plunkett, 'Modernisation Reappraised; the Kentucky Mountains Revisited and Confrontational Politics Reassessed', *Comparative Education Review*, XXII: 1 February 1978 (University of Chicago Press).

8. D. Crowley, A. Etherington and R. Kidd, *Manual on Radio Learning Group Campaigns* (Friedrich Ebert Foundation, Bonn Bad-Godesberg, 1978).

9. Tim Simkins, *Non-Formal Education and Development* (Department of Adult and Higher Education, University of Manchester, 1976).

10. Ibid., p. 17.

11. K. King (ed.), *Education and Community in Africa* (Centre of African Studies, University of Edinburgh, 1976).

12. Simkins, *Non-Formal Education*, p. 18.

13. Jane Thompson in a staff paper (unpublished) on 'Implications ... of the New Communities Project', 1976.

14. *Scope for Parents and Children, The First Year*, July 1976-1977, Southampton, July 1977.

15. 'Report of the Adult Education Committee of the Ministry of Reconstruction', 1919. An abridged version was reprinted in R. Waller (ed.), *A Design for Democracy* (Max Parrish, London, 1956) p. 59.

16. R. Peers, *Adult Education: A Comparative Study* (Routledge and Kegan Paul, London, 1972), p. 226.

17. Ibid.

EDUCATIONAL GUIDANCE FOR ADULTS

Linda Butler

Source: Copyright © The Open University 1983 (specially written for this volume).

The development of educational guidance for adults has been dramatic since the beginning of the 1970s, and has been reflected in the growth of literature on the subject. As late as 1974, Kelly's 'Select Bibliography'[1] had almost no references to educational guidance. By 1981, the National Institute of Adult Education (NIAE) had published a lengthy monograph reviewing existing research,[2] based on its own continuously updated computer-held file.

The growth in amount of literature reflects in part an increase in the variety of delivery points, and in part a change in the concept of educational guidance for adults itself. While many specialist and generalist agencies have long offered guidance to adults (the NIAE, professional bodies, some women's organisations, local education authorities (LEAs) Information Services, Citizens' Advice Bureaux and public libraries are examples), such provision has tended to be informational in emphasis and often a marginal part of the agency's activities. In educational institutions themselves, the picture has been much the same. Moreover, guidance as part of in-course activity has depended primarily on the voluntary efforts of individual tutors; even where specialist staff were available in the larger educational institutions, their services were designed mainly for enrolled students rather than outside enquirers, and for the younger student rather than the adult.

The 1970s, however, brought changes in three ways. The first was an expansion in the provision of vocational guidance for adults; while vocational and educational guidance are not synonymous, there are clearly areas of overlap. The 1973 Education and Training Act gave Local Authority Careers Services the power to extend their guidance and placement service to all students in full-time education and to other adults. Some Services responded by appointing full-time officers to serve adult needs. A Survey published in 1979 by the Institute of Careers Officers estimated that 135,000 people over 18 had sought advice from the Careers Service in 1977/8, of whom 42,000 received formal vocational interviews. At the same time, many of the activities of the Manpower Services Commission (MSC), which was also established by the 1973 Act, involved, directly or indirectly, engagement in the provision of vocational guidance. Its Occupational Guidance Units carried out nearly 50,000 first interviews and about 4,000 second interviews during 1978/9. TOPS (Training Opportunities Scheme) courses began to highlight the need for accurate pre-entry advice. WOW (Wider Opportunities for Women) courses were piloted in the late 1970s; focused on providing women with 'taster' experience of a wider range of employment, they again demonstrated the importance of guidance before, during and after attendance.

The second area of change arose within continuing education provision itself. The 1970s were marked by developments which had as their central concern the broadening of access to sections of the population previously debarred because of lack of formal qualifications and lack of appropriate kinds of provision. The Open University's commitment to ongoing counselling, informational and advisory support for its students was adopted by others.[3] Experience with adult literacy provision showed many students to have similar needs, and led the Adult Literacy and Basic Skills Unit (ALBSU) in the late 1970s to fund experimental guidance services geared specifically towards adult basic education. Most New Opportunities for Women (NOW) courses took account of the need for an in-built counselling element and a few, including the pioneering course at Hatfield Polytechnic, included a substantial assessment component. In the early 1980s, proposals for an Open Tech envisaged appropriate provision for promotion, information, counselling and guidance.[4]

These and other developments reflected many continuing educators' convictions that, even given more flexible entrance requirements and 'relevant' course content, adults considering re-entering the education system were deterred by difficulties in finding and understanding all the information they needed; by limited or inadequate assessments of their abilities (perhaps based on success or failure at school); by the difficulties of finding reliable advice on their best course of action; by the complexity of the task of marrying educational goals with personal and vocational needs, responsibilities and aspirations; and by the dauntingly bureaucratic nature of educational institutions. Such considerations suggested a collaborative model for the provision of educational guidance. By this means, the adult enquirer might be placed at the centre of the negotiation, able to select from the full range of institutions' offerings and aided by advisers free of institutional bias.

Hence, the third area of change; it was on this basis that many independent educational guidance services for adults (EGSAs) came into existence from the late 1970s onwards. Growth in the number of such services was rapid, with 45 listed in the Advisory Council for Adult Education's (ACACE's) 1982 directory.[5] Arguments justifying expenditure on these, and other, forms of adult guidance were an interesting mix of altruism and expediency. ACACE's 1979 'Links to Learning' Report reflected very clearly these two elements in the debate:

> Provision for education and training must be diverse; but diversity can build barriers to access. We argue that the way round this dilemma is a much more conscious and better-organised provision of educational guidance services for adults, which will inform and help people define their needs in relation to what the educational providers are able to offer ... Guidance services in continuing education should provide a two-way process, in which educators can promote their existing provision and learn about new demands. Selling what continuing education has to offer is an important reason for establishing guidance services, but it should not be the operating principle.[6]

The first independent guidance service for adults was probably that established in 1967 under the direction of Dr Dorothy Eagleson in Belfast. Significantly, the Service began life as the Adult Vocational Guidance Service,

> but it was soon apparent that a greater need was in broader educational information and guidance. When the vocational aspect was partially met by the setting up ... of Occupational Guidance Units, it was possible to shift the Service's orientation firmly towards adult education and in 1970 ... it was renamed Educational Guidance Service for Adults.[7]

From the beginning, Belfast EGSA has operated on a firmly client-centred basis; it has offered its clients the full range of guidance functions and, in particular, it has attended to the need to act as an advocate for them.

These two emphases, client-centredness and advocacy, find their clearest expression in the development in the United States of educational brokerages. By 1980, there were over 300 such centres. Educational brokering has been defined thus:

It means serving adult clients' interests as a broker for various educational opportunities. It represents a new configuration of educational services, and a new focus on the individual as a prospective learner with unique needs ... One distinctive quality of brokering agencies is that they aim to present adults with the complete range of educational and career alternatives and help them choose those most appropriate to their individual needs. Brokering agencies are neutral towards the choices made; conventional educational institutions usually aim to increase their own clientele or student bodies ... What is distinct about brokering is the packaging and delivery systems for these services — the ways clients are reached and served directly in the community — and, perhaps most important, the new educational role of client advocate. Client advocacy means placing learners' needs and interests above those of the institutions. This advocacy for clients' interests takes two forms: intercession on behalf of individual students, and efforts to change individual policies which hamper adult learners' re-entry and progress; e.g. scheduling, offerings, costs.[8]

These arguments for the autonomous agency with an interventionist role have found champions in Britain. Many of the guidance services set up in the early 1980s took over shops or other 'neutral' premises. The justification for such locations is not that it is only by such means that independent guidance may be offered. Rather, it emphasises to — and reassures — the educational institutions themselves that the guidance offered is bias-free and not a covert recruitment agency for any one host institution; it may reinforce the guidance workers' own feelings of independence from institutional pressures and thus facilitate the client advocacy role; and it is held to afford greater possibilities for reaching a clientele unlikely to approach an educational institution directly. In these respects, educational guidance services represent one facet of the client-centred and community-based advice and advocacy movement (e.g. in Neighbourhood Advice and Law Centres) which became established in the United Kingdom in the 1970s.

These fundamental issues about the stance that educational guidance should adopt *vis-à-vis* its clientele and the educational institutions have their repercussions on the other guidance functions: provision of information, assessment, advice, counselling and enabling or implementation activities other than advocacy. Those functions also carry with them their own inherent problems, both theoretical and practical. Debate on them is not confined to British practice,[9,10] but readers should beware of assuming that there is a consensus on terms such as assessment, advice or counselling. In Britain, the Educational Advisory Services Project (EASP) has conducted research into the provision of educational guidance by independent services and by public libraries, from the point of view both of the adviser and the consumer. It is on this work that much of the discussion of definitions, needs and operational problems which follows is based.[11]

Information

An obvious benefit in the creation of an educational guidance service is that it provides an opportunity to bring together all the information about learning opportunities in an area, whether 'hard' data (e.g. the time and venue of a particular class) or 'soft' data (e.g. the degree of formality characteristic of an institution's approach to the adult learner). Such a facility is of particular importance to the adult, who is unlikely to have access to the expert assistance and peer support often available to schoolchildren. Additionally, post-school education is very complex; there are more subjects, more types and levels of qualifications, more modes of attendance, complicated fees and grants structures to consider. These factors apply whether the intention is to develop a leisure interest or to pursue a career objective. Moreover, adults carry with them the accumulated benefits and burdens of their personal histories: commitments to people, to a job, to a particular area. Such considerations can rule out the better-known forms of provision, such as the evening class or the full-time degree course. Besides, what adults 'know' of contemporary educational provision for the mature person may be based on what they learned, or did not learn, at school 30 years before; innovations in adult education are seldom well-publicised.

Adults require educational information that is comprehensive, accurate, objective and readily accessible. Comprehensive information implies:

1.   Coverage of all local educational opportunities open to adults, whether vocational or non-vocational, is offered. While most adults want local provision, the definition of locality depends on each individual's circumstances and on the geography and transport network of the area. In addition, a regional and national perspective needs to be maintained, since a minority of enquirers are likely to want information on higher education outside the locality.

2.   Coverage that is prospective as well as current; knowing whether a course will be offered in the following academic year is essential in planning an educational programme.

3.   Offering a range of information irrespective of originating provider, since so many educational opportunities are offered by organisations other than the statutory providers.

4.   The range of information is offered regardless of mode of study; a correspondence course may be more appropriate to some adults than a course requiring regular attendance.

5.   Not only range but depth; adult learners need sufficient detail about individual courses — regarding their location, start-time, duration, length, costs, fees and grants, crèches and other enabling facilities, enrolment procedures, level (course content, required skills, qualifications), modes of teaching and learning, assessment methods, the usual recruitment profile — in order to identify the provision most appropriate to their personal circumstances.

Our second criterion is accuracy. It is at the very least discouraging and irritating to be given information which is inaccurate or misleading in part or in whole; but the consequences of misinformation may be irretrievably bad.

The third criterion, objectivity, is a particularly problematic area of educational information. A recent UNESCO Symposium emphasised this point: 'Legitimate publicity, including recruiting, should be distinguished from unscrupulous and misleading marketing.'[10] Nevertheless, the dividing line is a difficult one to draw; many brochures and prospectuses are primarily marketing tools. Such material may need to be supplemented with information about the quality of the course under consideration, in terms of content, teaching and student support, and reputation; its suitability for an individual's purposes and ability; and the recruitment needs and policies of the specific institution.

The final criterion, accessibility, implies both physical accessibility and the arrangement of materials according to user needs. Since adults are unlikely to possess a broad understanding of the structure of continuing education, arrangement by institution or on hierarchical principles is not always helpful. Lastly, accessibility of information also implies information which is comprehensible and inviting to read.

It is clear that the information requirements alone in educational guidance are daunting. Reviewing them, many of those engaged in guidance might respond, 'Yes, adult learners need this quality and range of information — and so do we.' Nevertheless, the quality of the information base determines to a very great extent the quality of all the other guidance functions, but most emphatically assessment and advice.

Attempts to address the problem of establishing and maintaining an adequate information base, while sometimes successful and occasionally ingenious, are beset with problems. The first is that there appear to be three levels of educational information: (1) public information is that which is made available specifically for public consumption by providing institutions, organisations and agencies. Obvious examples are brochures and prospectuses; (2) semi-public information is that which providers will normally offer if asked, most readily (although not exclusively) to co-professionals. A college's decision on the future provision of a particular course is an example; (3) private information is that which is not formally offered either to co-professionals or to members of the public, for example, views on the quality of a particular course or the competence of an individual teacher.

It is perhaps a characteristic peculiar to educational information that so much of what may be relevant to fully informing an enquirer is held to be outside the public domain. It is, of course, an obvious point that no guidance service operates without at least basic public information; some have developed a very comprehensive range of source material and great competence in obtaining, storing, retrieving and interpreting such information. Many services do feel, however, that the pursuit of semi-public and private information is rarely feasible (it can be very time-consuming indeed) and possibly unwise. Private information in particular is seen as problematic. It is often dependent on subjective judgements, and is potentially highly disruptive of carefully nurtured personal contacts. On the other hand, those who have been able to develop their access to private information tend to give it a very high value.

Secondly, there is dispute over the range of information which should be carried. As an example, many services give little or no attention to private sector provision, a decision which carries with it implications about the provision of information on alternative modes of study, since these often come within the private sector. It can be argued that the provision of a full range of information, regardless of originating provider, is one of the identifying features of the enquirer-centred as opposed to the institution-centred service. Some independent educational guidance services are under considerable pressure to demonstrate value for money, i.e. numbers of enquirers referred to each supporting public-sector institution (none is known to receive funding support from the private sector). Under these circumstances, and with the highly limited funding so often characteristic of such services, it is perhaps unsurprising that their efforts are concentrated on public sector provision. On the other hand, this stance may also be a matter of principle, to support the public sector wherever possible.

Thirdly, the question of who should be responsible for the provision of fully-adequate educational information is another problematic area. At the public information level, services show heavy reliance on individual institutions' brochures and prospectuses, while at the same time, their experiences with these sources demonstrate them often to be very imperfect. They are sometimes hard to obtain; they often arrive too late for peak demand; some of the information they contain will already be out-of-date on publication, and increasingly so as the academic year progresses; and in particular, they frequently lack the kind of information which those familiar with educational enquiries from adults know their public demands. In addition, they may be couched in language which is difficult to understand or prohibitive in tone, be unwieldy in format and lack internal logic or even an index. Thus, many services find one of their major tasks is supplementing and interpreting public-level information by direct contact with individual institutions. The resources, especially of staff time, available to collect, collate, verify and array information are, however, often limited. Moreover, services sometimes do not see information provision as an important function, viewing it as a low-grade clerical task; where staff time is scarce, it is seen as being better devoted to the 'professional' tasks of advice and counselling. Enquirers, it is felt, can reasonably be expected to be able to find information for themselves, but they cannot advise or counsel themselves. Some further justify this stance by arguing that it is ineffective in the long run to spoon-feed clients; finding the detailed information they need is an important test of the strength of enquirers' motivation.

Cumulatively, these three problems call into question whether it is possible, under current conditions, to offer educational information which is comprehensive, accurate, objective and accessible. This remains so even with such desirable developments as computerised data-bases and greater institutional awareness and co-operation.

Assessment

Assessment has been defined as 'making a diagnostic judgement about the client's suitability for certain options'.[12] Many adults' last exposure to formal public assessment of their suitability for certain educational options took place at the age of eleven years. Given the discrediting of the eleven-plus as a fully reliable method of selection, the predominance of early specialisation in the school system, the personal developments and declines specific to adulthood, differential access to educational, training and career opportunities, the enormous and continuing changes in the range and content of educational career opportunities open to adults, changing patterns of employment, and the difficulties inherent in self-assessment, the adult learner's need for assessment and reassessment facilities are very apparent. Those facilities imply, firstly, access to an appropriately-trained assessor and, where necessary, to psychometric tests and other tools to elucidate the individual's relevant personal history and circumstances, abilities, potentialities and aspirations. Secondly, such assessment should be offered in an independent context uncoloured by the particular provisions or recruitment targets of individual institutions or by the personal biases of the assessor. Thirdly, the assessor should be adequately informed about the range and nature of educational opportunities on offer. These three points are particularly important where adviser and assessor are the same person, and where, as a consequence, discrepancies of judgement are unlikely to be revealed in the process of case discussion.

The availability of educational assessment facilities of this sort is currently very limited indeed. There are a few independent fee-charging agencies and individuals which offer such a service. Some courses provide an in-built element of assessment (e.g. NOW courses). Some educational institutions offer to assess individual applicants' suitability for admission to their courses and advise them about suitable alternatives (e.g. the Open University, Open College). Institutions offering this facility tend to be those operating an open-entry policy and assessment is offered at least in part in order to minimise their own wastage rates.

There is, then, a critical gap in provision; how far are services able to fill that gap, and provide 'a diagnostic judgement about the client's suitability for certain options'? Two key issues here relate to diagnosis. The first is the way in which diagnosis is made. Most services rely largely on enquirer self-assessment and on the exercise of the guidance service worker's intuition, knowledge and experience. A few make occasional use of self-completion forms to test occupational interest, a technique borrowed from the Careers Service. Only in a minority of cases are facilities for psychometric testing offered to enquirers. Belfast EGSA, for example, argues that

> While testing is seen, not as 'magic', but as a useful tool giving clients objective information about their abilities, the service feels that it is of prime importance, particularly in assessing the potential of adults with little formal educational background or prior attainments, in examining special abilities and disabilities, and in promoting confidence in the accuracy of the assessments offered. The staff would be unwilling to function without this system.[7]

In contrast, many services object to the use of psychometric testing, claiming that the tests are unreliable, and that clients may well be fearful of them and hence deterred from using the service.

The second issue concerns what data about the enquirer are taken into account in the process of diagnosis. His/her educational and vocational history, aspirations, intelligence, aptitudes, personality and personal circumstances may or may not be given sufficient consideration. It is, of course, reasonable to exclude certain data from the process of diagnosis. The enquirer may not wish it to be included: several services have voiced scruples about intruding into the enquirer's personal domain. There are, moreover, a number of services which do not claim to offer assessment, but rather view them-selves as responding to enquirer self-assessment. On the other hand, it is in practice difficult to isolate and exclude diagnostic judgement about the enquirer's suitability for certain options from the process of educational guidance. Such judgements will form part of the process of information selection and of advice-giving, for example, and obvious dangers arise where a service's workers are not fully aware of making them or are making them from a partial understanding of the client's background. These dangers are magnified by the typically limited exposure which guidance workers currently have to training in the dynamics and skills of assessment. As an example, while many independent guidance services have made efforts to address the problem of institutional bias in their own personnel or network links, similar attention is rarely paid to sensitising service participants to their personal biases.

Consequently, the assessment process appears to be a hazardous one for assessors and clients alike. If services attract more enquirers without formal qualifications (with additional demands caused by the closure of all Occupational Guidance Units in the early 1980s), then these hazards will presumably increase unless greater attention is given to both methods and training. Yet, very few services have voiced more than minimal concern about their ability or inability to assess, so perhaps it is the case that intuition and experience are as valid, or better than, more measurable techniques, and that self-assessment and previous qualifications can be relied upon. Even if this is so, there is, nevertheless, a strong case for making assessment a genuinely open and interactive process. The need for re-evaluation of assessment practice and its impact on the enquirer is very plain.

Advice and Counselling

In the context of continuing education, 'advice', 'counselling' and the generic term 'guidance' are disputed terms. Some independent services have avoided using the word 'guidance' since it may connote in the public's mind that users have 'a problem' (cf., Marriage Guidance), and a similar consideration sometimes applies with the use of 'counselling'. Other services appear to use the term 'guidance' to indicate that counselling is not offered; one makes a distinction in its title between guidance, which is held to be directive, and counselling, which is held to be non-directive. The use of 'advice' is avoided by some services on the grounds that it suggests, misleadingly, that evaluations of the quality of courses will be made (cf., Consumer

Advice Centres). Others use the term to indicate that the emphasis in their provision is on helping people broadly to understand the variety of options open to them, rather than on providing detailed information or counselling. Yet others eschew the word entirely, feeling that it connotes imposition, partiality and directiveness.

Advice may be defined as the process of improving the learner's choice-making via a mediator who reviews and appraises the options available and who may suggest or recommend an appropriate path or paths. The following typology of advice-giving is suggested.

1. The arraying of the fullest range of educational options and an analysis of the advantages and disadvantages of each one may be termed complete and non-directive advice.
2. Recommendations on the most appropriate option to choose (from 1.) may be termed complete and directive advice.
3. The arraying of a narrow band from the full array of options and an analysis of the advantages and disadvantages of each one may be termed incomplete and non-directive advice.
4. Recommending as most appropriate an option from that narrow band may be termed incomplete and directive advice.

Such activities may be referred to as counselling, and certainly the distinction between counselling and advising is not easily made in this context. However, the advice-giving described here differs from educational counselling in a number of ways. Effective advice (and indeed information) depends on having as its base a client who is already at the point where he/she is able to be receptive to it. Educational counselling is appropriately offered to the client who is not yet at that point. In advice, the range of options from which selection may be made can fairly readily be determined, although they may not yet be fully clarified. Counselling is concerned with helping the client to identify the nature and extent of that range. The role of the adviser is to act as an expert resource mediator, with the client as a recipient, active or passive. The role of the counsellor is to act jointly with the client in order to facilitate identification and articulation of his or her needs. These three criteria demonstrate that educational counselling (but not advising) is characteristically developmental and long-term.

Thus, in theoretical terms at least, the distinction between advice and counselling is not that the former is directive and the latter non-directive. Advice-giving may well be non-directive; indeed, many independent services go to considerable trouble to ensure that it is so.

Moreover, counselling itself may be directive or non-directive. Non-directive counselling requires that the counsellor adopt a position of non-involvement and detachment. The counsellor is then concerned to reflect back the client's own input, and provide the means for the client to develop insight and thus be enabled to solve his or her problems without further assistance from the counsellor. In directive counselling, the client's attention is drawn to questions or areas which appear relevant and information may well be offered. The process also extends to directing the client into an appropriate course of action and enabling the client to pursue that course.

It is clear that much of the debate over advice is about services' concern to establish fully the concept of educational guidance as client-centred (a technique central to counselling) rather than about inadequacies in advice-giving *per se*. Anxiety not to appear institution-biased is reflected in the rejection of directiveness, with its connotations of imposition and partiality, conscious or unconscious. However, directiveness may actually be perfectly appropriate in practice. Recommending a particular option may be a perfectly reasonable response to directive advice-seeking and it is itself an imposition to refuse to give advice in certain circumstances. Moreover, it is not difficult to envisage situations where the giving of unsolicited directive advice, or even its imposition, is absolutely proper. An example might be telling someone making enquiries about studying 'O' Levels by correspondence to check whether he or she will be able to sit the examination locally.

I would argue, then, that advice is an integral part of educational guidance and that no one form of advice, directive or non-directive, complete or incomplete, is intrinsically superior to another. Certain conditions must apply here, however. The first is an adequate and easily-accessed information bank from which to draw out relevant options. Incomplete advice should be explicitly seen as an informed and positive judgement; the danger is that it may be passed off as a complete array or assumed to be so by an enquirer who is not informed otherwise. Second, competent advice-giving requires staff who are trained to recognise the processes of assessment in which they may be engaged. Third, directive advice should be seen explicitly as an informed and positive judgement and not be used as a vehicle for personnel's institutional partiality or biases. Fourth, staff should be competent to recognise the difference between information, advice and counselling needs, in so far as this is possible.

Formal strategies to deal with advice needs are often well-developed, particularly through the establishment of links with educational establishments. The importance of this form of agency outreach is very apparent. Few independent services have had sufficient staff continuity or expertise to be able to offer immediate and detailed advice themselves on the vast range of continuing education provision. Strategies to deal with counselling needs are much less well developed. In part, this is because the distinction between advice and counselling has not always been clearly made, with counselling appearing to be used to describe a process of thoughtful advice-giving, informed by some counselling techniques. Additionally, while it is relatively easy to discern an advice need, a counselling need may not be so easy to spot. In any case, few services and few educational institutions have trained counsellors available or sufficient time to adopt a counselling approach. The client is usually treated as autonomous, able to deal with the information and advice elicited with little further assistance. Although there is wide recognition that the client's initial or presenting enquiry may bear little relation to the one underlying it, this does not necessarily imply a counselling need; clarification of information may suffice. However, there has been an increased interest in counselling resulting from the growth of access provision for disadvantaged groups; courses for redundant workers and for women returners, for example, may well contain such an element. In addition, advocates of counselling maintain that decisions reached through moving from 'being-helped' to self-help may lead to better-motivated students in the long run.

It is difficult to determine the extent to which adult learners need counselling. Nearly all independent services report that such enquirers are in a minority. The extent to which factors like the pre-determined limitation of functions, lack of resources, and the use of personnel unskilled in recognising counselling need have contributed to this is impossible to assess. Anecdotal evidence suggests that educational counselling is very productive, in the sense of leading to a satisfactory outcome for the enquirer, providing institution and counsellor alike. On the other hand, this may be equally the case with information and advice enquiries, when follow-ups are much less likely to be made. The relative weight given to the functions of educational guidance may change however, as the clientele changes, most notably with the increase in the numbers of unemployed.

Implementation

Implementation, that range of activities intended to ease the learner's pursuit of the agreed educational goal, was earlier identified as a hallmark of the new concept of educational guidance. As well as advocacy, implementation also involves coping activities or sponsorship and feedback. Coping activities take two main forms. The first is helping clients learn to deal with the institutions and agencies they come into contact with in an appropriate and effective way. At its simplest level, this may mean being shown how to complete application forms, but it extends to teaching the client how to initiate change in provision, for example, making a complaint about a tutor. The second form of coping is helping the client learn how to deal with the educational demands of a chosen course of study. This may include help with study techniques or guidance on pre-entry learning, for example. Feedback may be defined as the discernment of patterns of need from client demand, based upon the systematic collection of data, and the presentation of this information to the providing institutions. Implied in this is the necessity of working with providers to effect changes in resource allocation, programme profiles, class times and so on. Sometimes, where institutions are unable or unwilling to provide, then a service may itself put on a class, though this is uncommon.

In practice implementation appears to be given the least weight of any of the guidance functions at present. Lack of awareness, lack of funding and facilities, and concern not to disrupt sometimes fragile relationships with providers, all contribute to this. The question of implementation activity is also debated on principle. Some services consider it inappropriate; self-directed pursuit of their education goal sorts the determined client from the half-hearted. Others view it as an inevitable extension of the guidance process; the greater the degree of educational and other disadvantage, the more the client needs assistance at the implementation stage. Furthermore, they argue that if access to many continuing education opportunities is closed, for whatever reasons, to adults, then they have a central obligation to try and effect change in the allocation of resources. Individuals are unlikely to be able to do this for themselves; they need an agency which can approach providers on equal terms.

While in theory, it is here that services have a crucial developmental role, in making coherent and amplifying the voice of the consumer, in practice activity is limited. Nevertheless, there have been examples of negotiated institutional change, often accomplished by force of personality, persuasive diplomacy and pulling strings. In such circumstances, the value of independent services' advisory committees, representative as they sometimes are of the major institutions in the locality, may be inestimable.

Conclusion

'Support services for adult learners ... are never as popular with administrators, government officials and other funders nor as visible to the general public as are the educational programs themselves.'[7]

At the same time, developments in continuing education (e.g. the Open Tech., credit transfer) and retrenchment in the area of vocational guidance are placing new demands on all those involved in the guidance of adults. Issues of this kind have led some educationalists to argue that educational guidance should become part of a new, reorganised and much expanded careers service. The majority view appears strongly against this; such a move is considered to threaten client-centredness and the advocacy role. For the adult learner, access points to educational guidance are becoming more plentiful, although such guidance is still concentrated almost exclusively on class- or course-centred learning. The independent or the self-directed learner is little catered for and calls for improved or integrated facilities[13, 14] have not received widespread attention. Thus, while services may stimulate demand for new types of courses, they are not necessarily from new types or groups of clients, a feature in common with American experience:

The area of outreach to clients is one where those of us without instructional programmes have not had, frankly, the impacts all have desired ... Specifically, we are faced with two barriers: people's capacity to *hear* our message, and their ability to *respond* to our message. The first one is a matter of information processing skills, and to some degree may be resolvable. The second is almost a matter of social psychology or cultural norms, and may be very difficult to modify. It also bears the most serious implications for long-range future planning.[8]

Notes

1. T. Kelly (ed.), *A Select Bibliography of Adult Education in Great Britain,* 3rd edn (NIAE, 1974).

2. M. Osborn, A. Charnley and A. Withnall, *Educational Information, Advice, Guidance and Counselling for Adults.* A review of existing research in adult and continuing education, vol. VI (NIAE, 1981).

3. K.A. Percy, M. Langham and J.G. Adams, *Educational Information, Advisory and Counselling Services for Adults: A Source Book.* Lancaster Series on Adult Education No. 3 (University of Lancaster, 1982).

4. *Open Tech Task Group Report,* Manpower Services Commission (June 1982).

5. *Directory of Educational Guidance Services for Adults,* Advisory Council for Adult and Continuing Education, 2nd revised edn (ACACE, April 1982).

6. *Links to Learning,* Advisory Council for Adult and Continuing Education (ACACE, 1979).

7. D.J. Ironside, *Models for Counselling Adult Learners* (Department of Adult Education, Ontario Institute for Studies in Education, Canada, 1981).

8. J.M. Heffernan, F.U. Macy and D.F. Vickers, *Educational Brokering: A New Service for Adult Learners* (National Centre for Educational Brokering, Syracuse, New York, 1976).

9. *The Development of Information, Guidance and Counselling Services.* A report of a conference arranged by the European Bureau of Adult Education in co-operation with the Europäische Akademie, Berlin, 23-7 Nov., 1981 (European Bureau of Adult Education, 1982).

10. *Ways and Means of Strengthening Information and Counselling Services for Adult Learners.* A report of the International Symposium, 22-7 May, 1977. University of Southern California College of Continuing Education in conjunction with UNESCO (UNESCO, 1978).

11. Accounts of EASP's work are available in the form of its reports to the British Library and to ACACE.

12. A.G. Watts, 'Educational and Careers Guidance Services for Adults, II: A Review of Current Provision', *British Journal of Guidance and Counselling, 8 (2),* July 1980.

13. S. Brookfield, *Independent Adult Learning. Adults: Psychological and Educational Perspectives,* 7 (Dept. of Adult Education, University of Nottingham, 1982).

14. S. Dale, 'Another Way Forward for Adult Learners: The Public Library and Independent Study', *Studies in Adult Education, 12 (1)* (April 1980) pp. 29-38.

Part 6

FUTURE

The final part of this Reader takes a number of glimpses into the future, always a dangerous and speculative task.

The first article, from the Advisory Council for Adult and Continuing Education's major report, *Continuing Education: From Policies to Practice*, details the main conclusions and recommendations of this body for the development of continuing education (this is the more formal and institutional part of the education for adults field, as Brian Groombridge points out in the opening article of the accompanying Reader) over the next 20 years. It is very much a programme for action, by which future progress may be judged.

Ritchie Calder's piece addresses itself to the implications of increasing automation for employment, training and education. Faced with the conclusion that most people have been educated or trained, and are still being educated and trained, for jobs and roles which will soon be irrelevant or non-existent, Calder remains determinedly optimistic about the potential for useful re-training and 'education for leisure'. It is difficult not to contrast his optimism with the pragmatic pessimism of Bryant's article in this Reader, which approaches the same theme, unemployment, from a rather different perspective.

The concluding article by John Lowe is also reasonably optimistic. Lowe opens out the discussion from the perspective of the United Kingdom and the Western developed nations to deal with the world as a whole and bravely speculates on the developments which might be expected over the next two decades in the field of education for adults.

6.1

PRIORITIES FOR ACTION

Advisory Council for Adult and Continuing Education

Source: Advisory Council for Adult and Continuing Education, *Continuing Education: From Policies to Practice* (ACACE, Leicester, 1982), pp. 181-96.

These are in summary Council's considered view of the 'priorities for action' which, taken together, could form a practical basis for a coherent national policy for the promotion of continuing education. To put these priorities into context we first of all briefly record the report's main arguments for the creation of a comprehensive system of continuing education and the associated need for consultation and collaboration among and within agencies and institutions, and we add a short account of the Council's conviction that policies must now be rapidly transformed into practice so as to provide continuing education and training for all adults at all levels of attainment wherever they may live.

Over the next 20 years this country will experience profound economic and social changes, largely as a result of the increasingly rapid spread of existing and new technologies. This could lead to unprecedented shifts in economic activity, and to marked changes in the patterns of work and leisure (or non-work), with less working time needed for much more highly skilled work. Quality will have to replace quantity. Adaptability will become essential. The present scale of these changes is small compared with the future effects of the accelerating speed of change which will reach in the next few years into many more sectors of the economy to affect far larger sections of the population. The idea of holding the same job for life is becoming increasingly untenable. Those with the greatest capacity to adapt will survive successfully; those least adaptable, nations as well as persons, will fail.

Continuing education offers one route to adaptability in a world where it is no longer possible to go on relying on the knowledge and skills acquired in youth. As it becomes more difficult to predict the knowledge and skills needed for adult life, the education of young people will have to concentrate on the learning skills to be used and developed throughout adult life. Thus education is not just an event

275

in childhood but an experience available at any time in life.

If it is to promote adaptability and creativity in the adult population, continuing education cannot be related solely to work. While economic success depends on the technical knowledge and skills of the working population, the success of specific job training depends on the general educational attainments of those being trained. Adaptability at work is also reflected in the ability to work co-operatively with others and to contribute to the shaping and taking of decisions. These abilities are most readily formed through the cultural and social aspects of general education. Just as good training for employment develops skills beyond the needs of specific jobs, so general education develops skills relevant to *all* the demands of everyday life including work. Continuing education must therefore be comprehensively planned to include all the forms of education and training available to adults beyond their initial education.

New technologies reduce the demands of work and enhance opportunities for leisure, but they also put a premium on the adaptability of knowledge and skills not possessed by those with only limited educational attainments. Particularly at risk are: those women whose level of educational experience and aspiration often put them at a disadvantage; members of ethnic minority groups who are often locked into multiple deprivations of poor education, poor housing and poor employment prospects; those manual workers who left school at the minimum age and have had no further education or training; young people entering the labour market for the first time, often with few skills to offer; and the retired, particularly the growing number of those retiring early, still physically and mentally active, but with far fewer opportunities to contribute to society in any satisfying and constructive way. A comprehensive system of continuing education would provide the poorly educated with much wider opportunities to improve their general level of education and hence their employability: it would remove people temporarily from the labour market, making room for others, particularly young people, to take their place; and it would provide opportunities for adults to play a more creative part in cultural and social activities. But it is among the least educated sectors of the adult population that continuing education has until now been least attractive; it has been the more educated adults who have demanded more education for themselves. If this pattern continues, the gap between the well educated and the poorly educated could become even wider. There must be a determined effort to attract back into education all those adults who have until now regarded it as irrelevant to their needs. The Council stresses the need to plan provision for priority groups, because it is all too easy to respond to the educational 'haves', who can make their demands known, and to ignore the 'have-nots', whose needs are generally far more difficult to identify and meet.

The creation of a comprehensive system of continuing education, which is efficient, flexible and effective in responding to needs, requires adequate arrangements for consultation and collaboration. The public education authorities, national and local, have a responsibility to ensure, within the resources available, the provision of a balanced range of educational opportunities to meet the needs of the whole population. This provision is generally made both directly by the local education authorities and through central and local government's promotion of educational activities by other bodies. But this important promotional function is at present not sufficiently exercised. While the Department of Education and Science, the Welsh Office and the local education authorities do promote the educational activities of other bodies through consultation in planning, through grants, and through the pooling of expertise and resources in collaborative ventures, these promotional activities are rarely part of any coherent plan of priorities and responsibilities for the education of the adult population.

At national level many government departments and statutory bodies are engaged in providing for continuing education and training. The separate responsibilities exercised by the Department of Education and Science, and the Welsh Office, the Department of Employment and the Manpower Services Commission can lead to unhelpful administrative and policy divisions between education and training, which are now being further divided as education budgets are cut and training resources are increased. No doubt there are arrangements for inter-departmental consultation and collaboration, but there is no mechanism for drawing up and carrying out a coherent national policy for continuing education, for assessing priorities, allocating responsibilities and promoting collaborative ventures.

The Regional Advisory Councils for Further Education have important responsibilities at regional level for facilitating the efficient use of resources through the avoidance of duplicated effort, the identification of new areas of need and the promotion of educational innovation. However the weight of their attention is on work-related rather than general education, and on students completing their initial education.

At local education authority level arrangements for consultation and collaboration among the different providers are not widely developed. Within educational institutions catering predominantly for adults much more could be done to build effective consultative and management links with students so as to help in assessing the best use of available resources and the nature and scope of the institution's activities in the education of adults in the local community.

The Council is convinced that it is imperative to begin work now to translate policies into practice in order to achieve, over the next twenty years, the comprehensive provision of continuing education and training for all adults. In support of that conviction we contend that:

1. Any highly industrialised country which cannot refute the charge that it is an under-educated society is condemning its own future.
2. Every country should ensure the highest possible levels of self-reliance and self-fulfilment among all its citizens, for both their individual and collective well-being.
3. A democratic society can only be sustained by its individual citizens' ability to take part in and contribute to economic, social and cultural change and growth.
4. The presently perceived inequalities in our society, which can adversely affect the relationships between government and people and between management and employees, partly reflect the inequalities in the past and present provision of educational opportunities. The widening of those opportunities would help to reduce those inequalities.
5. Education must therefore be regarded and planned as a continuing process throughout life. It is no longer sufficient to regard education as an early and finite process in preparation for adult life.

From this we conclude that:

(a) In this continuing process of education, the schooling of young people should be regarded as the initial preparation and encouragement to proceed to the much longer period of adult life, when the skills and enjoyment of learning acquired at school will be continuously exercised and developed. Nobody should leave school feeling that their education is finished.

(b) This continuing learning should comprise both education and training, as those terms are currently understood and applied, and a continuing education system should be built onto, in order to extend, the present provision of education and training for adults in the public and in the non-statutory sectors.

This leaves us in no doubt that it is of the highest importance for the development of continuing education that a clear national policy should be agreed. Without this agreement we will continue to lack the impetus needed to encourage and shape the local provision from which the whole system must grow.

In the Council's view, a substantial move can be made towards a system of continuing education through the reallocation of some existing resources, rather than through any significant additional funding, because the first and fundamental requirement is a shift in attitudes and organising arrangements. However, there are some developments which will have to wait on an increase in public education budgets. This will clearly depend on the prevailing analysis of the state of the national economy and the political determination to increase the public funding of the education of adults. When continuing education has achieved a higher political priority, the ways in which its growth might be financed could become more various and less constricted. Since the setting of priorities in the allocation of public funds for education must remain a political decision, many of the priorities identified in this report will depend on political decisions about the educational and economic appropriateness of their implementation both in size of funding and timing.

In the following paragraphs we bring together 'priorities for action'. This statement of priorities covers what we think are the main issues to be resolved in spanning the gap between the arguments in favour of a comprehensive system of continuing education and the policies and practices needed to transform them into the reality of adults' learning. The summary also contains our suggestions in relation to three questions about implementing the priorities — when should they be introduced, by whom, and at what order of additional cost?

However, it is neither realistic nor possible at this stage and level of consideration to be extremely precise about timetables and additional expenditure. We have therefore divided the proposed timetable for implementation into four broad periods covering the next 20 years: *immediate future* — meaning within the next couple of years; *short-term* — within the next three to five years; *medium-term* —

within the next five to ten years; and *long-term* — the following ten years up to the turn of the century. Clearly the proposed implementation period of some of our priorities does not fall neatly within just one of these periods; thus, we have indicated the full span of time when the proposed start and final establishment extends over more than one period.

Our judgement of the *additional* expenditure needed to implement the priorities is difficult to express in absolute figures. To provide anything but broad approximations would require detailed proposals and costings which would be premature. We consider it more appropriate and realistic to indicate the *relative* order of additional expenditure likely to be required. That is to say relative among the various priorities proposed, and relative for each separate priority to the current overall annual expenditure on the education and training of adults and to the very much larger total expenditure on all education and training. This has been shown in four categories. *Category I* signifies no more than some thousands of pounds; *category II* suggests additional expenditure of several hundred thousands; *III* a few millions of pounds; and *IV* all orders of expenditure above that. These broad categories refer to annual expenditure across England and Wales and include both current and capital costs. We would emphasise that these very broad orders of additional costs offer no more than relative indicators of the financial implications of the proposals and some measure of the economic and poltical decisions required to implement them. In our view none of the proposals would cost anything more than the equivalent of a *very small proportion* of the present total expenditure on education and training.

In ascribing responsibility for the implementation of the proposals, we have indicated only those organisations which, in our view, should be primarily responsible. However, the future development of continuing education will require co-operation and concerted action, and therefore none of the many interrelated aspects of that development can be the exclusive concern of any one body or institution. The following paragraphs group our priorities according to the issues examined.

Educational Guidance Services for Adults

Educational information, advisory and counselling services should be locally available to all adults to help in identifying their educational needs and in finding the best ways of satisfying them. These services would promote a more efficient use of educational resources and also provide educational institutions with information about local needs and demands.

Local education authorities and other providing agencies, including public libraries, should seek co-operative ways of establishing or supporting these services locally as soon as possible. Initially emphasis might be put on securing a network of information services with the subsequent addition of advisory and counselling elements. *Local education authorities and other agencies: II: in the immediate future and the short-term.*

The Department of Education and Science and the Welsh Office might fund a number of pilot research and development projects, the results of which should be made known to local education authorities and other agencies, with recommendations about the most effective ways of organising these local services. The results should be related to complementary research in the credit transfer feasibility study. *Department of Education and Science, Welsh Office: I: in the immediate future and the short-term.*

Access to, and Co-ordination of, the Full Range of Provision

All institutions in the post-school sector should actively encourage adult participation at all levels of their provision. A full sequence of attainment levels should be made available through co-operation, where appropriate, with neighbouring institutions. To ensure the accessibility of a full range of provision in each area there should be consultative planning at local, regional and national levels among all the relevant statutory and non-statutory bodies. *Department of Education and Science, Welsh Office, regional advisory councils, local authority associations, local education authorities, educational institutions and other agencies: I: from the immediate future.*

Co-ordination at local level is particularly important since many of the decisions about the practicability of provision are made there. There should be more emphasis on the local education authorities' role as promoters of continuing education. The establishment of local development councils for the education of adults in every LEA area, widely representative of all the education and training interests in the area, would provide the basis for local co-operation in disseminating information on local provision, co-ordinating provision, and reviewing provision to identify and fill any gaps. *Local education authorities and all other local interests in education and training: from the immediate future.*

Range of Provision

There should be the widest possible range of provision to ensure that as many adults as possible can readily continue their education. They need to be able to re-enter the education system at the time and level best suited to their own circumstances, and, after re-entry, to be able to proceed through the system according to their own requirements. The provision of this wide range of opportunities would allow more adults to build on their existing skills and knowledge, and would allow institutions to test the demand from adults for education. The re-entry of large numbers of adults to the education system calls for widespread provision of the following kinds:

(a) *Basic education* to equip adults who have a very low level of general education to take the first steps into non-advanced education. Developments in this field are already being promoted by the Adult Literacy and Basic Skills Unit, but longer term national planning and implementation is required. *Department of Education and Science, Welsh Office, Adult Literacy and Basic Skills Unit, Manpower Services Commission, local education authorities, educational institutions: III: from the short-term onwards.*

(b) *Post-basic* to span the gap between the basic level and the sorts of competencies required in the formal education system at GCE O-level and equivalents. *Educational institutions: II: from the short-term onwards.*

(c) *Return to study* to restore confidence in the ability to resume study and the skills to undertake it. *Educational institutions: II: from the short-term onwards.*

(d) *Bridging and access courses* to acquire the skills and knowledge required to enter higher academic and professional education. *Educational institutions: II: from the short-term onwards.*

Entry Procedures

The entry requirements normally used to assess young people's academic suitability are not necessarily the best indicators of adults' suitability. They take no account of the skills, knowledge and experience gained by adults outside the world of education; they may also not take account of adults' potential and determination to succeed. In view of this:

(1) All institutions of further and higher education should review their admission procedures for each course for which academic or professional entrance requirements are normally laid down. Where reasonable, a policy of open entry for adults to these courses should be operated. *All institutions: from the immediate future.*

(2) Wherever possible alternative admissions procedures should be available to adult entrants. *All institutions: from the immediate future.*

(3) A national credit transfer system should be set up to permit adults to offer alternative qualifications, either for entrance to a course or for exemption from part of a course. *Department of Education and Science, Welsh Office: II: from the short-term.*

(4) Research and development work should be set in hand on a range of adult alternatives to GCE 'A' level examinations. *Department of Education and Science, Welsh Office, Examination Boards: I: from the immediate future.*

(5) There should be a study of the feasibility of establishing a national framework for the certification of courses in continuing education. *Department of Education and Science, Welsh Office: I: in the immediate future.*

(6) Where adult candidates are unable to meet the entrance requirements, open entry courses should be available to provide the prerequisite knowledge and skills as quickly as possible. *All institutions: II: from the immediate future.*

(7) Information on all the forms of entry procedures should be made widely available. *All institutions: from the immediate future.*

Local Centres for Continuing Education

There is at present not enough accessible local provision. A key element in the creation of a comprehensive system of continuing education is the establishment of a comprehensive network of local centres to provide: ease of access to education, especially for those who cannot find time or money to travel long distances; attractive environments for learning in the front line of an educational system actively seeking to encourage hitherto reluctant adults to enter education; local bases within the community from which staff can provide education in other settings — at work, at home, in local clubs and centres — either directly or in collaboration with other organisations. These local centres need not be large and may sometimes be able to be accommodated in buildings surplus to requirements in the initial education sector. This will require:

(i) Preparation of plans at national, regional and particularly local level. *Department of Education and Science, Welsh Office, local authority associations, local education authorities: in the immediate future.*
(ii) Development of the network of centres at the local level. *Local education authorities: III: from the short-term.*

Rigidities of Time and Place

New modes of learning should be rapidly developed to overcome the limitations of physical attendance at set times in particular places. Priorities for action should include:

(a) Rigidities in the time-tabling of existing provision should be reviewed to find ways of attracting more adult learners. *All institutions: from the immediate future.*
(b) Development of more part-time provision and complementary child-minding facilities. *All institutions: II: from the immediate future.*
(c) Appropriate incentives to expand short full-time course provision. Adjustment of full-time equivalency ratios to take account of the additional workloads required for part-time education, and consideration of short full-time courses of up to two weeks duration as comparable to part-time provision for allocating resources through the full-time equivalency ratios. *Department of Education and Science, Welsh Office, local authority associations, local education authorities: III: from the short-term.*
(d) A study of the practical difficulties facing adult students, particularly those wanting to study part-time, to indicate how the existing structure of educational provision can be adjusted to overcome these difficulties. *Department of Education and Science, Welsh Office: I: within the short-term.*
(e) Positive support for educational release from work for those

working unconventional hours. *Employers, all institutions: from the short-term.*

(f) Development of modular courses. *All institutions: II: from the immediate future.*

(g) The provision of a national information service on credit transfer, as currently being examined by the Department of Education and Science, and development of operational arrangements for transferability of credit. *Department of Education and Science, Welsh Office: II: from the short-term.*

These developments within existing provision could be complemented by the exploitation of new technologies to provide new opportunities:

1. Open access systems, including both distance learning and independent learning, could be among the most important educational innovations in the next 20 years; the growth of independent study facilities and self-help groups should therefore be encouraged. These developments should be assisted through the setting up of centres for independent learning within established institutions, and consortia, or a national body, to provide centrally produced materials and ensure compatible systems and standardisation of equipment; and through the sponsorship of experimental studies and national assessment and support. *Department of Education and Science, Welsh Office, Council for Educational Technology, selected institutions, broadcasters, public libraries: III: from the short-term.*

2. Broadcasting has already proved to be a highly effective element in distance learning, but greater use should now be made of general broadcasting for educational purposes. Access to 'prime time' for educational broadcasting will remain very important, and the educational opportunities shortly to be available through the Fourth Channel, and through all the new video facilities for learning, should be exploited. *Broadcasters, all institutions: from the immediate future.*

3. The wider exploitation of educational opportunities through broadcasting and the new video technologies will continue to be limited by the strict limitations on recording under present copyright legislation. There should be new legislation to clarify the copyright position in favour of individual learners. *Department of Trade, Home Office, Department of Education and Science, Welsh Office: within the short-term.*

Financial Provision for Institutions

Decisions about the public funds to be allocated to continuing education should rank as of equal importance with decisions on the allocation of resources to the initial education sector. However, the increasingly tight limits placed on public expenditure over recent years need not prevent some developments in continuing education and, if there is increased public funding in the future, further developments will be possible. It is also therefore still appropriate to explore alternative methods of financing institutions for the provision of continuing education. Serious attention should be given to alternative financing arrangements in the form of collective funding, where there are various possible methods of collection — payroll tax, profits tax, insurance fund — but where the common object is to collect revenue from disparate sources for distribution to achieve agreed educational priorities. Thus, for example, it would be possible to allocate collective funding through the setting up of a 'continuing education fund' to allocate resources through a statutorily constituted board in accordance with predefined regulations and agreed purposes, to provide special assistance in the growth of continuing education. Studies are therefore required, and working examples of collective funding in other countries could be examined, to identify the most effective alternative means of complementing or revising the present system of financing institutions, with the object of encouraging the development of continuing education and training. *Treasury, Department of Education and Science, Welsh Office: from the short to medium-term.*

The link between financial provision for institutions and financial support for learners is the system of fees charged to students. There are four possible fee policies which could be operated, which we have summarised as: education should be free at the point of take-up; fees should be charged to meet some part of the cost of provision; fees should be charged to meet the full cost of provision; and fees should be charged according to a multiple pricing policy. In so far as this country has a national policy on fees, it is based on multiple pricing. That policy should be maintained, but more attention should be given to establishing principles about who should pay for what, if any, proportion of the costs of provision. Those principles should be related to broad categories of provision, for example, basic and post-basic education — no fees, and up-dating of knowledge and skills — approaching full cost fees. In addition to this formulation of a general policy, local education authorities should allow institutions, particularly adult education centres, some freedom in fixing fees, fees should be payable in instalments, there should be concessions for those on low incomes, and enrolment should be free for those who would otherwise suffer undue financial hardship or be debarred by reason of low income. *Local authority associations, local education authorities, and all institutions: from the immediate future.*

Financial Support for Learners

Educational opportunities beyond the age of compulsory schooling should be open to all without undue financial hardship, but lack of adequate financial means continues to be a major barrier to adults' access to education. It must be questioned whether the present methods of financing learners will enable the wider access of adults to continuing education over the next 20 years. It is therefore important that the present grants system should be modified and extended and that the feasibility of alternative systems of financial support should be examined.

The mandatory grants system should be extended to cover part-time and short full-time courses, for distance learning as well as face-to-face tuition, so as to enable adults to continue their education without undue financial hardship. Courses designated for mandatory grants should be categorised at three levels — basic, non-advanced and higher — and receipt of an award at one level should not affect subsequent eligibility for an award at a higher level. *Department of Education and Science, Welsh Office: III: over the short to medium-term.*

Attention should be given to the appropriate extension of paid educational leave in accordance with the ILO Convention 140, to which the United Kingdom government is a signatory. This might be seen as the first step towards a more extensive form of educational entitlement, since paid educational leave must by definition be confined to those in employment. The development of paid educational leave is most likely to be obtained through collective bargaining, which will lead to lack of uniformity. This could be minimised by enabling legislation to provide a general code of practice for the granting of paid education leave. *Department of Employment, Department of Education and Science, employers' associations, employers, Trades Union Congress, trades unions: IV: over the short to medium-term.*

The introduction of a system of entitlements to education would be a major advance in educational provision and would lay the foundations of an educational system capable of responding rapidly and effectively to changing needs. A system of entitlements should be regarded as the longer-term goal, which requires detailed studies of the various possible methods of collecting and allocating the required funds, including educational insurance, negative income tax, and student loans and mortgages. The Council therefore proposes to undertake studies of the feasibility of educational entitlement systems so as to provide an informed basis for discussion and subsequent policy decisions about the phased introduction of an entitlement system. *Treasury, Department of Education and Science, Welsh Office: IV: from medium to long-term.*

Staffing and Training

With at least 200,000 full-time, part-time and volunteer teaching staff at present employed in the post-school sector in England and Wales, the development of continuing education need not call for greatly increased numbers of staff, but it will require some redeployment of existing staff and the use of new skills. Concentration on quality through training and staff development will therefore be as important as maintaining the present staffing numbers in the post-school sector. Educators should continue their own education. There will also need to be greater flexibility in the use of staff time both inside and outside the conventional hours of full-time teaching, which will call for new forms of employment contracts for full-time staff and wider deployment of part-time staff and volunteers.

(1) There should be a continuing increase in the quantity and quality of training and retraining opportunities for full-time and part-time staff in the understanding and skills needed for the education and training of adult learners. This should be encouraged by the Advisory Committee on the Supply and Education of Teachers, and a National Forum on the training of further education staff should be established along the lines advocated by the Advisory Committee on the Supply and Training of Teachers. *Department of Education and Science,*

Welsh Office, local education authorities, all institutions: II: from the immediate future.
(2) There should be appropriate changes in the contracts of both full and part-time staff to permit more flexible hours of work, including evenings, week-ends and the conventional academic holiday periods. *Department of Education and Science, local authority associations, local education authorities: from the immediate future.*
(3) There should be more research about adult learners and in adult learning, an understanding of which should be central to the training and the knowledge and skills of staff engaged in continuing education. *Universities, polytechnics and other selected institutions: II: from the immediate future.*
(4) Some full-time staff should be given, and trained for, specific responsibility for staff training and development within their institutions. *All institutions: from the immediate future.*

Legislation

The necessary national lead for the development of continuing education should be made manifest in legislation:

(a) Sections 41 and 42 of the 1944 Education Act should be reformulated with the needs of adults as well as of young people in mind. The existing sections 41(a) and 41(b) should be amalgamated and the proviso to sections 41 and 42 deleted. The reformulated section 41 should contain a comprehensive definition of continuing education, and should make explicit the duty of local education authorities to secure a varied and balanced provision in their area to meet the needs of people of all ages in the community. The reformulated section 42 should make explicit the duties of local education authorities in regard to provision for further and continuing education including the establishment of: information, advisory and counselling services for adults; regular training for staff; networks of local centres of continuing education; and consultative structures and financial and other support for continuing education bodies in their area. *Department of Education and Science, Welsh Office: in the short-term.*
(b) Pending these statutory amendments, new regulations or memoranda of guidance should be issued by the Department of Education and Science and the Welsh Office, which will give due

regard to the educational needs of adults, will counteract the current interpretation of section 41 and its negative effects on educational opportunities for adults, and will set out the duties of local education authorities to secure a varied and balanced educational provision to meet the needs of adults. *Department of Education and Science, Welsh Office: in the immediate future.*

These priorities for action show that much can be done in the next few years at relatively small additional cost to achieve a significant shift towards a continuing education system. Changes in organisational arrangements, accompanied by detailed studies for more substantial developments, will encourage an increasing awareness of the actual and potential value of continuing education, with consequent shifts in the opinions and attitudes of political and educational decision makers and the general public. We believe that this widening appreciation of the need for, and the benefits of, continuing education will lead to an acceptance of the validity of our proposals, including those with substantial funding implications, and to their implementation through the provision of additional funds.

It may well not be possible to build, even in the next 20 years, a complete structure of educational provision capable of accommodating, within the available economic resources and social priorities of the day, all the educational needs of the adult population throughout life. But we must start now to lay the foundations by finding ways to encourage many more adults to enter education, remove the barriers to their entry, and improve the coverage and responsiveness of educational provision. When the measures proposed in this report are implemented, this country will have achieved the basis of a comprehensive system of continuing education throughout life.

The Council is in no doubt that such a system of continuing education is needed. Our education and training system must be developed and become fully accessible to the adult population, who will gain personally from its provision and become still more active and effective contributors to the country's social, economic and cultural wellbeing. It is now time for the comprehensive view of the future for continuing education and training, put forward in this report, to be transformed from policies to practice to the benefit of every adult in the country.

6.2

EDUCATION FOR THE POST-INDUSTRIAL SOCIETY

Ritchie Calder

Source: Neil Costello and Michael Richardson (eds.), *Continuing Education For the Post-Industrial Society* (Open University Press, 1982), pp. 11-21.

We know what we mean when we talk about moving from an agricultural society to an industrial society. In this country we have been through that historical process and can analyse it. We can go back to the Enclosures Acts, which expropriated the free grazing lands and drove the landless subsistence farmers into the towns to become the wage-slaves of the Industrial Revolution. We can quantify it in relative terms today by recognising that less than 5 per cent of Britain's work-force is now employed on the land. Farming itself became industrialised. The industrial processes replaced the traditional crafts. But the machines did not reduce arduous labour; they increased it. The machinery cost money and had to be kept moving to justify the outlay and maximise the profits. That meant long working hours and shift work. Labour — indeed life — was cheap and leisure in short supply. But industrialisation multiplied material goods for domestic consumption and for export. The be-all and the end-all of industrialisation was production. The quality of life was ignored. 'Where there's muck there's brass' was a boast, not a reproach.

Throughout the nineteenth century, Britain was the wealthiest, most powerful country on earth and those offshore islands controlled an Empire covering a third of the map.

Out of the political struggles to redress the social cost and redeem our public squalor, the private profits of this prosperity were with difficulty tapped for public services. After 200 years of industrialisation we have the Welfare State in which the basic human needs are safeguarded. That is the climax of our industrial society. But, as we are so vociferously reminded, that and much more depends on maintaining and increasing industrial productivity, and we are constantly told that we are falling behind our competitors. It is called 'The British Sickness', the lethargy of the layabouts.

Bernard Rossiter, an American economist who is London correspondent of *The Washington Post*, offers a more sympathetic diagnosis and a more encouraging prognosis — as you can gather from the title of his recent book *Britain A Future That Works* published by André Deutsch. His conclusion is that Britain is not sick but a more or less affluent society. It will grow less slowly than other industrial countries and this trend — richer, but less rich than some other countries — will continue. His diagnosis of the *malaise* is shrewd.

> The preference for leisure over goods applies chiefly to those toiling in the mines or on the assembly lines, labouring at routine tasks in huge white collar bureaucracies, public and private. Their work does not, cannot, enlarge personality; quite the contrary; it diminishes it. They work because they must to earn enough to support themselves and their families. It is the workers who have decided that there are limits to how long and how hard they will labour for extra goods. *Britons, in short, appear to be the first citizens of the post-industrial age, who are choosing leisure over goods on a large scale.*
>
> Why this preference should appear in Britain before any other industrial country is not clear. It may prove as hard to answer as that perennial exam question 'Why did the Industrial Revolution first come to Britain?' Perhaps the two are related.

I think they are. We have worked our way through the Industrial Era to the Post-Industrial Society. We cannot clearly see or define it because we are part of the process. We are like tourists without a guide book and without a language. Certainly I can attest to the latter. Judging by the many and weighty debates in the House of Lords with learned economists, successful business men and practised politicians taking part, we are talking an archaic language and the gobbledegook of discredited text-books. Of course they mention things like silicon chips in passing but without a glimmer of their portentous significance. The logical meaning of silicon chips and of the computers and cybernetic techniques which they sublimate is that, in terms of productivity, they make human labour redundant. In terms of 'efficiency', that hallowed word of the board rooms, human operators are not only superfluous; they are a positive obstacle. We are going through a painful transition.

The sobering truth is that *Homo faber*, Man the Maker, has confounded his *alter ego, Homo sapiens,* Thinking Man. Ingenuity in creating things has exceeded the capacity to manage them. Our political, social and economic institutions are inadequate. We discover the innermost Secret of Matter and we release it from the nucleus as an apocalyptic bomb, for the military, political and psychological consequences of which, 34 years later, we have found no reassurances. We discover the code of the Secret of Life in the molecule of DNA and acquire the capacity, through genetic engineering, to change the nature of living things, including Man himself. But who will write the prescription for posterity? Or more important, how can we prevent it being written? We have broken the gravitational forces of the Earth and have landed on the Moon but the nation which accomplished this is queuing up at gas stations. The electronic senses have not only reproduced but have excelled the human senses. The microphone is more tireless and more precise than the human ear. The photoelectric cell is more tireless and more precise than the human eye, and far more sensitive than the human touch are machines which can operate to precisions of a millionth of an inch. Those artificial senses, as the Space Programme has shown, can reach out their nerve endings to the planets, survey and chemically sample the surface of Mars or Venus or Jupiter and televector their findings back to earth. But we cannot get our mail delivered. The computer has become a misnomer. It is not just a glorified abacus, albeit doing in split seconds calculations which would have taken a Senior Wrangler with pencil and paper a life-time to figure out. It is now capable of simulating the logical and analytical faculties of the human brain, and cybernetics, the feed-back responses of the central nervous system. A computer can be equipped with a prodigious memory so that today with silicon chips and microprocessors we could store all the knowledge of all the libraries of all the world in a casket no bigger than the human cranium.

Far short of ultimate automation, the modern industrial workers, with a flick of a switch, can summon electron slaves to do prodigies of work no human being would attempt. The better-off housewife has in her gadgets more servants than *Upstairs, Downstairs* could muster. In his machine-shed, today's farmer has more slaves than were ever the property of the plantation owner. The owner of a modest motor car has a hundred horses harnessed under the bonnet.

The process of automation in the production of goods is irreversible. Human beings have to conceive the machines and, with the refinements of technology, construct them and maintain them.

Ideally, they have to remove the risk of human error and the way to do that is to remove the human beings who could make that error. A human being is a stutter or a stammer in the production process [...]

The Machine can efficiently produce our material needs but there is a catch in it. It is epitomised in the famous exchange between the President of General Motors, Charles Wilson, and the head of the Autoworkers Union, Walter Reuther. In a pay-bargaining row, Wilson threatened to automate the entire production. 'And', he warned, 'electrons don't pay union dues'. 'No', said Reuther, 'but will the electrons buy your automobiles?'

That is the present quandary: purchasing power depends on earnings and earnings depend upon work. But what is 'work'? What are the imperatives and what are the incentives?

The work ethic, that hallowed virtue, we are told dates back to Eden when Adam delved and Eve span for sheer subsistence. Its modern version, productivity, or surplus creation, dates back to Cain and Abel when Cain, the settled tiller, killed Abel the nomad, and the pastoral life of the food-gatherer. The husbandman with his food crops and his domesticated animals could produce beyond family subsistence. The farm surplus became the basic commodity of trade. The tiller could acquire his special needs — better tools than he could make himself, better pots, better baskets, better fabrics and luxuries which became necessities. These were custom-made by specialists; craft workers who in turn produced their own kinds of surpluses. The settled farmers, to appease their gods, supplied the tithe-barns of the temples and maintained the priesthood and its clerks. Surpluses of food and artisan artefacts went into trade not only within a community where barter could work reasonably well, but also with other communities where it was more awkward. So merchants came into being and merchant bankers, converting barter into money exchanges. And money became itself a commodity. Cities grew wealthy and attracted envious marauders. So there were armies and warrior kings. Wars and conquest provided slaves to do the muscle-labour.

In the age of the Greeks, the divisions of work were clear. Slaves provided muscle-labour. Craftsmen contributed their skills and philosophers had leisure to think. Plato made the distinction clear when he upbraided Eudoxus and Archytus when by unseemly recourse to instruments they solved problems which philosophers regarded as impossible. He accused them of 'making use of matter which requires much manual labour and is the object of servile trades'. Whatever Plato worked at it certainly had nothing to do with productivity.

Ever since the invention of the lever, the wheel and the pulley, Man's ingenuity has been directed to the reduction of muscle-effort. The Industrial Revolution was a mechanical revolution which mechanised craft-skills into mass-production techniques. But it did not increase leisure for the working classes; it increased productivity. Today machines, apart from the muscle-functions, have taken over other human functions and rendered acquired skills obsolete. Every innovation which changes the nature of work threatens somebody's livelihood. It is only natural for a human personality to resent being rejected — jilted for a machine. And that is the ongoing struggle between the skilled unions and the new technology which micro-processing can only intensify. Electrons are more efficient but will they pay the grocer's bills?

What we need is a non-work ethic. It is heretical but it is logical. If productivity is the aim and machines are more efficient in achieving it, we have to revise our meaning of 'work'. If, as we are told, the GNP is what matters and the product is better supplied and increased by The Machine, what is the role of the human being and what is his entitlement to a share of the product?

I use the term 'non-work' deliberately. It comprises retirement, redundancy, unemployment, a shorter working week, a shorter working day, longer holidays with pay. It is not slothfulness, that deadly sin in terms of the work ethic. It removes the stigma which has become attached to compulsory idleness — unemployment — giving the victim robbed of the use of his skills a demoralising sense of inadequacy. It is what is usually called 'leisure', doing what one wants to do, which might be personally productive (like do-it-yourself) or creative, like inventing or painting, or writing, or music or physical recreation.

We all think we work and some of us think we are overworked. But obviously 'work' means different things applied to different people. The Queen is hard-working. The Cabinet Minister, taking his dispatch-box home at the end of a crowded day, is working overtime. The director, taking a client out to lunch or for a game of golf, is working. His personal secretary, filing his papers, keeping his diary and stalling importunates, is working. So is the copy-typist tran-scribing his disembodied voice. The financier on the phone to Zurich is working. The manager, making duodenal-ulcer decisions, is working. But the craftsman's work is something different from the process worker's; the teacher's from the research worker's; the doctor's and nurse's from the actor's or the fashion-model's; the spider-man's on a high-rise, the miner's in a pit. And so on.

Work was something which used to end when the ploughman homeward plodded his weary way. Now it ends in a traffic jam, in a commuter train or strap-hanging in a tube.

Work used to be, at worst, drudgery or, at best, job satisfaction — the craftsman's sense of self-merit in handling his own creation. Indeed, if there is real job satisfaction it is not really 'work', it is a kind of self-indulgence, nothing to do with clocking-on and clocking-off, or differentials or productivity agreements, like the writer burning the midnight oil or the research worker ignoring the night-watchman.

But what about non-work? If The Machine, in the ultimate refinements of microprocessing and computerised management, can produce what we need more efficiently how are we as individuals going to come to terms with what Daniel Bell has called 'post-industrial culture'?

John Maynard Keynes foresaw it in 1930 in an essay 'Economic Possibilities for our Grandchildren'. As he put it:

> The economic problem, the struggle for subsistence, always has been hitherto the primary, most pressing problem of the human race. If the economic problem is solved, mankind will be deprived of its traditional purpose.
>
> Will this be of benefit? If one believes at all in the real values of life, the prospect at least offers the possibility of benefit. Yet I think with dread of the readjustment of habits and instincts of the ordinary man, bred into him for countless generations, which he may be asked to discard within a few decades ... Thus for the first time since his creation, man will be faced with his real permanent problem — how to use his freedom from pressing economic cares, how to occupy his leisure, which science and compound interest will have won for him, to live wisely and agreeably and well.

Julian Huxley put it another way: 'Beyond the Welfare State, the Fulfilment State in which the individual, his basic needs taken care of, will be free to develop his own personality and his talents.'

He saw, of course, that the average person would be a bit lost and that there would have to be social investment in education and facilities to foster the talents. But what would be the effects on individuals and society when not only basic needs but machine-produced affluence were available without the galley-whip of work?

One gets no reassurance from Freud who was hooked on the work-ethic:

Laying stress upon the importance of work has a greater effect than any other technique of living in the direction of binding the individual more closely to reality. In his work he is at least securely attached to a part of reality, the human community. And yet the great majority work only when forced by necessity and this natural aversion gives rise to the most difficult social problems. (*Civilization and its Discontents*)

Britain, not without difficulties, has spliced together the raft of the Welfare State so that from the womb to the tomb everyone has available social security and social services. The community has thus provided the basic needs of the lowest paid workers and the unemployed, the aged and the handicapped. From Freud's 'great majority with an aversion to work' the sanction of subsistence has been removed but it is this 'great majority' who still contribute to the GNP which makes the Welfare State possible. The standard of living of even the lowest brackets is many times higher than it was a generation ago; luxuries, like cars and television, have become necessities for the average family. Technology devised by brain-workers and machines still made by skilled workers with a lot of help from technology itself can maintain or increase that mass-consumption. It can do it by managerial and technological efficiency with a diminishing work-force.

We have the harbingers already. When the power shortage compelled a three-day week, the pundits were surprised that production did not seriously drop. Jack Jones, as General Secretary of the Transport and General Workers Union, suggested a shorter working week as a relief from unemployment, redistributing the work available. Prime Minister Callaghan gave a four-day week his blessing for the same purpose. Unions wanted earlier retirement age and longer holidays with pay. Cynics said it was a device to get a guaranteed weekly wage as a basis for overtime or for moonlighting and that the unemployment situation would not be significantly improved. But the idea of planned non-work was not dismissed as preposterous.

If we take the working year as about 1,900 working hours we could cut it to 1,100 working hours. We could have a $7\frac{1}{2}$-hour day; a 4-day working week; 39 working weeks a year; 10 bank holidays; 3-day weekends and 13 weeks vacation a year. Thus one would spend 40 per cent of one's days on a vocation (working for the GNP); 40 per cent of one's days on avocation (doing one's thing); and 20 per cent on vacation (just relaxing). And meanwhile The Machine would be carrying on and having a chance to demonstrate its efficiency.

This, in the days of microprocessors and computerised machine supervision and control, is not the frolic it sounds; it is well within the bounds of feasibility.

As in the days of Ancient Greece, when they had human slaves instead of slave electrons to do the work, we can choose to be either epicureans or stoics. As the first, we can opt for self-indulgence and 'cultivate our gardens and our friends'. In the second, we can seek virtue in our duty to our fellow men and in service to good causes; we can choose the active, and not the contemplative life.

One thing is painfully clear: our educational preparedness is pretty inadequate. Our young people leaving school are entering the uncertainties of the transition to the post-industrial society. They want to get jobs; they want to have careers; they want to marry and get homes and, in turn, to create a meaningful life for their children. They might or might not have got as far as 'O' levels; they might have gone on to technical colleges or to polytechnics or to universities. They might have acquired paper qualifications but to what careers will these provide the openings? Some may be potential Nobel Prizewinners looking for facilities to fit their inspirations. Some will be looking for academic careers in universities which are being constrained to practise austerity. Some will be taking their degrees and high qualifications into the growth areas of energy. Some will be going into the developments from our oil windfall in the North Sea. Some of them will go into the activities which are generating the possibilities and problems of the microprocessors. They will be creating the machines which will be doing jobs that in traditional industries would have meant paid employment for hundreds of thousands of their contemporaries.

What is going to happen to the school-leavers who every year swell the unemployment figures? It is apparent, to me at least, that whatever jobs they are trained for will change in character at least half a dozen times in the next quarter of a century. How do you produce that versatility? Only by helping them to understand not only the 'How' but the 'Why' of what they are doing. What used to be a radio mechanic wiring up a birdcage of circuits has now to become not only an electronic engineer but a solid-state physicist in order to cope with the developments.

Our educational system has to take this need for versatility into account not by producing specialists at an immature age but by broadening the natural curiosity of pupils so that they are sensitised to new ideas and given the capacity to recognise their own talents. [...]

The education and training (and I make a meaningful distinction between the two) for the oncoming generations of the post-industrial society must become a present concern to ensure a viable pattern of living, social and economic. Naturally, that education does not end with school. It is an ongoing process which if neglected produces an impoverishment of the spirit which is more serious than a depleted wage packet.

Now that ongoing education has become all the more important because people must develop innate resources to cope with the surfeit of non-work which has come or will be coming to them. We reached out for it in the past. Even in the struggle for existence, workers had a craving for what they had been denied, seeking enlightenment, lighting the lamps in their own minds, kindling the flames of their own interests.

That was in the Industrial Era. In the post-industrial society we have again set the world an example — the Open University. When Rossiter is looking for his markers for Britain's entry into the post-industrial society he will find that one of them was the Open University. As Britain pioneered the Welfare State with the National Health Service so we pioneered the Fulfilment State ten years ago.

6.3

THE FUTURE OF ADULT EDUCATION WORLDWIDE

John Lowe

Source: Copyright © The Open University 1983 (specially written for this volume).

Introduction

To discuss trends and prospects in adult education within a world-wide context might seem presumptuous but there is a valid reason for it. Education in general and adult education as a distinctive sector thereof is one social institution that has evolved since the Second World War under the influence of public aspirations and pressures that are common to virtually all countries. At the most recent world conference on adult education, held at Tokyo in 1972, delegates from capitalist and socialist countries, from advanced industrialised and less developed countries, from the Northern and Southern hemispheres, experienced no great difficulty in understanding one another's aims and problems and shared a common terminology. In the words of the book commissioned by Unesco to commemorate the Conference:

> This mutual understanding might partly be attributed to the high percentage of adult education specialists who were present. The same explanation cannot be invoked to explain why at the Tokyo Conference the Director-General of Unesco could justly claim in his concluding address that the delegates belonged to 'the same intellectual universe', for the majority of them were politicians and administrators, generalists rather than specialists. The explanation lay instead in the rapidity with which information about educational practice in general has spread from country to country, so that to a considerable degree many ideas, experiences, problems and aspirations are shared in common.[1]

In this paper it is proposed to consider the most important trends and

300

to reflect on the prospects for adult education as mankind approaches the beginning of the third millennium.

Changing and Expanding Functions

Growing national importance is attached to adult education as an essential social service in the modern world, especially in the less developed countries (LDCs). Most governments have sharply increased their support for it, though still to only a small extent by comparison with the support given to other sectors of education. In many countries public co-ordinating bodies and national working parties or committees have been set up to examine the strengths and weaknesses of the existing provision and to make recommendations for its expansion. The awakening of interest in adult education is due to the fact that social, economic, political and ecological changes, accelerated by the impact of technology, have led policy-makers, together with many employers and community leaders, to the conclusion that life in the modern world for the great majority of people is intolerable without the appropriate knowledge, skills and attitudes to cope with it. In the new rhetoric education is seen as 'necessary and life long', just as the authors of the British 1919 Report[2] had desired. Education of the young is no longer considered a once and for all preparation for life. The education of adults is perceived as a powerful instrument of innovation and adaptation, not as a frill but as a contemporary imperative.

In LDCs, governments give priority to economic development and national integration and are concerned about the contribution which adult education can make to the overall process of nation-building. Since national resources are scarce, they can hardly afford to finance adult education programmes except in so far as they are relevant to national development plans for increased economic production. Given the shortage of skilled manpower, the adult population must be trained to become more productive. In drawing up schemes for economic development, in building reservoirs or locating factories, it has become vital to take into account the size and quality of the workforce that will be required. But nation-building does not depend on economic progress alone; it also necessitates the formation of informed, articulate and active citizens and the creation of new institutions. In countries bedevilled by ethnic, tribal and linguistic divisions, there is the additional need to consolidate national unity.

Against the current background of economic recession and rising unemployment rates all governments have been obliged to select their priorities. Should preference be given to élite or under-privileged groups? Should rural areas be given preference over urban areas? Should support be restricted to specific types of programmes? The very process of raising such questions and trying to seek rational answers has proved to be of benefit to adult education in two ways: (a) it has made at least some economic and social planners aware of the untapped productive capacity of the adult population; (b) it has led some LDCs to look at adult education as a key factor in national growth. One very striking illustration has been the switch of emphasis in LDCs from general literacy to functional literacy programmes that fit in with overall development plans, and entail focusing upon local areas and economic sectors which have high development potential.

Most of the LDCs are currently particularly concerned about the impoverishment of rural areas and the urgent need for agrarian reform. Even though masses of people, especially the young, crowd into urban areas, the majority continue to live in small villages and isolated homesteads. Agencies administering international aid, such as the World Bank, now also treat rural development as the key objective. Though the chief justification is to alleviate the effects of under-nourishment and disease by raising rural incomes, it is notice-able that many countries which strove to achieve rapid industrialisa-tion are now persuaded that national prosperity depends first and foremost upon the maximum utilisation of land resources and on the generation of capital surpluses for investment. Given their concern to harness adult education to developmental goals, governments in LDCs are far more interventionist than governments in advanced industrialised countries (AICs). Some of them control every aspect of adult education.

Educating adults as a means of dealing with collective local and national problems is, however, shared by the LDCs and AICs. The bad effects of material progress — poverty amidst plenty, urban decay, intensified racial conflicts, loneliness, alienation, vandalism, drug-taking — have caused some governments and many communi-ties to turn to adult education instruments as a means of combating them. The blame for social disorder has been ascribed to a lack of sound planning and the inadequacy of existing educational provision. The most constructive solution has been to apply the community development principle, stimulating people to tackle their social problems through political and co-operative action. Thus, a new function for adult education in community action has been indicated. Programme planners seek to identify the problems besetting their communities with a view to devising courses and projects that may help to solve them.

Adult education programmes were traditionally designed to give the individual the opportunity to study the formal curriculum of the schools and the universities. More recently, there has been a move towards the construction of programmes directly corresponding to the different needs of adults at different stages in their lives, giving them the knowledge which will enable them to make rational decisions and the skills which will enable them to adapt efficiently to their changing roles.

Adult education is not regarded as a national priority in the AICs. Not merely is it a minor or non-existent factor in economic or, for that matter, social planning, it is commonly a conspicuously marginal sector of national education systems. Such stress as exists is on continuing formal education and on vocational training, most of which takes place under the aegis of government departments other than education ministries and at the workplace. Nevertheless, the position of education is generally much stronger than it was.

A Broad Definition of Adult Education

The old and divisive antithesis between vocational and liberal education which used to bedevil international meetings on adult education is almost a dead letter now. Unfortunately, however, while leading adult educators have arrived at a broader definition of adult education and classified its wide-ranging activities, confusion about its scope and functions still reigns in the minds of others. In several countries the tendency persists of equating adult education with a particular programme, such as literacy or vocational training or evening secondary schools. Some government officials, not least in ministries of education, are also vague about what adult education constitutes. The continuing use of a variety of terms to describe its realm of concern, for example, *social education and further education*, leads to misunderstandings. Some authorities distinguish between education geared to qualifications and so-called 'non-formal' education.

Many adult educators argue optimistically that the whole problem of definition and terminology will evaporate once the idea of life-long learning has been universally adopted. But that is still a distant prospect.

Rationalising Resources and Legislation

In the past, the provision of adult education was most uneven across regions and countries. Today it is more evenly, though still far from equitably, distributed thanks to two reasons: first, the statutory assumption of responsibility, or of greater responsibility than in the past, by public authorities at national and local levels; secondly, better arrangements by providing agencies to co-ordinate their activities.

When the public authorities assume responsibility for adult education they are obliged to take account of the scale and distribution of the existing provision and ask which groups of the population are being served and which are being neglected. Since the Second World War many national authorities, having taken stock of the situation, have expanded and rationalised the public service. In doing so they have been aided by the increasing administrative competence of providing agencies and their willingness to collaborate in offering wide-ranging programmes. Measures taken by national authorities have included the clarification of policies and the setting of planning goals, the enactment of enabling laws, the creation of co-ordinating machinery and new sources of financing, investment in buildings and equipment and staff development.

Systematic planning of adult education has been largely associated with the LDCs, whereas in the AICs there is sometimes no mention of adult education even in general educational legislation. Most countries, however, have not gone beyond enunciating a policy for adult education, usually couched in general terms and lacking any mandatory force. Only a few have enacted laws specifying that adult education shall be provided under prescribed conditions. Two areas have significantly benefited from binding legislation — literacy and vocational training. In some countries, illiterates are entitled to attend literacy classes during normal working hours. In others, the law guarantees those in employment the right to paid educational leave under certain conditions. It is also to be noted that in a growing number of countries the law requires that all educational buildings, and sometimes other public buildings, should be put at the disposal of adults outside normal working hours.

The General Assembly of Unesco recognised the necessity for official backing and material support in its recent 'Recommendation', which calls upon every member state to remedy the prevailing penury of provision.[3] New structures and goals should be developed, the fundamental object being to define and then cater as broadly as possible for adult needs, aptitudes and problems. In most countries this very wide policy objective would imply seriously rethinking and reorganising the existing financial and legal framework. Thereafter constant and close evaluation of the changes introduced would be essential. To ensure appropriate programming it would be necessary to bring about effective collaboration between national and local government in consultation with all those bodies and representative associations, whether privately or publicly funded, which might be concerned. In planning and conducting programmes, maximum advantage should be taken of the ability of adults to apply their own knowledge, skills and experience to facilitate fruitful interaction between the classroom and the outside world.

It goes without saying that implementing new policies is more easily said than done. To create a framework so well conceived that it can respond in practice to a vast range of adult needs, be suitably integrated into the general system of educational provision, and still count on adequate legal and financial support is certainly no mean ambition.

The co-ordination of adult education provision at national and local levels is, however, becoming more common. At the national level, co-ordination by the public authorities is sometimes assured by a statutory board, as in Kenya, or by an advisory body. In most countries the leading adult education agencies have formed national associations, the influence of which over both public policy and practice in the field varies, but an increasing number of them are becoming more powerful as they acquire greater resources and master information and public relations skills.

Experienced adult educators aver that, from a pragmatic standpoint, local co-ordination is much more important than national co-ordination. Local co-ordinating machinery is often totally lacking or less efficacious than that at the national level. It is surely significant that, whenever a local education authority takes on responsibility for co-ordination, the rate of participation in programmes usually rises.

The Financing Factor

By what means and on what scale adult education is financed is obviously crucial for its stability and development. Yet the financing factor remains a territory largely unexplored by practitioners and researchers. They cannot fail to be aware, of course, that adult education is the least supported sector of education and the one most vulnerable to cuts in times of economic recession. Only in those few countries where private agencies flourish, most notably in the United States, is the aggregate expenditure on adult education at a high level. Even then, the greater part of the expenditure is incurred by industrial and commercial firms on occupational training. Adult education provision can be maintained at an adequate level only by attracting a fixed annual percentage of the gross national expenditure on education.

In the current worldwide economic recession, a few governments have decided to maintain educational expenditure at its present level in real terms, but the majority have reduced or propose to reduce it. It is noticeable that most countries wish particularly to cut back their expenditure on post-secondary education. Words like 'efficiency', measured in terms of output, are being invoked in connection with the universities. Many countries, genuinely alarmed at the phenomenon of graduate unemployment, have put a ceiling on entry to those disciplines which seem to offer a narrowing or closed exit into the labour market. In theory, this might be countered by the expansion of recurrent education provision. The reality is, however, that despite the lip-service paid to recurrent education, most politicians and educational policy-makers still adhere to a 'front-loaded model' of education. They are not disposed to invest in adult education.

From the student's point of view, there is a case for charging those in employment more than others and for having differential fee structures. The difficulty is that, whereas in a few countries there is a tradition of adults paying their own way, as in North America, in most countries adult education is either free or subsidised. If the pressures to introduce Paid Educational Leave schemes continue, it may be that in the course of time governments or employers will be prepared to subsidise adults to attend both full-time and part-time courses to a greater extent. Consideration might also be given, at least for post-secondary courses, to the possibility of introducing voucher systems, so that adults could choose which kind of institution they wish to attend. One danger is that many governments might decide that part-time study is to be preferred to full-time study simply because it is supposedly cheaper to provide.

Staffing, Research and Development

Historically, adult education services were planned and organised very largely by part-time administrators, the great majority of whom were unpaid volunteers. In many countries part-time and voluntary workers still constitute the majority of staff. Nevertheless, the percentage of full-time staff is on the increase, especially in the LDCs and in those AICs where public provision is rapidly expanding. Simultaneously, the qualifications and functions of adult educators are being more precisely defined, and the growing body of professionals is trying to exert influence on policy-makers and the general public, often with some success. In most communities a positive correlation exists between the number of administrators and organisers employed and the volume of activity.

The increase in full-time staff has led to a demand for pre-professional and in-service training. Adult education departments have been created in many universities and they typically offer diploma and degree level courses. Professional conferences, workshops, seminars and training courses are organised in ever-increasing numbers by these and a variety of other agencies.

Research in adult education still looks weak alongside research in education in general. None the less, there has been a surge in research output since about 1970 which would appear due to three causes: (a) the professionalising process which has led some practitioners to wish to define and develop adult education as a discrete field of knowledge; (b) a limited but increasing demand for information about the extent and impact of programmes by the public authorities and educational foundations; (c) independent initiatives by scholars attracted to what appears an unresearched phenomenon. Most of the research is undertaken by university faculties. A growing interest in comparative studies in adult education is of particular interest.

Attitudes and Participation

There is currently a measure of disenchantment with education as an intrinsic material good. It is no longer seen as the Mecca it was in the 1960s and early 1970s. As a result of redistributive incomes policies, many individuals can see no advantage in pursuing their education, or are more conscious than heretofore of the earnings they will forego by devoting time to study. Thus, if governments decide to introduce cuts in adult education, they do not have to fear a loud public outcry. This means, in turn, that adult education institutions have to be constantly at pains to preserve an attractive image.

It is still reasonable, however, to predict that the demand for adult education will increase, but the market is not limitless. The majority of adults in most countries will participate, at best, only fitfully in programmes. But there is plentiful evidence from the experience, for example, of the Open University, the outreach programmes in Sweden, and the mass post-secondary education movement in North America, and to a lesser extent, in Australia, that anywhere between 30 per cent and 50 per cent of the adult population are likely to seek learning opportunities, providing the functions and goals of adult education are interpreted in a broad sense. If countries where the adult participation rate is currently low, or relatively low, were to borrow from the experience of those countries where the rate is high, they would undoubtedly witness a rise in their participation rates.

Yet it would be naïve to anticipate the advent of such well-founded and ubiquitous systems of adult education as would enable any adult to satisfy a learning need whenever he or she so wished. Very few countries could afford to maintain systems of mass adult education. Some selection would nearly always be necessary.

It is hard to make predictions about participation rates in the LDCs. In the AICs, on the other hand, it seems safe to predict rising rates because of participation trends in the formal education system, and changes in the work and leisure relationship. In nearly all the AICs there has been a great increase in the take-up of secondary education within recent years. This has occurred for two reasons. First, there is obviously a genuine individual demand for it. It is notable that girls are showing a particular tendency to stay on and, indeed, in Scandinavia they outnumber boys in upper secondary education. Secondly, there is a strong social demand, which arises mainly from the present high rates of youth unemployment. These not only prick the social conscience, but also raise fears that a really large percentage of disenchanted young people might revolt against the societies that appear to have betrayed them. So there is much talk of youth guarantees and of ensuring that, after compulsory schooling, young people should have the right to three or four years of education or training or both. Much of the concern is, and will continue to be, with vocational training, but there is in addition a new trend which stems from the realisation that young people are most employable on the labour market when they have general knowledge rather than narrow knowledge and general skills rather than narrow ones. The content of vocational courses is therefore becoming more general and liberalised, thereby leaving open the possibility of access to further levels of education. Some countries are now so structuring upper secondary education as to leave open in the vocational branches the possibility of students reverting, at 18 or 19, to a post-secondary institution. At the same time, although they may receive only lip-service in practice, the concepts of equality and social justice are still dominant in the political rhetoric of governments. So long as these concepts are *de rigueur* there will be no relaxing of the pressure to do more for the 16 to 19 year age group. The implication of the expansion of secondary education for adult education is clear. Any increase in the participation rate at one level of education is immediately or very soon followed by a rise in the participation rate at the next level.

The conventional age cohort attending post-secondary institutions has diminished, is diminishing and will diminish more rapidly in the 1980s and 1990s. There may be one or two minor peaks but essentially the trend is downwards. The pressure is accordingly on these institutions to seek a new or, at least, greatly enlarged clientele of adult learners. It can be confidently predicted, therefore, that present education policies of AICs, combined with strong, individual demand for secondary education and a decline in conventional university enrolments will ensure a rising demand for adult and continuing education.

Training, Work and Leisure

However insecure the status of other branches of adult education, there is, in AICs and LDCs alike, an increasing expansion of facilities for continuing education and training linked to the needs of the labour market; if only because governments, employers and trade unions share a common interest in maintaining a high rate of employment and the efficiency and mobility of the work-force, whether on the land, in industry or in the service sector. Indeed, continuing education and training is the only function of adult education universally acknowledged as a priority requiring adequate financing from public funds.

There has been an enormous transfer of workers in all AICs and some LDCs from the primary and manufacturing sectors to the service sector. Fundamental adjustments in the structure of the labour market are taking place which mean that most employees are going to require less knowledge and skill in order to do their jobs, whereas a limited number will require more knowledge and skills. But people will also be obliged to change jobs more often than in the past. The need for retraining will therefore become more, not less important. At the same time, unemployment is likely to be a fact of existence for the foreseeable future, since it is not a temporary but a structural phenomenon. Yet no government that values its political survival can afford to tolerate a high level of unemployment for an indefinite period. Thus, one way or another, governments must devise means of masking its impact and reducing its visibility. One counter-instrument is to adopt an active training policy, which implies that governments will deliberately encourage the development of training or further education, legislate in support of Paid Educational Leave schemes, and urge employers and employees to negotiate contracts guaranteeing workers the right to sabbatical leave, on condition that they undergo some form of education or training. There is also the likelihood that professions will protect and control entry into their ranks by using their own screening system, which may take the form, as in the United States, of licensing, applicable not only to initial entry but to periodic tests of competence to continue in a profession. For example, every five years or so a dentist or an actuary or a lawyer may be obliged to undergo two or three months' training.

All this leads to the conclusion that structural changes in the labour market will lead to a sharp and progressive rise in the demand for training courses of all kinds. This will be reinforced by other labour market factors. There will be shorter working weeks, partly in response to trade union agitation. Trade union negotiators are less exclusively concerned with obtaining higher wages and salaries than with longer holidays and earlier retirement. There is also the prospect of more job-sharing schemes. The upshot of all these developments is bound to be an age of greater leisure. In theory at any rate, more leisure ought to entail a greater demand for adult education.

If adult education is to flourish during the coming decades it appears essential that institutions should offer more open access to opportunities and more flexible systems — more active marketing policies and sophisticated information systems are required. Those centres that have introduced information networks, such as Toronto in Canada, have experienced remarkable success in raising participation rates. Other desiderata are: part-time as opposed to full-time courses, modular courses, credit transfer systems, flexible hours, flexible methods and vacation courses.

Conclusion

Adult education occupies a less marginal position than in the past. In several countries the scale of government support and the rate of public participation are satisfactory. Even so, three major problems continue to cause concern. The first is the reluctance of many governments to treat the education of adults in practice as an integral part of the State's provision for education. Secondly, in the majority of countries, it is those who were most successful in the initial education phase who take most advantage of organised learning opportunities. The problem of how to assist the mass of adults who experienced little or no initial education is currently the dominant concern of adult educators almost everywhere, as witnessed by this declaration:

> Experience shows that the provision of more education in most countries tends to favour most the already well educated; the educationally under-privileged have yet to claim their rights. Adult education is no exception to the rule, for those adults who most need education have been largely neglected — *they are the forgotten people.*[4]

The third problem is the risk of adult education being subjugated more and more to the exigencies of economic productivity. Occupational training will receive every encouragement from the public authorities whereas other activities will be neglected.

Notes

1. J. Lowe, *The Education of Adults: A World Perspective*, 2nd edn. (Unesco, Paris, 1982), p. 14.
2. *Final and Interim Reports of the Adult Education Committee of the Ministry of Reconstruction 1918-1919* (1980 Reprint), Department of Adult Education, University of Nottingham.

3. *Recommendation on the Development of Adult Education* (UNESCO, Paris, Nov. 1976).
4. Third International Conference on Adult Education, *Final Report* (UNESCO, Paris, 1972), p. 19.

References

Botkin, J.W., Elmandjra, M. and Malitza, M. (1979) *No Limits to Learning: Bridging the Human Gap*, Pergamon Press, Oxford

Bown, L. and Olu Tomori, S.H. (1979) *A Handbook of Adult Education for West Africa*, Hutchinson Educational, London

Coles, E.K.T. (1977) *Adult Education in Developing Countries*, 2nd edn, Pergamon Press, Oxford

Coombs, P.H. and Ahmed, M. (1974) *Attacking Rural Poverty: How Non-Formal Education Can Help*, Johns Hopkins, Baltimore, Md.

Cross, K.P. (1981) *Adult Learners*, Jossey-Bass, San Francisco, Calif.

Hely, A.S.M. (1962) *New Trends in Adult Education: From Elsinore to Montreal*, UNESCO, Paris

Lowe, J. (1982) *The Education of Adults: A World Perspective*, 2nd edn, OISE Press, UNESCO, Paris

Organisation for Economic Co-operation and Development (1977-81) *Learning Opportunities for Adults*, vols. 1-5, OECD, Paris

Peterson, R.E. *et al.* (1982) *Adult Education and Training in Industrialized Countries*, Praeger, New York

UNESCO (1972) *Final Report*, Third International Conference on Adult Education, Tokyo, Japan, 25 July to 7 Aug. 1972

UNESCO (1976) *Recommendation on the Development of Adult Education*, Records of the UNESCO General Conference, Nineteenth Session, Nairobi, 26 Oct. to 30 Nov. 1976

INDEX

313

interaction and non-formal
education 249; problems and race
relations 161-2; relevance and
race relations 159-60; science,
radical education as 28-9
socialism *see* Labour Party
Society for Diffusion of Useful
Knowledge 22-3, 27
Society for Promoting Christian
Knowledge 3
Society for Promoting National
Regeneration 32
Society of Arts 8
Sophia of Birmingham 30
sponsorship 93, 97; *see also* finances
staff *see* teachers
stages of adult life 174
Standing Conference of University
Teaching and Research in
Education of Adults 63
Stapleton, J. 211
state education criticised 21, 23, 27,
31
Stephen, D. 165, 169
Stobart, J. 41
Stock, A. 55
Strathclyde University 6
structure of National Extension
College 198-9
students *see* social characteristics;
target groups
Sunday schools 4-5, 10, 25, 27
support: for individuals 179;
inflexibility 106, 109
Sweden 197

Tanzania 244-5
target groups and students: literacy
schemes 115-29; local centre 225,
241; Open University 174-6,
184-5; unemployed 130-44;
women 145-58
Tawney, R.H. 17
taxonomy of providers 94
teachers and tutors: future 307; local
centre 228-32; National Extension
College 199-200; non-formal 250;
part-time 146, 148, 199, 228-9;
priorities for action 288-9; quality
and conditions 106, 111-12;
radical 25; training 77-8, 229-32,
288-9; university 251; WEA 251;
women as 146-9
technical approach to race relations
study 165

technology 292-6
telephone referral service 50, 197
television 44-52; *see also*
broadcasting
television literacy 203-22; audience
217-20; ideology 216-17; images
220-1; ownership, control,
production 215-16
theatre 67
Third World/developing countries:
LDCs 301-2, 304, 307-10;
National Extension College and
189-90; parallel with non-formal
education 244-5
Thompson, E.P. 32, 36-7
Thompson, J.L. 113, 143-5, 156-8,
254
Tight, M. 70, 225
time rigidities 284-5
Tokyo conference (1972) 300
TOPS *see* Training Opportunities etc
Townswomen's Guilds 64, 80
trade unions 61, 64; broadcasting 51;
North-West 94-5, 98, 106, 109;
priorities for action 288; women
and 156
training: future 307-9; staff 77-8,
229-32, 288-9
Training Opportunities Scheme 17,
68, 100, 127, 133-4, 256
Trenaman, J. 48, 52
Trust, National Extension College
199-200
tutorial class 13
tutors *see* teachers
typology of agencies 96, 99, 101

Ulster People's College 87
Ulster Polytechnic 84-6, 89
unemployed, educational
inititatives for 89, 130-44, 298,
308; community education
138-41; finances 134; principles
131-3; prospects 142-3; provision
133-42
Unemployment Centres 61, 141-2
UNESCO 260, 271, 300, 305, 312
UNICEF 246
United States 166, 197, 258, 270,
310
University Correspondence College
191-2
university extension and extra-mural:
departments; broadcasting and 40;